Some Are Born Great

by Adela Rogers St. Johns

Some Are
Born Great

Adela Rogers St. Johns

DOUBLEDAY & COMPANY, INC.
GARDEN CITY, NEW YORK

The author and publisher are grateful to the following publishers and individuals for permission to include in this book the selections listed below:

From "There Are No Islands Any More" by Edna St. Vincent Millay. Harper & Row. Copyright 1940 by Edna St. Vincent Millay, 1968 by Norma Millay Ellis. By permission of Norma Millay Ellis.

From "One Perfect Rose," "Resume," "Godspeed," "The Maid Servant at the Inn" in *The Portable Dorothy Parker*. Copyright 1926, 1928 © renewed 1954, 1956 by Dorothy Parker. All rights reserved. Reprinted by permission of The Viking Press, Inc.

From "Over the Rainbow". Words: E. Y. Harburg, music: Harold Arlen. Copyright © 1938, renewed 1966 Metro-Goldwyn-Mayer, Inc. Rights controlled throughout the world by Leo Feist, Inc. Used by permission.

Acknowledgments

As the controlling factor of the world's destiny, all women are born great. Greater. Greatest.

My first acknowledgment of help goes to Mary Kennedy, wife of Dr. Robert E. Kennedy, and thus First Lady of California Polytechnic State University, San Luis Obispo, California, of which he is President. For Mary, in a conversation at the Madonna Inn, insisted that I *ought to* write about great American women I have known.

Then to my son Richard for being the Irritant that produces whatever pearls I may generate. And to his friend Victor Palmieri, who for over twenty years has been another son to me. It was Vic and his gracious wife, Tita, who finally turned up the house by the side of the ocean where I managed to complete this book. To my son Mac, who takes time out from handling labor disputes for TV and what is left of The Movies to talk stories—he likes to as well as I do. To my physician, Dr. Robert Loveland, he agrees with me that there is no need to grow older and is willing to accept any prayer help in healing we can get from such devoted ministers as Dr. Fletcher Harding, Dr. Frank Richelieu, and Dr. Beth Newton, as well as Father Hilary of the San Miguel Mission. A special vote also to my granddaughters for keeping me eager for their future. Kathy, Tracey, Kris, who likewise gave me my great-granddaughter Jessica, and also to Liz, Bernadette, Ashley, and Julie, whose love sustains me. Come to think of it, I have two daughters-in-law, Barbara and Anna, and two granddaughters-in-law, Kathy and Pam—and I've learned a lot about women from them. Special mention to my grandson-in-law Frederick Wolf, Coordinator of Special Programs at Cal Poly; his good word for me to Director L. Harry Strauss, Ruth Spenser, and Joy Berghell of the Cal Poly Library gained me their kind, clear-eyed, and invaluable assistance. And to another great American woman, Miss Peggy Lee, often and often on the telephone she sang me back into confidence, inspiring ideas I wouldn't have come up with otherwise.

All writers are restless. Before I came to my lovely house by the ocean I was blessed by being able to do various parts of this book in various hospitable places for which I am truly grateful. To the Madonna Inn and its staff under Alex and Phyllis Madonna. I spent a year in San Luis Obispo surrounded there by beauty and good friends such as Peggy, Doris, Maxine, Irma, and Edna. To the Huntley House in Santa Monica and its manager Elizabeth Crook. To the Paso Robles Inn where Lynn and Harriet Chandler made me welcome, where the echoes of Paderewski's melodies linger on; he lived there and restored the genius in his hands at the Hot Springs.

Of course to Ben Reddick. Having achieved that dream of every big city newspaperman, Ben now owns a paper in a small town, *The Paso Robles Press*. Ben talked me into and out of great women as I was making my selections. We were together, in tears, when Harry Truman died and we realized what a *great* woman he'd had as a wife. To my friend Nancy Bender who is also my typist. I can never tell you—or her—how much freer I am in writing because I know she'll eliminate the major spelling disasters.

Sam Vaughan—how do I say this? As head of the publishing division of Doubleday & Company, Inc. of Park Avenue our Mr. Vaughan has *class*. No synonym, no substitute possible. It allows you to hold your head up higher, to be published by a man like that.

Now, beside my Elaine, I owe whatever this book may do in reaching other women to Ferris Mack, my editor at Doubleday. I rely on his judgment as the British did on Gibraltar, it's never failed me. Judgment. He can reject the maudlin, any slipping too far back into the sob sister, *but* he can be moved by sincerity, suffering, or salvation. *Or story*. No one can ask more of an editor. I don't. I'll settle for Ferris for the rest of my life.

I was warned by my editors and publisher to keep these acknowledgments *short*. I'm sorry. I came to realize what a team it took to make this book. I'd like to give the whole line-up card; if I've left out anyone please know it was lack of space and not lack of loving gratitude and appreciation.

Adela Rogers St. Johns
Malibu, California
July 12, 1974

FOR
My daughter Elaine St. Johns
to whom it already belongs. Without
her enthusiastic encouragement to
start it, her determination that we
finish it, and her final inspired editing
this book could never have been begun,
finished, or fit to print.

Some Are Born Great

Chapter One

That is *another* story.

I have another story to tell, this time many in one, yet all one story really. A gallant story of the irrepressible spirit of American women I have known.

Sitting on the curb, all the kids in the neighborhood around me in days before television—Tell us a story? So I begin, the Tin Woodman said to Dorothy do you think the Wonderful Wizard of Oz could give me a *heart?* Or I make one up as I go along beginning Once upon a time—

Once upon a time in the United States of America were some women of irrepressible spirit who accomplished nothing less than miracles. One of them actually was canonized as the first American saint, but the others were no less remarkable. These women were born some in gutters, in mansions, on farms in Kansas or northern Italy, some had greatness thrust upon them by cops with axes in New York and some by standing steadfast before juries in Boston or flying a spy mission for their country.

Mostly, they fought our battles and these stories are not just of what they did in the past but of what, with the hope and confidence they give us, we can do in the future. They stood for a safer happier life for everybody but especially women and children.

The thing I find they had in common from Carry Nation to Judy Garland to Bess Truman to Amelia Earhart—*gallantry*. This is defined in my dictionary as dashing courage and heroic bravery but to me it means much more than that. It means high-spirited defiance in the face of danger, it means they were quite unaccustomed to fear and got up off the floor if they had to and they had to, you'd better believe it! Marie Dressler or that naturalized American citizen, Maria Francesca Cabrini, whose name comes first on the list of famous immigrants at the Statue of Liberty, and with the *gallant* smile I saw on Miriam Van Waters' face when she was on trial in a Boston courtroom. Same as that with which Rachel Carson from her death bed faced the indifferent and unbelieving world she was trying to save from disaster.

If I were asked, a famed Frenchman said around 1840, to what the singular prosperity and growing strength of the Americans ought to be mainly attributed I should reply: *To the superiority of their women.*

I am about to prove that to you.

"Allright, Swifty, what've you got?" That's Howey, our most terrible and wonderful editor. He wants my story about the Dempsey-Tunney fight or the Leopold-Loeb murder or Elsie Parrish before the Supreme Court. Or it's Mr. Hearst from the Hearst Castle at San Simeon and *he* wants my series about the First Family in the White House named Roosevelt.

Now I'm on my own, but I've got stories I know I must tell because some of them nobody knows but me and because today the American Woman is the hottest story there is anywhere and *she*—Today's Woman—ought to know a good deal more than she does about the irrepressible spirit and the gallant character and the never-say-die methods of her predecessors.

There are so many!
Which ones shall I select to tell you?

Damon Runyon, the greatest reporter who ever lived, used to say There is a Tavern at the End of the Road, where we shall all meet again, renew our deep friendships and swap yarns once more as we have done in so many places and at so many times around the globe and over the years. Between innings, between halves, between rounds, between sprints of the Six Day Bike races at Madison Square Garden, waiting for juries or election returns or reports from the FBI about a kidnapped baby. At Fisherman's Wharf or Dempsey's or Nellie's Taproom in Flemington, New Jersey, at the Lindbergh Trial of the Century, at "21" or Chasen's of Hollywood, or the Savoy Grill in London or the Ritz Bar in Paris or Alfredo's in Rome or the Brown Hotel in Denver or the Royal Hawaiian in Honolulu or for me above all the Occidental in Washington. I know I have friends waiting for me in that Tavern, I've made dates with a few of them, like Fulton Oursler who wrote *The Greatest Story Ever Told*, but the other day I realized with horror and amazement that there isn't a woman at the table in that Tavern and none has ever been invited. Not one. For now or past or in the future.

What kind of a thing is that?

A girl called Nora, brought up in her father's law offices, knew little of women and practically none of it good. *I wish she'd drop dead, she's driving Papa crazy*, those are the words the girl I was then used about her mother when at last she came to write the story of her father Earl Rogers and herself as Earl Rogers' daughter Adela. Not a good introduction to women, is it? It was the only one I had.

In many areas where I worked as the first woman reporter I naturally worked with men only. Quentin Reynolds, O. O. McIntyre, Ring Lardner, Paul Gallico, Russel Birdwell, Fulton Oursler, H. L. Mencken, George Jean Nathan, Arthur Brisbane, George R. Holmes, L. B. Mayer, Victor Fleming and Clark Gable, and they were all helpful, humorous, kind and nearly always interesting. One way or another, I didn't miss women. Everybody had to fight hard to have By-Lines on our copy in those days, and I wish to go on record that in this or any other matter I was never discriminated against. *Tout au contraire*. I had a card to the Press Box at Churchill Downs in Louisville for the Kentucky Derby, the hardest one to come by. At the Hauptmann trial I sat at a side table with Ray Block, from the Trenton paper, which had first call on seats since it was in their jurisdiction.

No women around anywhere.

So it is perhaps natural when from the mountain I am laboriously —sometimes with *grace* more swiftly—climbing toward the Desired Country when I see the table at the end of the road I can see clearly my son Bill, my father, my brother Bogart, Mr. Hearst to be sure, Damon himself, Mark Kelly and my best friend Clark Gable.

Where then is Mother Meyer, my Mrs. Valiant-for-Truth, the

more-than-friend who took the place my mother never wanted, who meant more to me than anyone but Papa? Then I realize I would never have thought of her *there* because she is always with me *here*, not then but now.

Somehow, I keep her beside me always.

In Sacramento not long ago where I'd gone to attend a Prayer Breakfast given by Governor Ronald Reagan, I read a headline in the *Bee* which said that Mrs. St. Johns (me) is Anti-Woman. I get mail along those lines, too. Some of it agrees with the views I've expressed, some is in decent opposition, some in indecent and threatens dire punishment. The truth is, has been, always will be, I am too Pro-Woman. I am the one who is sure woman's gallantry in covered wagons, transatlantic flights and having the babies has never faltered. And will save the world again and again and again if she understands her place, power and the need of her irrepressible spirit, *not* just her nudity which she had in the Garden of Eden and got thrown out of.

After all, God made man and then said I can do better than *that* and made woman.

Like Jane Addams.

Who described herself to me as an ugly, pigeon-toed little girl who grew up into an ugly little woman and never had a proposal of marriage. Thus she could (then) have no children. This would have broken her heart except that she thought of the idea of founding the Social Settlement called Hull House, for children with no mothers. *They all became mine*, she told me. And she, with what the Encyclopedia describes as her *practical methods*, her hard-working talent for organization, executive gifts and indomitable spirit, became the pioneer of social settlement work in America.

Often, when I hear of all these women in America today with much time on their hands I think of Jane and of what—of all people—Tennyson once said:

> If time be heavy on your hands,
> Are there no children at your gate?
> Oh teach the orphan-boy to read,
> Or teach the orphan-girl to sew.

Or baby-sit for some poor young mother who can't afford to *pay* one!

Probably women who have too much time on their hands don't really care for children?

In 1931, this funny-looking obscure little woman won the Nobel Peace Prize.

Nobody discriminated against her nor denied Jane Addams her right to serve her country as the first citizen of Chicago, as she was called, sometimes even the first citizen of her nation, and she was able to push labor legislation and protective bills for women and children through the state legislature.

I think this was because Jane Addams was always thinking of the children, never of herself.

As one labor leader shouted at a meeting where she had spoken, "I wish the Protestants had saints, for Jane Addams could be one."

And, as you know, when the church which does have saints decided to so honor an American, it was to be a woman. In her, as you will find, was the irrepressible spirit that as we travel with her will seem indeed to be beyond human strength and will alone.

Re-create.

I want to re-create some of the women it has been my good fortune to know. Who would have known Cleopatra or Mary Magdalene or Barbara Fritchie or Betsy Ross or even the Blessed Mother herself if somebody hadn't re-created them in the time-space continuum. They *continue*, because of what others have said or written of them, as do the senators in John Kennedy's *Profiles in Courage*.

I did not realize at the time I was walking up that small perpendicular hill back of Burbank, California, with a *saint*.

The first time, I mean.

Maybe I should have, the truth is I didn't. For that matter, neither did she.

Yet the front page of the New York *Times* only thirty years later said in its biggest, blackest type:

AMERICA'S FIRST SAINT
MOTHER CABRINI

I like the word *mother* being there, don't you?

The Devil's Advocate had examined the life of this little Italian nun, who arrived penniless, without a word of English, in America, and they had found no flaw in her miracles either before or after she became an American citizen. But it was not this, either, that brought me to a realization of her official canonization and *that* wasn't why I was swept off my feet by this thought.

She is a saint to me because, as I will show you, she continues.

In 1916, when I was a young reporter and went to see her, I had no idea. In 1972 I knew.

No no, everybody said loudly.

We stood in the bright noonday sun, gazing up at the little white chapel atop a small peak in the first range of California foothills. Bonnie McCarthy, now in charge of this beloved Shrine, several ladies of the Cabrini Literary Guild, my daughter and I, *and* a uniformed guard. Though he was a most courteous one, I did not think Mother Cabrini would approve of him there. The nun who in 1903 wrote, ". . . get a piece of land donated so we can build a nice mission from which the Sisters can go to convert even the Indians . . ." placed her reliance only in heaven. However, the red tape that now seems to be trying to separate Saint Frances Xavier Cabrini from ordinary people, as it was never able to separate Mother Cabrini from ordinary people, or wayward girls, keeps the chapel where their own saint used to pray now padlocked, chained and bolted! The trail up to it is rough and stony, overgrown with cactus and tumbleweed and matted grass, often it twists and turns sharply and always it goes *up* at a stark angle.

My daughter Elaine who, as usual, was beside me when the going was stark and steep, said No louder than anyone.

Not at your age. They weren't saying this aloud, from within their thoughts I could hear it however as plain as though they'd shouted it.

Mrs. McCarthy, a beautiful and shining lady, was willing to lead the way but she, too, was reluctant, and as I followed her gaze upward I saw it was quite a hill and sympathized with them. I had climbed it many years ago with Mother Cabrini when she had just finished building the little white chapel so that she and the Missionary Sisters of the Sacred Heart would have a place to pray and meditate above beautiful downtown Burbank which wasn't as noisy then as it is now. At sixty-five, one year before her death in 1917, she climbed up to it, always a step ahead of me, small and frail and slight; that airy step showed no effort at all. And all the way up she kept smiling serenely. I remember that smile, the blue eyes filled with light, a golden light; should I have known by that light that she was a saint? If as a *reporter* I was so all-fired omniscient as I thought I was, as all reporters know they ought to be, why didn't I know?

It is necessary to admit I didn't because the point I must make is that *later* I did. This present incarnation, not that.

For as I started up the hill over all the protests, in spite of all the big Nos, I knew I was floating without any weight of my body or protest from my bones and muscles. I was floating as Mother Cabrini had always done when *she* was old, as I now was. I knew she was walking it with me once more and *this* time I understood.

I felt my daughter beside me in watchful attention. I had a moment of knowing what it means to have a daughter who walks up hills with you when you insist on going against all *sense—*

"You all right?" she said and I agreed I'd never been more so.

"Well," she said, "I'm not."

We got to the top. Me first. They will all bear witness that I was not out of breath, though the Southern California air pressed against the hill heavy and smoggy. I wasn't sweating one drop though the sun of Southern California had grown hot. The others were breathless and gasping and sweating, even the exquisite young Mrs. McCarthy, even my slim daughter.

The saints purify on sight, says the Mahabharata.

She did.

Saint Frances Cabrini, the first American saint.

When I was a cub and she was an old nun, she hadn't bothered. Now I had returned to make this pilgrimage, to *re*-create for others, and she came with me, timeless and *loving*, to help me up her hill.

To let the uniformed guard turn a rusty key in the padlocks

and break chains he'd sworn couldn't be broken, to open sealed doors so that we could go in and kneel where she had knelt so often.

There was one small statue of Mother Cabrini there—and none of the ladies knew where it came from, and would I care to have it? I said I would, and so it stands on my special shelf with the balcony picture of Mary Baker Eddy, my favorite photograph of Mahatma Gandhi, the one of Bobby Kennedy on his knees with his rosary during a strike, and one of Amelia Earhart about to take off—and when I tell you all about her you will understand why she is *there*. What did Saint Joan of Arc do except die for her country?

I knew then, that second time, about Saint Frances Cabrini.

It's wonderful to grow old enough to recognize a saint when you meet one.

Nothing you can remember is ever lost to you. Remember that!

So I can and will re-create Mother Cabrini for you.

I have a special point of view from where I now am on the road of life—and from that point of view I have a few thoughts I'd like to share with you so we will know each other better.

Let me not deceive you. Personally, I liked it better when the moon was over Miami. That is my privilege, one you maybe don't have because you never knew it when it was over Miami and nowhere else. You don't have Moonlight Bay, you only have that sort of Death Valley landscape up there with little Munchkins from the land of Oz jumping up and down on it.

At my age, I can live in all life's dimensions.

And now at last, I have time. And space. The crowds around me, big and little, keep their distance a little better. I adore crowds, I like campaigning for a candidate or a book or a new law, but I also like the crowds to do what I want them to do.

From up here as I climb the mountain I can see the past—I only have to get out the strongest of my memory binoculars to see it clearly—so clearly—like the day I said good-bye to Amelia, or the time Margaret Mitchell showed me the pages on which she had changed "Dorothy O'Hara"—imagine!—to Scarlett O'Hara, in the manuscripts of *Gone With the Wind*. And Pearl Buck in her Chinese garden.

Because of all this I am as frantic as a hostess who had forgotten to ask a beloved son's mother-in-law to a party.

I want to get out my invitations to that Tavern at the End of the Road! Even Runyon and Mark Kelly and Mr. Hearst will approve of my new guests. Hell's bells, Mr. Hearst sent me to interview or assigned me to write about them, once or twice just to find them! Like Elsie Parrish. And he did love the Follies girls and loved to see the one-and-forever-only Marilyn Miller dancing in the Great Hall at San Simeon—after all he'd first seen Marion Davies when *she* was a Follies girl. For all those magnificent years when I was a reporter in his Service, the greatest that ever existed, following the stories as they broke and writing about the notable newsworthy exciting people of that moment, my good fortune was that I was assigned by him to most of these women.

He recognized gallantry and irrepressible spirit when he saw it, even from a distance.

Go and find out, Mr. Hearst said, *find out* what is so shocking about the dances of this young woman Isadora Duncan that they are expelling her from Boston for indecent exposure. (When I got there she had on enough veils to cover a harem.)

Go down to Twenty-eighth Street and *see* why they keep on arresting this Margaret Sanger, perhaps she should not use the words Birth Control quite so freely. But the first sound I heard when I got there was the police axes crashing through the windows of her bare little clinic where she was trying to lower the death rate of the miserably poor women and their babies. And Margaret Sanger looking like a blazing forest fire as they dragged her to the Black Maria—and once again to jail.

You have to know how much she has affected your day and mine!

One woman whose name is part of the English language. Emily Post. *According to Emily Post* . . . Her book is still a bestseller in a time when there is little enough etiquette about. Why was I so fortunate as to see her dunk her doughnut when I went to have tea on the terrace of her Madison Avenue penthouse? Is then there a time when it is correct for you and me to *dunk?* This, too, I found out.

The first song the superlative Ethel Waters ever sang was "Jesus, Lover of My Soul," at age eight, and she is still singing it with Billy Graham in this hour of what so many young people believe to be the Second Coming. (They do, you know—and there are as many of them as the heroin users.) That was also the song Ethel sang the night her gallantry held a drinking mob still and silent in a club where a fire had broken out and panic, such as had caused a holocaust in a Boston cafe only a short time before, was rising like a volcano.

Bess Truman.

Now there's a girl.

Until I met Mrs. Truman it seemed to me that all *wives* were burdens and disasters—it was difficult to think of Eleanor Roosevelt as a *good wife*, though she was and once told me she put that first of her duties in life. But there was so *many* other things.

And I know now that it was as a *wife* the Press of Washington selected Bess Truman as their all-time All-American First Lady.

Go down, W.R.H. said, to the courthouse (courthouses it turned out over the years) and see what this young woman—a very young woman I am told—is doing about organizing what she calls a *Juvenile* Court. And forty years later I had to fight and thank God defeat my own Service for this same Dr. Miriam Van Waters, a name that ought to be shining in great letters of gold. I was glad when I got to Gardner Auditorium in the basement of the State House and saw Miriam fighting not only for her own life but for the reforms she had brought about in Women's Prisons which up till then had been indistinguishable from the Black Hole of Calcutta. Believe it or not, one of the accusations I heard leveled against Dr. Van Waters in that courtroom was that she had taken three girls whose problem was alcohol to an AA meeting. That, said the male authorities, was *pampering* them.

Elsie Parrish.

Elsie WHO?

Allright, allright, only the woman to whom never-have-so-many-owed-so-much, not even to the few but to one. One Woman.

A middle-aged chambermaid from Spokane, who came to stand in the Supreme Court of the United States before the Nine Justices in their black robes.

> Anyway you look at it, the decision of the United States Supreme Court in this state's minimum wage and hour law for women is destined to rank alongside the famous *Dred Scott decision* in the shaping of this nation's future.

So said the Wenatchee *World*—in the State of Washington—on its front page.

And quite right, too. As you'll agree when we review the Elsie Parrish decision. Perhaps the women of today who keep *losing* all the time should study this fight by a *lone*, courageous, unknown, unfinanced woman with only the help of a brilliant young Irish lawyer she got to carry her case all the way.

Lone gallantry always has so much of the Irresistible and Irrepressible Spirit—maybe because there is more *room* for the Spirit.

This is getting to be quite a list to select from, isn't it?

I've never been any good at guest lists. Mine get tangled. I mean between the people I want and the ones I ought to want and the ones I mustn't forget because I love them and the ones I mustn't forget because they are important—besides, a cocktail party is to me the final relic of the Rack. Or the ducking stool. Dinner parties as a rule are nature's elemental din, still rooted in savagery or a modern version of the old-time wake. My social instincts are primitive, centering around a fireplace and a pot of chili and beans.

Then it came to me in an inspired flash.

I may be lousy at this social swing but my best friend after quite a number of years is a *genius*. At social swings and guest lists, I mean.

When she was fourteen or fifteen, her uncle, the great Walter Howey, sent his little niece Kathleen Morrison out to Hollywood to his pal D. W. Griffith, because she wanted to be a Movie Star.

And, as Colleen Moore she not only became one but the biggest one, and in *Flaming Youth* changed a lot of things around our country. But after the talkies came, she married Homer Hargrave

of Chicago and for thirty years was known as *Mrs.* Chicago.
Not only did she invent the Debutante Cotillion, so that the vast
sums spent for the debuts of young Chicago Social Registerites
could all be put together and given to her favorite Passavant
Hospital, but she was chairman of practically everything in sight
from the Republican Party to the Children's Hospital and the
Opera, Symphony and Casino Club.

To be invited to one of Colleen's parties—morning, noon or
night—was a *must* if you had any pretensions to social standing
in the city by the lake.

And many a time I had seen her, on my brief visits through,
manipulating her own notebooks, the Social Register, and the *Wall
Street Journal—*

So now, said I to myself, she can just give me a hand with my
guest list of women to be invited to the Tavern.

She won't let me leave out anybody I should have . . .

And sure enough that's right where we started because she
said, "We will start with Clare Boothe Luce," and I said, "No we
won't" out loud but to myself I said You see? Of course we must
have Mrs. Luce but *you* would never have thought of her in a
thousand years.

"I always wonder why you don't like her," Colleen said.

"She dressed down to the delegates, a simple little blue dress they
could have bought in Macy's basement, when she was keynote
speaker at the Republican Convention."

"Maybe," said Colleen, "but she was the only woman ever to be
the keynote speaker at a presidential convention."

"She's always being something no other woman has ever been,"
I said crossly. "And Bernard Baruch let her come sit with him on
his park bench when he was advisor to the White House and she
had Jim Londos pinned down when he was world's champion
wrestler and the most romantic Greek up to Aristotle Onassis.
Baruch and Londos were both in love with her."

"If they were," Colleen said, "it means that both brains and
brawn couldn't resist her. I can't imagine that unless she was a
remarkable woman."

"She's so remarkable and successful it's repulsive," I said. "In
my father's office I got the habit of being most moved by the
underdog. That's something she never was."

"A very good case can be made out for Mrs. Luce," Colleen said with her nose in the air. "She came from nothing and nowhere just as much as Cinderella. True, Clare was born on Riverside Drive, but it was after it started to be a marble slum and smelled of stale cabbage. I defy you to find any American man whose career has the breadth and depth of Mrs. Luce's. Society leader, editor, smashing Broadway playwright, Congresswoman, Ambassador Extraordinary, two *big* marriages, founder of magazines that changed the world—I mean to say!"

I changed the subject. I said, "and of course Judy Garland—"

"Judy Garland!" said Colleen in as definite denial and disdain as I'd used about Madame Ambassadress Luce. "Surely not."

"You mean," I said, hoping to make my voice menacing, "she's déclassé and derelict and as outside the gates as though she was the last woman on earth?"

"Well," said Colleen noncommittally, "it's certainly a long time since she was invited anywhere."

"Except to heaven," I said. "Much is forgiven genius."

"Genius," said Colleen. "Judy Garland?"

"Listen!" I said.

She said she didn't hear it but I know she did.

> *Somewhere—over the rainbow—*
> *Way up high—*

Oh yes, all God's women have wings, Judy forgot to use hers, but she had 'em.

Even Carry Nation, who went on wrecking expeditions throughout Bloody Kansas demolishing any place where they sold Fire Water and when they clubbed her she kept right on gallantly brandishing her axe, smashing glasses and bottles and plate-glass windows and mirrors and challenging the Devil himself to come out so she could hit him.

When you know *why* she did this—and that baby born dumb and deaf which started her on this campaign of destruction—you know it was *Heart* that throbbed her on her way.

You have to have *heart* to begin with.

In time, it adds the glow of soul.

Marie Dressler had it to a supreme degree. I saw it shine from her when she was dying and determined to follow George M.

Cohan's favorite song, "Always Leave Them Laughing When You Say Good-bye."

Rachel Carson's *Silent Spring* is a book by a biologist on the subject of pollution by pesticides. *But* she made every reader long to hear those songs the birds weren't singing any more in the spring. So that is why the top English naturalist Peter Scott told the House of Lords, "Future generations will regard Rachel Carson as a great benefactor of the human race for the impact of *Silent Spring*." We have another obscure young woman with a heart benefiting the human race.

They say very young and very old people suffer from loneliness. But here old people have the advantage. They have built their old age with Character, even maybe with gallant character, with at least a desire for the irrepressible Spirit. I, for instance, can never be lonely. If my large family take off in all directions, if they get too busy to see me, or we're too broke for plane fare or gasoline, no one whose character has been taught to build memories can be lonely.

That is the glory of the rest of your life—or mine—from our viewpoint of where we now are.

I am not, I cannot be limited to what I can see, hear, do or compound *now*. I have a choice. And what a choice! I do not have to limit myself to a ball game where the Dodgers of today do not seem disconcerted by making five errors per nine innings. *I* can go back and watch Sandy Amoros make that catch to save a World Series, or the Jackie Robinson—Pee Wee Reese infield at play. If Barbra Streisand seems to me considerably unfunnier than Fannie Brice of the Follies, *I* can still watch Fannie and spend the evening with her afterwards at the Drake in Chicago where we were in adjoining suites the day of the Taylor murder! If I miss my son Bill sometimes till it hurts, I can help with my memory cassettes and movie slides and watch him get his wings in Toronto or see him get a home run against the House of David with men on bases of course—Curt Gowdy was talking about the House of David only the other day on my favorite TV show, "The Game of the Week." It took me back.

We take Remembrance with us and that is why it is wise to learn to remember. To record. To save those things you will love to find some night when otherwise you might be lonely—a sunset off Malibu, the opening night of Helen Hayes in *Victoria Regina*, finding sons Dick and Victor's names in the list of those who'd passed their Bar Exams, watching my granddaughter Tracey take her first steps or great-granddaughter Bernadette saying grace in a high treble that everyone in the lunch room of the Beverly Wilshire Hotel Drug Store stopped to hear.

Of that first moment of knowing that God IS and is available because He loves us. Which gives you a shot of irrepressible Spirit.

The most exciting thing about this book is that all these friends, these remarkable women, these great Americans, these chambermaids and stars and lawyer-doctor-merchant-chief and yes, in one instance, thief, will walk with me in Remembrance as clear as the thing itself all the Rest of My Life.

My grandson Sean, when at four he saw his mother setting a buffet table in the big glass porch at Malibu, began to whirl like a dervish, jumping up and down with joy and excitement and shouting, "People coming! People coming? People coming!"

They are indeed.

You come too.

Chapter Two

::

This is the End of the Search for Amelia Earhart.

Amelia Earhart went on a so-called round-the-world flight as a cover-up to see if she could find out how far along the Japanese were in their plans to drop bombs on Pearl Harbor and/or the Santa Barbara Island and San Francisco Bay.

A Navy pilot who was fooling around Midway and Wake about then told me later that they saw the entire Japanese Navy on parade. "And," he said, "I told my co-pilot, I said, 'Buddy, if we don't hurry up it's going to be too wet to plow.'"

Amelia was to be "off course" in trying to land at a new airfield on Howland Island of which no one had ever heard before—or since. The Japanese caught her over Saipan, naturally didn't believe that tale, captured and did what all nations do, have done, and will do world without end as long as there are wars or rumors of wars—they executed her. As the Germans did Red Cross Nurse Edith Cavell and the French did German dancer Mata Hari. This was a calculated risk on Amelia's part for which she must have been entirely prepared.

Many people have given their lives for their country in many different ways. Amelia was one of them and should be given the glory of and for it in spite of Geneva and International Law and whatever.

This I know from two sources.

One, the secret files of the United States Navy which I saw with my own eyes. Naturally, it was a Marine officer who showed

the Amelia Earhart files to me. You know how different the
Marines are from the Navy when it comes to Public Relations.
When the Marines have Landed, you always know about it. The
Navy started out trying to keep Pearl Harbor out of the papers.

Second, I know from Amelia herself.

Don't worry about me.

On the airfield in Oakland, May 20, 1937, a few minutes before
she took off on what proved to be her last flight, that was what
she said to me. Holding my hands in hers, giving me that up-we-go
smile I never can forget. There is no way Amelia Earhart could
have said *those* four words about *flying* any place any time anywhere,

No way!

You might as well expect Jerry West to say them before going
onto the basketball court or David Rockefeller about to enter a
bank.

That's the other way I know it had to be more than an airplane
flight and one of the times and places I love to go back to, to live
over, to see and hear again is that good-bye to Amelia.

Like to come?

A slim boyish figure—nobody would have dreamed her next
birthday would be forty—moving with a long, free stride always
quite sure the earth was something she could leave at any moment
for the sky which was her real home. We'd had a radio interview—
one of the early ones, she'd talked vaguely about flight plans, introduced and kidded the man she had chosen to be her co-pilot on
the flight, big dark good-looking Fred Noonan, patted my shoulder and moved toward the big shining silver plane that was waiting
for her to take the controls. I thought idiotically of David and
Goliath, she seemed so small, not as tall as my own five foot four,
the bright uncovered head, she never put on her helmet till she
was inside the plane, she swung it in a sort of dancing rhythm—
and she had that little *David* isn't afraid of *Goliath* big as he is
which is the height of gallantry.

Suddenly, on the second step, she turned and came back to me.

"Don't worry about me," she said and ran to the plane, climbed

aboard—in seconds we were standing there watching it go up—up
—up—and far away until it disappeared into the blue universe.

She left behind her the echo of her very low clear voice, it had
always been heart-lifting to me since the first time I heard it when
I was sent to interview her as she crossed the Atlantic—the first
woman to fly that ocean.

Don't worry about me don't worry about me don't worry about
me.

Amelia Earhart?

So I knew this couldn't be just another flight. Whenever in all
those years since her disappearance people ask me if she just made
a landing in the ocean, or was captured by the Japanese and held, I
always hear those words and I knew and know that Amelia was
telling me—*this one is different but always remember I know what
I'm doing.*

Not until I saw the Navy Files did I know she'd received her
orders from the Commander-in-Chief himself, President Franklin
D. Roosevelt. But as I began to *think,* after she failed to return, I
remembered she'd been to see him not long before, I remembered
that he was her idol, her hero, a former Naval Person himself, of
course.

Today we all know of the U2 adventures. We have familiarity
and awareness of secret espionage flying missions. Since I said
good-bye to Amelia Earhart we have all read about a million
books on spies, spying, espionage in and out of the cold, we know
all its aspects and are instantly alert to science fiction possibilities.

That wasn't true when Amelia took off that day in May.

Just the same, because of her own words, I wondered.

Already in Washington, where I had been for some time covering
the Roosevelt Administration for the *Times-Herald* and INS, there
were rumors of wars. Already Mr. Hearst's headline warnings
about the Japanese peril and their intention to drive us out of the
Pacific and take control of the Pacific Coast were repeated
quietly in the War Department and by the Chiefs of Staff of all
the services. No one could any longer dismiss them as wild Hearst
journalism or shrug them off as ridiculous exaggerations. The old
sense of security, our conviction of our invincibility between the
two big oceans, on which we had so long based our stand of isola-

tion, our refusal to think in any terms but Entangling Alliances against which we'd been warned, had to be gone. Aviation and speed had reduced those oceans to little more than the creek that ran under the bridge at Lexington.

Who better fitted to fly around and about in a plane given her by Purdue University, where she had once taught, than our most famous woman? Our heroine of so many airborne firsts, our Amelia of the cold, chill nerve and the friendly girl-I-knew-in-high-school smile? Looked to as the greatest pilot in the United States—for Lindbergh seemed to lose interest after he flew the Atlantic (he'd avoided all publicity and public contact as soon as he could)—Amelia, though there was a certain reserve in her public appearance and personality, loved people, above all loved aviation; she was always bursting to show everybody what its future could be.

She became more and more a public figure after she married George Palmer Putnam, head of a big and highly successful publishing house. For G.P. was, we all knew, a lens-louse, a headline grabber, and we soon became aware that he didn't care what anybody said about Amelia as long as they mentioned his name too. It was put forward to me later that the United States would not have sacrificed Amelia on such a risky mission, one of the reasons being that her husband would never have permitted it. The latter is doubtless true. George Putnam had a gold mine in his famous wife and a standing with the Press because of her, but frankly I never thought he knew anything about said mission. By that time I do not think Amelia consulted him about her flying business. Much as I am inclined to like and be grateful to publishers, I myself thought George Palmer Putnam at least a bit of a bore, and perhaps finding herself married to him gave Amelia an added impetus to take her big chance for our country, to seek excitement and adventure outside the home as it were.

She couldn't have the man she really loved.

Some of us can't.

Things happen to reporters.

Probably it is because we attract them that we *are* reporters.

A combination of a nose for news, an observational power so trained it is strong enough to seem part of nature, an inner conviction of power granted because without Freedom of the Press

none of the other freedoms are safe for a minute, a psychic vision
of what people have a right to know. *We, the People.* They are *our*
courts, *our* public servants, *our* diplomatic policies, *our* wars.
How else can we know about them except through the Press. So it
must be *free* to tell us.

One of those moments granted to each of us came on that Oakland airfield and of course it also came partly because Amelia and I
were friends—and we were friendly partly, but only partly, because she was always *news*. I want to tell you how it came about
that we were friends.

She was so one-point-dedicated that she didn't have as much
time as perhaps she would have liked for the usual social life and
friendships. We had a common heartbreak and discovered it, by
chance, in our first conversation. Our lives had been changed,
keyed, developed, timed, we were the kind of independent women
we were in many aspects, we saw things the way we did, we had
made certain moves and gained some strengths and taken certain
then unusual steps in our teens because of the same thing.

Our fathers drank.

I mean they drank more than was good for them or us. Her
father was a lawyer too, and as girls at about the same age we
had lived under those dark clouds of the same fear, that dread of
disbarment and disgrace, we had fought, bled and been ready to
die so that no one—*no one*—could hurt that one human being
to whom all our love was given. All of it. We fought and even
disliked our mothers, our families, our clients, to protect and preserve those who were to us the first responsibility of our hearts. I
called mine *Papa.* Amelia always said *my father* when we talked of
him and I think that was what she called him.

We both came out of this childhood-girlhood way of life already determined on independence, already strengthened and experienced beyond our years as are most youngsters who have an
almost parental responsibility to their own parents. Amelia didn't
dislike her mother as I did mine, in fact except that as a *wife* for her
father she considered her a failure, she was fond of her pretty,
gentle mother. I was not quite eighteen when I got my first job on
a newspaper and Amelia wasn't yet twenty-one when she made her
first solo flight. She had tried other things, never having seen an
airplane. I wrote a book about my father because writing is my

profession, but I don't think Amelia ever talked much about hers until she found we spoke the same language and had carried the same cross.

I have to go back to that Oakland airfield for a moment and explain why that man named George Palmer Putnam was leaning against a building looking extraordinarily distinguished and obviously part of the momentous occasion. Some of us thought Mr. Putnam took more credit than we were willing to give him for we knew he hadn't really conceived this take-off, arranged this trip, mapped the flight and he wasn't in charge of Amelia Earhart and the works. He was there because he was married to Amelia Earhart but you got a funny feeling that he had long ago decided that Amelia Earhart was there only because she was married to him.

> The people people have for friends
> Your common sense appalls,
> But the people people marry
> Are the queerest folk of all!

I may have been the only person there at the time who knew why Amelia Earhart had married the queerest folk of all, George Palmer Putnam.

It was because her father drank.

I know, I know, but it's the plain unvarnished truth. For she had fallen in love as romantically, passionately and completely as Cleopatra on her barge at the sight of Anthony. And the man Amelia had fallen in love with she couldn't, *wouldn't*, marry.

He drank.

Girls who haven't had much experience often marry men who drink in a golden optimism that *if he loves me he'll stop drinking*. And sometimes with the help of God, prayer and AA he does. But to Amelia hope had been deferred and defeated too often. She'd been daughter to all that, she wasn't about to become wife to it, which in some ways is even worse. A husband who drank and especially a pilot, for inevitably the man she really loved was a pilot. In those days, pilots were a race apart, they spoke another language, they had different lives, they were in worlds of their own. To her, drink for a pilot seemed even more deadly than for a railroad lawyer like her father, a pilot's feet aren't on the ground to begin with.

To be Mrs. Putnam—*Mrs.* anybody for that matter—put her beyond the temptation on one of those moments when the world might seem well lost for love. Amelia Earhart Putnam—*Mrs.* Putnam—she was marrying respectability, responsibility, security, stability, all things that may seem directly contrary to her nature and her desires and in certain aspects were. Yet she had them all, or she could never have made the flight she did, which took steady nerves and great self-discipline and the need to take responsibility for grave decisions. Being Mrs. Putnam, she explained to me, would give her a life, interests, friends away from flying.

A life away from flying!

When you see a gold cup know you cannot separate the cup from the gold. They are one. So was Amelia Earhart a woman pilot. They were one. You couldn't separate the woman from the pilot, either.

Don't worry about me.

Two scenes with Amelia appear to me instantly, always, they get mixed up and I hear the words alternating.

This is as good a time as any to insert an apology and an explanation. By my father, later by William Randolph Hearst, I was early persuaded that a good memory was essential to success and accomplishment whether in the White House, the laboratory, the courtroom, house and garden, aviation, navigation, writing poetry, Wall Street bulls and bears, or quarter-backing the Stanford Indians. From Plato to Johnny Carson no man could be tops in his field without it. I was trained by my father to memorize from Shakespeare through Kipling so that their words would be part of my brain-blood-stream and my unconscious using-without-direct-quoting vocabulary. By W.R.H. I was taught to take a Q. and A. in a murder courtroom without pencil and paper, which I did last at the Overell trial in Santa Ana.

Nevertheless let's face it, on *dates* I am unethical and lousy.

So that while I know my two most vivid memories of Amelia are separated by years I do not know how many or when and thus it is difficult to look up even in an Almanac. Actually, does it matter much? Time has been going on so long that where we were or are in it I can't make important.

I've given you the first scene in the Oakland airport.

The other one that made those four words spoken then and there so powerful and convincing took place a few years prior to that at a table in the quiet, rather austere dining room of the Hotel Seymour on Forty-fifth Street in New York City.

Today unless you are going to the moon or beyond, airplane flights or rockets are pretty routine. Also women's achievements are less and less news. But each woman has to be judged according to the times in which she lived; it's no use judging *Elizabeth* for cutting off *Essex*'s head when as her lover he began to annoy her against *our* background of No Capital Punishment, not even for drug pedlars who sell to little kids on school grounds. Amelia, a woman who had flown all those sensational hops across continents and oceans for the first time, in the early days of aviation, was perfect casting for the heroine of her times and to this day we never think of a woman aviator without *seeing* Amelia. She was always noticeable. We had intended that day of our first interview to lunch at the Algonquin, then the most *in* restaurant in New York where Dorothy Parker, Bob Benchley, Alexander Woollcott and James Thurber often sat around the table together and thus it didn't occur to us that Amelia Earhart would cause a riot in the lobby we regarded as celebrity proof. But she did, so we ducked and as passers-by spotted her and began to stop on the sidewalk we ducked again up a side alley which ended on the next block and there we slid unobtrusively into the Seymour Hotel and the maître d' with no more than a dignified "Good morning, Miss Earhart" showed us to a corner table. This became our meeting place for occasional interviews and talks.

I can perhaps best show you Amelia's outstanding personality in any crowd by saying she and Kate Hepburn always reminded me of each other. In fact even in *Coco* I somehow expected Kate to be swinging her helmet. I once did a movie for Hepburn in the early days at RKO called *Morning Glory* (I think) about a woman pilot and from then on I have always been confused in my memories of Kate and Amelia and which is which.

On the one day that left me with so strong a conviction that it had to be connected with her last words to me and gave them their special significance, we were celebrating her preparation for

an around-the-world flight—this was the first one that cracked
up on the take-off. Out of it comes some casual conversation
and the surprise I felt that Amelia had thought of doing and being
so many things before she saw her first airplane.

Born in Atchison, Kansas, in 1898, she had gone to grammar
school in Kansas City and then to high school in Des Moines,
Chicago and Detroit, and she never did get to graduate from any
of them—which was another thing we had in common. Just at
the time when she was about to once again, she took off for
Toronto where her sister Ruth, who was a little older, was at
a Canadian college and there, seeing the agony and devastation
wrought by the First World War, she stayed to work as a nurses'
aide in the hospital to which wounded men were being brought
on Mercy ships from the battlefields in France. This turned her
as soon as the war was over to Pre-Med courses at Columbia,
then to some time spent in Medical Research, and during that
period she had about decided to devote the rest of her life to that
work. Especially in the field of Medical Research for children.
But here destiny took a hand. Her father and mother and her
sister, back from her war service, moved to California and of
course Amelia went along and there by what seemed mere chance
at an airfield near Long Beach she saw her first Air Circus. Actually
I think, her first airplane. There hadn't been much flying in the
Middle West, her home ground before, and at once she inveigled
her father into paying for a passenger ride and it was all over.

"I wonder how people can stay on the ground," she said to me
once. "Why should they? I knew instantly like turning on the
light in a dark dark room—all that mattered in life was to learn
to fly as soon as I possibly could."

To pay for her flying lessons, she took a job as a telephone
operator. Soon she soloed. Since at that time no pilot's license was
necessary she was an *aviator* in a few weeks. Piling up firsts—
records—the Atlantic, the Pacific, cross-continents, and all this she
had done when we sat together at the Seymour and she began
to say those things that built up the background against which
I heard

Don't worry about me.

"Promise me," she said, "that you will never show any fear
of flying. Promise me that you'll pray not to have any. Get over
any fear you have—you have to, it's only fair."

My daughter Elaine, still in her teens, had just begun to learn to fly and remembering her utter recklessness when at the age of six she had learned to jump a horse I couldn't help wondering if she might carry that disregard for her own neck into flying.

"Let's hope so," Amelia said fervently. "The one thing in flying or riding a horse or a lot of other things that can destroy your timing and do you in is fear."

"Aren't most of us afraid to fly at first?" I said.

"I—perhaps," Amelia said, "but you can overcome it."

Today of course there isn't any way not to think of Jonathan Livingston Seagull—who learned to fly. Who overcame everything and thus became—the national American hero.

Some people you can always see, some you can't.

Amelia Earhart wore a dark blue suit of some rough silk, a short jacket and a pleated skirt in the summer, it gave her a schoolgirl look. Her face was all lit up—no other word is adequate. "We now live in a world where man can fly!" she said. "It has to be a different world and from now on it always will be. When the world changes we have to change with it. I saw an eclipse of the sun from the air once on a flight to Catalina and I knew then I was in the Universe. Don't you see what this means and will mean? Queen Elizabeth knew the world was round because Sir Walter Raleigh kept on going off to places and he told her so. But as she walked in the gardens of her palace at Whitehall or was carried in a sedan chair along the streets of Oxford I don't expect in her stomach she believed it. Lots of people still don't. But God made a Universe for us and we now live in a world that is part of it and where men, women and children will and must fly."

And seagulls!

"It says," Amelia told me quietly, "that we *abide* in the place of the Most High. So the higher we are maybe the better we abide? Your children will never remember that there was a time when we didn't fly and you dare not give them one single flutter of fear or reluctance. It's not just that it's more beautiful, more godlike, to see all its wonders from the air, but it's all

God's world and worlds opening up to us, all new." After a deep breath she said, "Promise me that you will stand against letting any kind of fear get into your mind about flying. Pray about it!"

Don't you see that the woman who said those things *to me* couldn't possibly say *to me*

> *Don't worry about me—*

> > because she was *flying?*

She had more joy in flying than anyone I've ever known and I've flown to New Orleans for dinner with Captain Eddie Ricken- backer and seen Catalina from the air with Pappy Boyington and watched the curve of the earth at dawn with Eddie Bellanti at the controls of a Boeing coming out of Winslow, Arizona, and Dick Merrill once set me down in Raleigh in a thunderstorm. Amelia had a belonging-in-the-air beyond anyone. So you see it would have been impossible for Amelia to use the word *worry* —to feel uneasy or anxious or fearful; torment oneself with dis- turbing care and apprehension—

> about *flying.*

Spying is another matter, as Edith Cavell knew. It takes gallantry because it is so secret, so without credit or applause.

It's an odd commentary on Amelia's contribution to the history of American women that she created a lasting and omnipresent fashion dictate. The trousers, or slacks or pants, the sweater worn with grace over a shirt that opened at the throat to show a bright scarf, the walking shoes and wool sox, believe me when I say that no one had ever worn this costume before Amelia Earhart and everyone has worn it ever since and apparently always will, I hope. It was another of her *firsts.*

> Courage is the price that life exacts
> > For granting peace,
> The soul that know it not knows no release
> > From little things.

That is a poem *By* Amelia Earhart, you will find it in Bartlett's Quotations.

It might well be our theme for these great women I am telling you about, as you can see.

She had that kind of courage, release from little things which build into apprehension and anxiety, when she took off from Oakland that day. On her last great gamble—and I realize now that the passion to gamble on adventure lay at the bottom of her heart always. I'm going on a mission of risk—don't be apprehensive—don't be tormented by any mystery that comes of it —I know what I'm doing! That, I know, is what she said to me and I cherish it.

Somewhere still in the files of the United States Navy is the full complete story of Amelia Earhart.

This the Navy cannot and will not reveal because it breaks all kinds of Codes, Conferences, International Laws and agreements —sending our "lady flyer" on such a mission in the first place, as I said in the beginning.

This Amelia understood full well.

I suppose the farthest she got was that—Don't worry about me.

I didn't, Amelia.

I don't.

I'm sure by now she has wings of her own up there among the seraphim and the cherubim.

I'm also sure the wings are not too big for her to sit a moment at our Tavern.

Chapter Three

Two people in America can say *I did it with my little hatchet*.

George Washington and the cherry tree may be a myth invented by a P.R. man of that day, but they are part of our tradition.

What Carry Nation did with *her* little hatchet is beyond peradventure of a doubt. By the time Carry got into the stride in pursuit of the Demon Rum, roaming hatchet in one hand and the Bible in the other from the coast of California to the court of Edward VII, the entire population of the United States could bear witness to her raids on red eye, rotgut and BOOZE, as she familiarly called them. For Carry operated always in the center of the stage with whatever spotlight she could find, fulminate or invent focused upon her.

For a woman who had never, as far as we know, been inside a *theater*, Carry's sense of drama was as pungent and pointed as P. T. Barnum's, but perhaps the daughter of a *lady* who literally believed she herself was Queen Victoria and drove about their home state of Kentucky wearing a crown of cut glass and chandelier pendants would both by heredity and environment be violent, dramatic and theatrical.

In the Name of the Father, crash-bang kerboom, In the Name of the Son, rippityracketyrowdydow, In the Name of the Holy Ghost, tantivitantivitantivi get thee behind me Satan—and then the gutters of Kansas, or Illinois or Iowa or California, ran with the rarest Bourbon. Barroom floors were soon ankle deep in shattered glass, jovial bartenders and their even slightly inebriated patrons often found themselves stretched prone on the sawdust with bloody noses as a result of an unexpected and uninvited visit from Carry Nation, and that's the way she used to make war on Alcohol, the curse of a free nation in her eyes, heart and imagination. She terrified an entire country border to border and darn near got herself *lynched* for her pains. Men did not wish to stop drinking red eye, rotgut and BOOZE in 1886 any more than they did in 1918 when we passed that so-called Prohibition Amendment nor than they do today when what Carry called *guzzling* is at its all-time peak.

No wonder Carry became our first nationally famous woman.

Her sense of drama and of public relations was far in advance of her time. You cannot leave a trail of destruction, devastation and drama of which you are the dramatist and the acting star without becoming famous. To this moment I am not sure how much of this Carry understood and did with guile and gusto and how much was just plain inborn genius. I am sure of one thing, however. All this would have been possible only to someone with a passionate conviction in the rightness of her cause and this is why in our wishy-washy times she still can steal the spotlight and turn her rip-roaring career as the first real Temperance Leader of all time into her own personal extravaganza.

Destiny, I am convinced, took a hand early, and continued all her life to deal her the right cards.

Look at her marriage to a man named NATION.

Any marriage for Carry Amelia Moore seemed problematical.

Her mother, not to put too fine an analysis upon it, must have been mad as a hatter—but in such a picturesque exciting way. There she rode, in her carriage with black postilion outriders, scepter in hand, crown on head, bowing to the populace or the trees or the barns or whatever. I knew a man once who thought he was Napoleon, and another who was convinced that he was J. P. Morgan—this got him in a lot of trouble like with bad checks and such. But in those early days in the South life was magnificent, terrible and always dramatic and nobody seems to have bothered much about Carry Nation's mother and her delusions. Who cared, actually?

Queen Victoria's prince consort in this version was, unfortunately, a drunk. Unfortunately because, as with more stable and less dramatically inclined girls than Carry, this can mark a character. And when Her Majesty got around to making a matrimonial alliance for the Princess her daughter, David Nation drank too. BUT, I still believe, it was because of his name—his last name —his to-be-forever-engraved-upon-our-history last name—that he was chosen to wed Carry Amelia Moore.

For thus she became *Carry Nation*, and not Sinclair Lewis himself, with his obsession with names to become part of our language such as Babbitt, could better that one.

Carry Nation could carry an axe—and knew it.

She never missed a trick, that one. And the majority of Youth today know that NAME, though whether she was an early Channel swimmer or the sixth wife of Brigham Young they aren't sure. But I have found they are *fascinated* when I use Carry to prove that Doing Your Own Thing did not originate with them in the Twentieth Century. In one of my favorite books, *Tracy and Hepburn*, Garson Kanin lists the true American Originals: Thoreau, Jane Addams, Edison, George Washington Carver, Margaret Sanger (with whom we'll come to grips later), Carry Nation, my great-great uncle Robert Greene Ingersoll, Charles Ives, Dashiell Hammett (I hope Dashiell knows, he'll be so pleased), Eugene V. Debs, Samuel Gompers, Jackson Pollock and Ralph Nader.

Exalted company for our first nationally known American woman.

She rates it. And while her fame rests upon her campaigns against alcohol, upon her role as our greatest temperance leader who inspired Emma Willard to start the WCTU, let us not think of her as a dull or drab character—she is flamboyant, hammy, all-star and irresistible!

Lit by an inner fire, a blazing dedication to save men, she was able to crash through the swinging doors of many a barroom and hold men with one foot poised above the brass rail and one hand frozen with a lifted glass as her rich contralto rang forth:

> "Father, dear Father, come home with me now
> The clock in the steeple strikes ten
> You promised you'd come straight home from the shop
> And here you are spending your paycheck again"

> (Or words to that effect.)

Exalted company or not, we must always remember that this was a Kentucky-born *lady,* reared *on* a plantation, *in* a Southern mansion, *by* a Mammy named Jerusha and—recall this—a mother who thought she was Queen Victoria. All this proves the overpowering obsession and possession of her Crusade. Go down to Louisville, *Kentucky*, even now to see the Kentucky Derby, which took me there the last time, and you'll find it is the only place in the world where they can still make a Mint Julep. This is hearsay evidence because myself I haven't had one since the year I saw Citation win, but I know the tall silver chalice handed down by Grandpappy with a long white mustache who fought with Jackson at Antietam helps some. Still, how could *Kentucky* have produced such a violent, temperance leader when the Temperance Cause was yet a mere gleam in the eye of the No. One suffragette, Emma Willard? Few women themselves drank in those days. In an early bestseller by Robert W. Chambers—along about 1908 or so—the heroine's drink problem—considered so serious she had no right to marry and have children—consisted in dropping wine on a lump of sugar and eating it.

When, at nearly forty, Carry Nation started on her militant operation against Rum she had much feminine charm which, as we shall see, kept her from being lynched. And—try this speech with a Southern accent. It is one delivered by Carry in Mart Strong's saloon:

> You women of America, listen to me.
> Your husbands bring their money HEAH,
> to this heah Mart Strong and his luxurious
> and gilded barroom and Mart Strong isn't
> a-smilin' at the faces of your under-
> nourished children and wan-lookin' wives,
> all of them being undernourished and
> wan-like because of him and his BOOZE
> that they spend all their money to buy
> and do not bring it home to their wives
> and their babies. The faces at which he
> smiles are those of devils and BOOZERS—

and following
that you may picture her butting Mart in the stomach with her head and, as he went down, belting him a last blow with her Bible *and*, with her axe, demolishing the rich voluptuous picture of a naked harlot leering from the wall behind the bar counter.

Carry's aim at these whores of Babylon, as she called them, was accurate and demolished their charms entirely. The final scene of this barroom drama was Carry doing a war dance like an Indian squaw with a fresh scalp. Oh, in her own way Carry A. Nation enjoyed herself and taking a good look around today who is to say she didn't have a point in this glee?

Came a day when men, beginning with a judge, got fed up with Carry and her ceaseless crusade against their favorite indoor occupation. A judge began it by pronouncing sentence—

> The JUDGE
> Ninety days for disturbing the
> peace and destroying private
> property and God forgive me for
> not strangling her with my bare
> hands . . .

She could arouse *passions*, could Carry.

There she was, locked up in jail and the Vigilantes who marched to get her *out* didn't mean to rescue her—they meant to *hang* her to a nearby tree and thus really eliminate her. No other American woman as far as I can find has ever been as near being lynched as Carry Nation.

Not perhaps what you'd called a lovable character, yet when you know the whys of her actions your heart must go out to her. I wish we had her back for a couple of weeks! It would be something to have one American woman who had the *guts*, who *cared enough*, to take an axe to drug pedlars who sell drugs to teen-agers on the streets, or to butt in the stomach and hit over the head with a Bible or a hatchet any of the criminal cowards who sell rotgut and BOOZE to high school children. It is then I love Carry Nation because I am sure she would! Could I suggest to some of the Women Libbers who are so busy knocking a boyfriend down if he tries to open a door for them or designing unisex toys or stampeding to be allowed to liberate their bosoms like the cows that here is a Crusade for Our Children that needs doing and that would bring them hot sympathy and support from every age, color and sex?

How, actually, were we lucky enough *then* to have anybody like Carry Nation happen to us?

The leading obstetrician of the New York Hospital, recognized as one of the greatest in the world, told me that without exception in his work every woman says the same words as soon as she knows her baby has been born.

Is all well with the child?

The right number of fingers, toes, eyes and ears—is the baby all right?

Carry Nation had married late and then only because she wanted a child. Moving in the extraordinary unreal world of her mad Mamma, the Queen, she had never had the usual beaus. At last the words Old Maid reached her as a warning signal that unless she got a husband soon she would never become a mother—and this she found truly heartbreaking. And so she got up her courage and asked her mother to arrange a match of some kind. Somehow David Nation, a part-time lawyer and man-about-town, was selected, the marriage took place and was finally, after some initial difficulties, consummated.

Today of course psychiatrists would have a good deal to say about Carry's mother and about this arranged marriage for her daughter. But arranging marriages was fairly common at the end of the Civil War and there didn't seem to be anything unusual about Carry's. Even a sheltered Southern lady knew a husband was a necessary preliminary to a child—but all too soon Carry found that she had married a problem that, as of our day, would be frankly faced, discussed and solved with less soul anguish and possible aftermath. David Nation turned out to be what we today call an alcoholic—then his fellow drinking companions called him a drunk. What Carry called him came out of the Old Testament. In many speeches later Carry cried out to women, as she swung her little hatchet, that drunkards soon lose their sex impulses, that her own husband had been almost impotent from the curse of whiskey, that his sex relations were soon what Shakespeare refers to as coming often to lame conclusions. Carry shrieked aloud later that in order to become pregnant, to conceive the child she longed for with such real passion, she had to go to him. She had to be the aggressor. With hanging head she would warn other wives and potential mothers that she had taken the First Steps toward motherhood herself. If David Nation—or any other husband —allowed the Demon Rum to slow him down, cause him to pass out before he had performed his marital obligations—well, a woman must do the best she could to keep him awake. Humiliating and painful as it was, this was her *duty* if she wished to become a mother.

Having by these means conceived a child, when that child was born dumb, unable to speak because of locked jaws, Carry blamed it entirely upon her husband's drunkenness and regarded it forever as the curse RUM had transmitted to her poor little baby girl.

Medically, I have checked with Dr. J. R. Spencer, one of California's finest physicians, and I know this is totally impossible. J.R. says that a man is born with his sperm complete already. Nothing can be added to it nor anything taken from it. David Nation, like every other male, was without any power to alter the seeds of his fatherhood; his alcoholic content at the moment of conception could have no effect of any kind upon his child.

Nothing and nobody could ever make Carry Nation believe this. The medical ignorance, the old wives' tales, the misunderstandings of every kind that were prevalent then seem incredible to us in this more enlightened age—but we do know by some experiences of our own that they existed.

Carry had married to have a child; her husband was a drunkard.

Is all well with the child?

No, perhaps it would be better for this little one if she returned to heaven at once. She will never be able to speak.

Six days after this birth, Carry got out of her bed against the pleas of doctor and Jerusha. This time, the first pitched battle of her career, Carry was armed with an umbrella snatched up as she went through the hall. She met the merry men coming home down a snowy lane, a land of lovely fantasy in the moonlight. Merry men they were indeed, singing at the top of their lungs the postwar hit tune, "When Johnny comes marching home again, hurrah, hurrah"—a song that was to follow Carry around the world. Mad mad mad with booze they may have been but it was as of that moment a merry madness—they were capering in the newfallen snow. Only David Nation seemed to be having any trouble. As usual, David had taken one more than his capacity; it rendered his legs something like Charlie Chaplin's. It also made him lift his voice louder than anybody and detached his mental processes from what was actually going on.

Must have. For when he saw his spouse bearing down upon him with her umbrella held high he gave her an affectionate hail.

How ya doin', Carry-baby, he shouted, or something similar.

Carry-baby soon showed him.

If by chance there had been an *axe* used as Carry used her umbrella it would have reduced silly drunken David Nation to hamburger and the lynching of Carry Nation would have been carried out legally.

Shortly thereafter she found her hatchet and set forth to save men—and therefore their wives and children—from the bitter curse that had fallen upon her.

In her middle forties now, she had superabundant long silver-blond hair, which was never quite what was in those days called tidy, she was under five feet and weighed only a little over a hundred pounds and she never wore anything but the most feminine clothes. Laces, ruffles, and pretty colors. A *pretty* woman, observers said, when for a few moments she was quiet enough so you could *see* her.

And we must never forget the enchanting Southern accent. It has some kind of hypnotic influence, as I heard it used by Wallis Warfield Simpson of Virginia on the King of England.

Soon Carry made the front page of a Chicago paper with a cartoon, it showed a bartender crouched behind his counter regarding Carry Nation, brandishing her axe with all-out terror. The caption read:

BUT, MADAME, LIQUOR IS LEGAL IN CHICAGO.

As far as Carry Nation was concerned liquor was never legal anywhere, and she did always what she herself believed.

"You are a madwoman," a judge said to her when she was hauled before him on the usual charges of destruction of property and disturbing the peaceful drinking of American citizens.

"Of course I am," Carry cried. "*One*, because I am a woman. *Two*, because I am sober. *Three*, because I believe it is possible for a sober woman to change the face of the world."

The story moves on from there. Whatever else changes in towns, states, the country, Carry remains the same.

Held in prison once again, three thousand men marched with the avowed intent of getting her out of there so they could get rid of her by the then all-too-often used method of lynching. It was, believe it or not, the men within the prison who saved her. They'd been inside long enough to get sober and Carry turned loose upon them all her charms, all her feminine appeal and apparently some of her seldom used but very effective tears. Standing in the corridors, as the jailors permitted her, she pleaded through the bars from cell to cell—she told them her own story—she spoke to them of their own wives and children. And when she had finished with her rare and fervent eloquence they called her a Queen—they said she ought to be Queen of the World. Her tactics must have been different in this setting and with no hatchet in hand for she so moved the jailors and wardens that they opened all doors and helped form battalions to protect her and soon the so-called Vigilantes had to turn back.

When she got out she moved with the same magnificent inner compulsion, wielded her axe with the same strong hand and sure aim.

Side by side with this is the wonderful, heartbreaking story of the daughter who had been born with jaws locked so that speech would never be possible. All Carry's money went to hospitals and doctors for the girl, she herself often went with love and prayer to see her daughter as she grew into a beautiful young woman—and, in the end, through a series of far-ahead-of-their-time operations, the girl could not only speak but sing. So that Carry could believe the Lord had come to her rescue because she had spent her life upon his work against alcohol.

I never knew Carry Nation. I wish I had.

The entire story about this daffy, difficult, distinguished and dedicated woman came to me, except for one small personal detail, from the brilliant research done for a screenplay by my good friend, Robert Thom, whom you will remember for the Emmy he won for his "Defenders" script on TV and his New York play Compulsion. Robert not only brought me his screenplay but encouraged me to use his material because Carry had fascinated him across the years with her irrepressible spirit and her never-failing gallantry against probably the strongest attack any woman ever had. He found she wasn't just a shrieking virago and insisted she *belonged* in my company of gallant women.

"At a Tavern?" I said. "Might she be too sensational? Suppose she bops Mr. Hearst in the ear. He loved the big tankard of ale, where you took a long drink and it went down a peg and then you passed it on—and I understand Carry Nation wouldn't put up with any booze at all."

"She was an extremist, no doubt," Bob said. "Aren't most of the women you're talking about one-pointed in a cause? Probably Carry left her hatchet on this side and the way I've heard you talk about bars that serve whiskey to underaged children you're one that might pick it up. You ought to have a warm fellow-feeling for Carry and her crusade; you've suffered a lot from alcohol as I understand it. She was trying to do a job you want done. And, while Mr. Hearst may not have had any trouble taking it down a peg and passing it on, he *did* have a drinking problem, didn't he?"

"I—yes," I said, "the name of his drinking problem was Marion Davies. I remember her saying to him, 'I never get cross with *you* when *you* drink,' and to this Mr. Hearst replied, 'No, you only get cross with *me* when *you* drink.'"

"How true that is," Bob Thom said. "Amelia Earhart had *two* drinking problems as you tell her story. The name of one was Father—and of the other The-Man-I-Love, wasn't it? And—surely your best friend Colleen—she'd have great sympathy for Carry even if she brought her hatchet to one of Colleen's elegant scintillating Japanese dinners."

If Colleen Moore hadn't told in detail in her excellent autobiography *Silent Star* how alcohol broke up her first marriage to John McCormick I wouldn't bring it up here. This irrepressibly spirited little Irish girl had married early, a newspaperman who became one of the top producers of his time, finally head of First National Studio, and this was a true love match and one of the finest professional partnerships I ever met up with. It looked ideal but . . .

> The day that was to be the turning point of my life came a couple of weeks later on a Thursday afternoon. I went to the Bel Air house as usual. The servants were off, as well as John's day nurse. The night nurse was due at six. Why I took my chauffeur inside the house I will never

know. But I did, asking him to wait in the hall for me while I went upstairs to John's room.

John was sitting in his large, gold brocade overstuffed chair, his face red and bloated, his mouth hanging loose, his eyes blank and staring straight ahead. He bore no resemblance to the man I had married six years before.

Sitting on the edge of the bed taking in this picture, I said, "John, I want a divorce."

As the words sank in, he turned to look at me. Getting up from his chair, he came over to me and grabbed me by the throat, pushing me back on the bed shouting, "You'll never divorce me!"

Before I could make a sound, his hands closed tight around my neck. The room began to spin. In the hall below, the chauffeur heard John's shout. He rushed upstairs and pulled him away from me. Gasping for breath, I tore down the stairs, the chauffeur following. When we got in the car I was trembling so I couldn't speak.

I was still shaking when we arrived home. My mother made me drink some brandy, saying, "You must never go back again." Then she went to the phone and called our lawyer, telling him to file for divorce.

Right here I remembered suddenly that I had used the name *Carry Nation* as a part of our language to be easily understood by any reader. As we use lynching—which came from a Judge Lynch who recommended it. Or Sandwich from the Earl who invented them. Somewhere in my life story of my father Earl Rogers, called *Final Verdict,* I'd referred to Carry Nation, so I got the book to look it up:

> . . . they were standing there watching Papa and the singer. I think her name was Lou, she was a real nice girl and had no idea what was going on, she was laughing merrily and why not? She and Papa each had a drink in their hands and were about to toss them off when I came in.
>
> Everything stopped. The singer saw something in Papa's face, I guess, she swung around and saw me and Ketchel right behind me. I hadn't had such an easy evening myself, my stomach was still going up and down from being shot at and knocked out and I was fit to be

tied or I probably wouldn't have behaved the way I did. I just walked over and knocked the glass out of his hand and then I turned and knocked the glass out of hers. Like Carry Nation. Then I smacked Papa longside the ear . . .

Fortunately I didn't have a hatchet or an umbrella.

Are there any women, or men for that matter, who have *never* for a moment wanted to have Carry Nation's fire against this curse, as she called it? Never had that frantic anguish and uncontrollable fury of frustration ending with an impulse at least to reach for a hatchet?

It was Isadora's downfall. If Carry had been down there on the Riviera with her little hatchet maybe the first American woman to win European fame could have fulfilled her dream of the Isadora Duncan Schools for children of all races and colors, maybe today we would have more peace and understanding between those nations who danced with their hearts and with irrepressible spirit.

Judy Garland—as great a genius as Hollywood ever produced— maybe if she'd met Carry and Carry could have spoken from her heart to Judy's, maybe Judy would have been able to fly over the rainbow.

So—you can see—when I read Robert Thom's screenplay, after I had finished it and sat shaken by its impact, I knew that, Tavern or no Tavern, there was *no way* to leave Carry Nation out of this cast of gallant American women.

"She cared," I said to Bob. "She *cared*. I am so tired of people who don't care."

"They don't mean much, do they?" Bob said. "I love the way she died. How people die is, to me, very important. They should be allowed to die in their own time and their own way and not be degraded by a prolonged keeping of the body half-alive by mechanics, after the soul has winged its way—all right, over the rainbow. Wherever that is."

"I think," I said, "death has a right to its own courage and dignity and self-respect."

"Carry's last words ought to be immortal," Bob said. "When you read them, you are compelled to believe she knew she was doing God's work."

"You've written that she said them with an *enchanting smile* and *Papa* said it was an enchanting smile . . ."

"Do you mean your father knew Carry Nation?" Bob said.

And so I could contribute my own bit to this saga.

"Papa went somewhere once in California to get Carry Nation out of jail. I must have been too little to know about it, because I don't remember it at all. She came to California early in her career, I think, long before she went to Europe. Is that scene in your play where she supposedly got into the Throne Room or somewhere and delivered her irrepressible spirited speech to King Edward VII true or entirely your imagination?"

"It could have happened," Bob said. "She was there, so it probably did. You know Carry by now. Did your father admire her work?"

"He—wouldn't admit it exactly, would he?" I said. "But of course my godfather Jack London wrote the best book of all time against alcohol—*John Barleycorn.* Except perhaps Robert Louis Stevenson—you have to see that his *Dr. Jekyll and Mr. Hyde* was actually about alcohol—the drink Dr. Jekyll took that turned him into Mr. Hyde was what Carry Nation called BOOZE. I've seen it do just that many a time. And I do love the way she dies," I said and read it from the script:

> CARRY (with an enchanting smile): Early in life, I decided that the way to die was as the flowers did. Standing up! I think I can do that now. I am standing up like a flower and say to you—*I have done what I could!*

"You have to love her for that," I said, and found it a little difficult to speak.

"You can ask her how she managed it if you invite her to the Tavern," Bob said.

"If—" I said, "but of course I will."

And quite literally I find myself having cold chills at the thought that I *might* have forgotten to ask her. As sometimes you do forget to ask your best friend or something.

She has to be a best friend to me. I haven't had a drink in thirty years but I am an alcoholic myself.

Chapter Four

This—is Hollywood!

And its gallant lady who belongs among the greatest.

Does this girl belong? I said to myself, remembering the depths, dangers, disgraces and disaster on her record. Does she belong with this goodly company of saints and successes, angels of mercy and ministers of grace and philanthropists and pioneers? Oh yes, that very track record is *why* Judy Garland has a number one right here, for hers is no untested spirit, no phony gallantry displayed like a flourished cape. With her life, as with her song, she gave us love—and hope. Without an ability to get up off the floor swinging, without courage which kept her in there in spite of the pains and perils that beset genius, she would have vanished early and been forgotten.

She did, as a matter of fact, vanish a goodly number of times—she was fired, she tried suicide, she spent months in hospitals—and then suddenly there she was again, the most beloved of stars.

Also in those jammed and jostled years she produced two daughters who are now stars—Liza Minnelli and Lorna Luft—*and* one of the two immortal movies—the other is *Gone With the Wind*. Judy Garland's is, of course, *The Wizard of Oz*.

Little Judy Garland is dead. As things go she died young, worn out with living. But *Dorothy*, Dorothy of Oz, will never die, thank God. Every year as long as the world lasts millions upon millions of children, some for the first time, some repeaters, some grown-ups like me, who look forward to it all year long, we all still see

Dorothy on the Yellow Brick Road with the Tin Woodman and the Scarecrow and the Cowardly Lion.

And Dorothy is always Judy Garland and had to be; I can think of nineteen other actresses who could have played it one after the other, a new one every few years, and people would say Oh yes, I saw it with so and so or this one or that one, as they do of Peter Pan, and pretty soon it would have been forgotten.

Every year we have heard, do hear and will hear, we hope, that warm throbbing moving voice that is so much too big for her, as a robin's song seems too big for him, puff up his little throat as he may. She tells us from a full heart that somewhere over the rainbow way up high there's a land that we heard of once in a lullaby and we believe her. Then when she holds out her hands and cries *Birds fly over the rainbow, why—oh why—can't I?* our hearts break and we rush up and climb over the footlights as we never have for anybody else and say Oh you can, Judy, we love you so, Judy—we'll help you fly over the rainbow—

The very first time she walked onto a stage she held out her hands just that way. She was two and a half years old that time. For over forty years she kept prancing onto stages everywhere, in studios, in movie theaters, on Broadway, in London, and always by her own magic she made you believe it was unexpected and unrehearsed and for real.

As it was that first time when at two and a half she stood in the dark wings and watched the Gumm sisters, Sue and Virginia, who were in reality her own sisters as well as a vaudeville team, out there where it was so beautiful and where the footlights gleamed and glowed. And out there also were people, people to love, people to sing to, people to applaud and love you back—and so *tiny* Judy-Garland-to-be decided that was the place for her, not back here in the dark. So out she went, prancing, dancing, and singing the only song Frances Gumm knew—

> "Jingle bells, jingle bells,
> Jingle all the way,
> Oh what *fun* it is to ride
> In a one-horse open shay—"

A Star Is Born!
From then on she kept doing the same thing—different songs, to

be sure, "San Francisco" and "I'm Going to Love You" and "I Can't Give You Anything But Love"—but it was the same thing!

"All the years I was on the stage," Judy told me once, "I was always waiting to make that entrance and I could hardly *wait*." And always, until that one terrible night in Las Vegas I can hardly bear to remember, with the same result.

The audience loved her!

Judy's story is hard to follow and you will soon see why.

Most of it happened in Hollywood, but even when it was *out* of Hollywood, it was still *Hollywood*, not the Hollywood of today, which has only a few stars scattered in its heavens. Not the Hollywood of TV and commercials and more realism than you really want to know about and less romance than your hungry heart longs for.

The Hollywood of which Clark Gable was King.

That Hollywood had heroes.

It had *a* heroine. One of America's gallant spirited women who was undefeated and undefeatable.

Her name was Judy Garland, as I've already told you, and in that Hollywood of love, laughter and tears Judy lived *nine* lives. Nine different people, she was; in her short span as a shooting star she managed to cram more living, loving, singing and dancing, mothering, ups and downs and, unfortunately, uppers and downers, than any other woman of whom I have knowledge. I mean, Amelia Earhart only had one life to give for her country, but Judy somehow personally or professionally—and those lives are so interwoven you will see how difficult it is ever to separate them—managed to die and live again in every one of her lives.

A Star.

A Star was born when she sang "Jingle Bells." Always whether she was two and a half or twenty-nine and a fourth or as on that historic night at the Palace when she made the first of her great comebacks, or that last time at forty-seven-going-on-forty-eight—when she sang "Somewhere, over the rainbow" at the Palladium in London—

How can you have a rainbow without rain?

There was rain in all of Judy's lives but—every time she sang *Somewhere*—A Star was born again—and again—

The first time I ever saw her she was prancing again, this time around a football field, and I wasn't sure whether she was a drum majorette or the left guard. My brother Bogart Rogers was making this football picture called *Pigskin Parade* for Twentieth Century-Fox and he was shooting on the gridiron at Hollywood High School where he and our kid brothers Thornwell and Bryson had all played on the team. Soon I saw the little girl waving a baton, as far as I could see she was perfectly square, then I heard her singing a fight-on song in a voice that *literally* sent shivers up and down my spine. But I said to myself, all college songs do that to me—"Cheer, Cheer for Old Notre Dame" and "Sons of the Stanford Red" and "March, March on Down the Field, Fighting for Eli." Just the same I went and asked my brother Bo who she was.

He said Oh some kid that's been around singing at Elks Club Smokers and Chamber of Commerce banquets in small towns and bum vaudeville—she's only about twelve or fourteen, or some such, he said, and she's got a voice all right, poor kid, if she was only a little more *attractive*—I suppose if somebody told her to take off about forty or fifty pounds—

Ida Koverman, Louis B. Mayer's other self, heard her in *Pigskin Parade*, and Mr. Mayer told her to take off those pounds and showed her *how*.

Now begins another of her professional lives.

Let me stop to identify all of them in one, as her true status in the overall history of Hollywood and the final, to date, picture of the Movies.

I quote the best authorities there are, as you will recognize.

Fred Astaire, on the set of *Easter Parade* with Judy:

> "Judy Garland is the greatest entertainer who ever lived or probably ever will live."

Noel Coward, one time in New York, referring back to the night he'd seen Judy at the Palace in the first of her comebacks:

> "There have been three great entertainers. Al Jolson, Frank Sinatra and Judy Garland. Of course the greatest of these is Garland."

President John F. Kennedy during his term in office, and Judy's advent into television:

"We have changed our dinner hour at the White House so we can watch your show," President Kennedy, who knew a great deal about TV himself, told her. "Everyone at Hyannis Port listens, too. It is our favorite show. It is everybody's favorite show."

Louis B. Mayer, top Hollywood producer of all time, and production head of the Metro-Goldwyn-Mayer studios during Judy Garland's eleven years there as a top star:

"There has never been any other motion picture star to equal Judy Garland in genius and love of the public. The bitterest moment of my life was when I had to let her go."

To try to be chronological, Judy had spent the years between "Jingle Bells" and the day Ida Koverman saw *Pigskin Parade* and walked her onto the MGM lot doing whatever she and her sisters could find to do. Now, with *Love Finds Andy Hardy* and *The Wizard of Oz*, the youngest Gumm sister became a Movie Star of magnitude. During those eleven years at Metro, Judy Garland married briefly first a young bandleader named David Rose, chiefly because he was a bandleader as far as I could see, and then Vincente Minnelli, a sensitive, idealistic musical director-composer, and that lasted long enough for Liza to be born. Later, in another life, she married Sid Luft, an ex-RCAF pilot, and had two more children.

While it is out of sequence—and I defy anybody to put Judy and her nine lives in sequence—I would like to put something here that is true all the time, that never falters or alters no matter what men, money or merchandizing is going on. Judy Garland was always the most loving, the most *caring*, the most devoted and thoughtful and concerned mother of any professional woman I ever knew.

My grandmother used to say, and I have quoted her perhaps too frequently but it seems to apply so often, that the modern woman is trying to drive three mules and that in Ireland there is a proverb that this is impossible. Of those three, husband, children, and job or career, as Judy was trying to drive them, she told me that the happiest time in her personal life was once when she wasn't

working in London and could take the three children, Liza Minnelli and Lorna and Joseph Luft, to Battersea Park every afternoon
to play with the dogs. The children always came first, she said,
and then her work—we didn't talk about the husbands.

It was along about 1949, when Liza was four or five, and Judy's
magnitude as a movie star was at its most brilliant, that one day
Howard Strickling, then head of Metro-Goldwyn-Mayer's publicity, came to see me.

I was under contract to MGM at the time as a story writer and
consultant for Clark Gable. And as my work was fairly easy I am
sure Mr. Mayer felt I'd be glad to do something for him and he
was right. Moreover he knew that, like everybody else, I adored
Judy.

"You worked for Harry Anslinger in the Federal Bureau of
Narcotics in Washington, didn't you?" Howard said. "We thought
maybe you knew some of the narcotics boys here—and Mr. Mayer
wondered whether you'd give us a hand with Judy."

Judy?

Judy Garland?

I had been through all this once before with that other genius,
Mabel Normand—then, too, rumor had loved a shining mark. Of
late I'd heard some tales that Judy was fooling around with the
stuff. In fact, a scandal sheet whose name I've forgotten had
printed a few facts and figures, times and places to show she was
hooked, but I still couldn't figure *how* and I didn't want to believe
it. Now looking at the lines of pain cut into Howard's face I had to
know there was something.

From the terrace of my house on the Hill, where Howard and
I sat, I could see my beloved rose garden. Clark had started it by
bringing me a rosebush to be planted there instead of a box of cut
roses—those dark red General MacArthurs were his, and the
Peace Roses were from little Liz Taylor who'd been to lunch one
day, but the pink-gold Radiance was from Judy.

I sat thinking, wondering how many of the great public that
jammed the magnificent Movie Palaces all over our country at that
time realized that all the gold and glamour and truly fine motion
pictures being made at MGM then, all the stars who were created
and publicized and worked for by huge staffs, all the operations of

the biggest motion picture lot ever known, making four hundred pictures a year, all this was based on two very young stars. Mickey Rooney as Andy Hardy. Judy Garland sometimes costarring with him but mostly singing "Over the Rainbow." They were the foundation, the rock, on which the Art and the Industry of that biggest studio in Hollywood were built, because of them all the more spectacular stars and features were possible.

"We used to get off in a corner," Judy told me once, "and see if we could figure out a way to get the best of Mr. Mayer. He was a Grown Up. We tried to think up Mischief—with him as the target."

Judy followed the Yellow Brick Road and Mickey Andy Hardy Rooney walked up the street of the town where he went to school and his father, the Judge (that much loved actor Lewis Stone), had his courtroom there and his mother baked apple pies.

It was pretty doggone pure Americana as it was then and America loved it and paid real money at the box office to see it.

"We were *actually* only kids," Mickey Rooney told me when he was a grown man. "When we were making Andy Hardy—Judy played my girl in some of those, remember—we used to brag about our salary checks. Neither of us could count up to a hundred or multiply, or divide it—we had allowances and Mr. Mayer was trying to put our money in trust funds for us."

Afterwards, when disaster struck, there was a charge that Mr. Mayer worked her too hard, but that isn't—never was—true. I was on the MGM lot myself a lot of that time, close to those who were there all the time like Joan Crawford and Spencer Tracy, and though faults Mr. Mayer as its head may have had, working a box office gold mine into a danger zone wasn't one of them. His protection of his—and Metro's—properties was the best in the business.

True, Judy was burning the candle at both ends and she was at the studio twenty hours a day sometimes. You couldn't get Judy to *go home*. Matter of fact, she had no home to go to, in the sense of a place that was hers, that was open to guests, that offered her what we called a home life. Despite her two attempts at marriage the only life she knew, the only place she had, the only friends or social circle that were ever really part of her life then was the Studio. On the lot, was our trade term for it. That was bad. More than anything, Judy wanted to sing and dance, she needed people of course to sing and dance with. Nobody gave her any of this comradeship or conversation or gaiety off the lot, in what was, I suppose, The Private Life of Judy Garland, so she came back to the Studio—or stayed there, more likely.

When I try now to associate Judy with a *home*—with a regular life away from the great sprawling studio which was alive, active, and working twenty-four hours a day—I find I can't.

I think of Jean Harlow—and there's that glorious all-white castle on a hill where she lived. I think of Clark Gable and remember at once the little ranch and friendly home-like farmhouse out in the San Fernando Valley. Of Crawford, and a Beverly Hills mansion and a most distinguished Crawford apartment ready on Fifth Avenue opposite the Park. Of Colleen Moore and her Bel Air estate with the pool, tennis court, small theater in which to run movies. If you think of Marion Davies, there is the Hearst Castle at San Simeon, her own Beverly Hills mansion and the beach house on the ocean front at Santa Monica that later became a hotel.

I can't remember any house or home where Judy Garland lived. I just telephoned Howard Strickling at his ranch in Chino where he now lives and neither can he. What I connected Judy with, and still do, was the super-plush bungalow Mr. Mayer built for her on the lot when she *wouldn't* go home.

At the studio Judy was always with the Musicians, wonderful in their way but troublesome. Judy suffered from insomnia. They all had insomnia too. Never knew what was going on outside their small world.

"Who actually ever came to any harm through overworking?" That was what Spencer Tracy said when I asked him if he thought Judy had been overworked. He said, "There are always contributing factors outside the work." At that time, Mr. Louis B. Mayer was the highest paid executive in the nation, not just in the motion picture industry, in *any* industry. Only a brainless idiot would have killed off a star with a long prosperous future, and I was there a good deal of the time and I know Mr. Mayer was always trying to protect her.

How *did* she get hooked?
The contributing factors?

"You might," Howard Strickling had said, "have a talk with her. You've always been a good friend of hers. And—honestly, you'd be surprised how ignorant and—sort of unsophisticated Judy *is*. Do you know she's never even been to New York?"

If I was to help Judy, before I went to see her I had to try to answer those questions. Here is what I found:

First—No home and no philosophy of life of any kind.

Second—A little girl trying to grow up without either and, as I will prove to you, an inferiority complex of all things.

Third—The constant hourly day and night fight against weight, which we didn't know as much about then as we do now.

Fourth—When she really did fall in love, poor baby, she picked the wrong man, or he picked her.

Some of this I found out from others, some I knew myself, but when I took the most important, the first step in trying to understand what philosophy of life she had been taught, what inner impulses or influences we could appeal to—

I couldn't find any.

I moved as quietly as I could. I realized she hadn't been taught any religion, any philosophy, nothing like that. The four women, she and her mother and her two sisters, just went hurrying and scurrying around the country trying the best way they knew how to make a living. No home except her studio bungalow. No education except what she got in the MGM school after she came to Hollywood. No wonder Judy always kidded about being a *bad kid*. I'm a bad kid sometimes, she used to say.

This was a strange child-woman, half-grown-up as a star, trying to grow up as a girl—that I had seen for myself.

Let me show you what I mean.

It happened at a party at Eddie Mannix's house when Gable came home from the war. Judy was there.

Judy, just turned twenty but still not looking out of her teens, Judy in a long black dress with *sequins* no less. Long black gloves and her face painted like a signboard. At first I thought the outfit had to be from Wardrobe and then I saw that far from being a *gag* this was Judy done up to make a play for Clark Gable. Like

every other female from six to one hundred and six on or off the
MGM lot, Judy had a crush on Clark, now that Carole was dead
in that shocking airplane accident on a tour selling war bonds,
every woman alive felt he needed a good wife and was willing.
Thinking back, if Judy had come as Little Girl Lost or Dorothy
of Oz, Clark's heart was so empty of his only love, he was such a
sentimental pushover and about as sophisticated himself as the
Man of La Mancha . . . As it was, he took one look at little Miss
Sequins, put her over his knee, literally, and spanked her. In answer to which she made the best-selling record "Dear Mr. Gable."
If you can find a copy anywhere, play it—then you'll understand
exactly what I mean.

Two people always. Dr. Jekyll and Mrs. Hyde. Split personality.
Judy Garland Movie Star, and Little Girl Lost in a lonely world.
Both had irrepressible spirit, and Judy was doing her gallant best
to stay on her feet between them.

JUDY GARLAND

IN

STRIKE UP THE BAND   MEET ME IN ST. LOUIS

EASTER PARADE

Idolized by vast audiences. How could she have been hooked
on and with that absurd idea called an inferiority complex?

Note this. Star or no star, on the same lot at the same time were
Elizabeth Taylor, the most beautiful girl born since Helen of Troy,
Joan Crawford the most spectacularly gorgeous of all Our Dancing Daughters, the incomparable Garbo, the all-time platinum
blonde sex symbol, Jean Harlow, the Swedish Norse maiden Ingrid Bergman—this is as first class competition as ever gathered
in one place, men being what they are.

It was Joan Crawford who told me that Judy had grown up
convinced that with her forty-nine-inch fanny (which was always
on her mind since she was always trying to *reduce* it), and her
funny face, she would never get a beau.

"She told me when she first came on the lot that she thought
she looked like a polliwog about to become a frog," Joan who
was devoted to Judy said sadly, "and it had a sort of *cartoon*
truth about it."

"But Judy—Judy had lots of beaus," I said.

"Musicians," Joan said, "that's no good."

"Everybody adores Judy," I said. "It's ridiculous."

"Nothing a girl with Judy's imagination can convince herself of is ridiculous," Joan said. "Could be those two musical marriages of hers were just to prove something to herself. If Judy ever finds the right man— But I don't like this young New Yorker that's hanging around there all the time now."

"Around where?" I said.

"Her dressing room," Joan said furiously "where else has she—or is she?"

"Who is the man?" I said.

"He's a writer or producer or something. I've known his type in New York for years. What's he doing with *Judy?* If I'm not mistaken—"

Joan was rarely mistaken about men. She wasn't mistaken about this one.

She'll have to take off some weight, Mr. Mayer had said—and he was absolutely right. And who, in those days, had ever heard of amphetamines—a drug taken to help *reduce* and "to stimulate the central nervous system"?

Certainly neither Mr. Mayer nor Judy Garland. For years Judy dieted and exercised, and went *hungry* and *sleepless*.

But the sophisticated young man from New York told her later. No need, he told her, to go through all this hell of diet and denial. I don't care whether or not Mr. Mayer says No Pills. That's just because he is so entirely provincial. A girl I knew in New York lost forty pounds in two months without all this fuss. It's so easy, he said. In no time you can be as slim and elegant as she was.

And there was Little Girl Lost running around as a top Movie Star trying to lose weight.

Insomnia.

Weight.

And then the young man from New York.

I had a talk with Mickey Rooney, surely he could give me a better line on Judy than anybody. Not only costars but best

friends. A little wearily, he agreed that somebody better look
after her. He didn't name any names but I remember that he gave
me a long classic speech about how this world perils young genius, how often it is preyed upon. If, he said, you look back you
can see it happening to Byron, Shelley, Keats, Mozart, even Le-
onardo da Vinci. Playing on young people's weaknesses is a profession like picking pockets or drug running, he said.

I wanted, of course, to talk to the narcotic agents I knew; from
my knowledge of the Washington policies directed by Harry
Anslinger, they wouldn't want to destroy Judy and I soon found
they didn't. All they wanted was to help her get off the stuff—
they wanted the sellers, not the poor deluded users. Then we had
none of the present-day illusions about *drugs* as a pastime. The
Drug Traffic has spent billions—sometimes Mafia billions per month
—to promote all sorts of fairy tales about drugs and how harmless
and sophisticated and *up* they can be. We knew then that they
were a deadly menace to health, morals, happiness and success.
Anslinger, a great man, wanted the Big Guys. Jack White, head
of the narcotics squad in New York when I worked there, never
got over the shock that after Lucky Luciano was sent back to Italy
his place as head of the Drug Syndicate was taken by a woman. He
arrested her one night on a roller coaster in a Palisades Amusement
Park and told me later he shouted at her. There should be Capital
Punishment for you!

At once, I found out that all the agents wanted was for Judy to
quit using phony prescriptions, or forged doctor's signatures. They
wanted to know, if possible, how high up she had contacts.
They loved Judy. It hurt them. One of them said to me, "We'll
put away everybody we can find. But that's no good if she's still
hooked. *Do something.*"

> But there were no flowers as beautiful as these big scarlet
> poppies. "Aren't they beautiful?" the girl asked as she
> breathed the spicy scent . . . and so they kept walking
> until Dorothy could stand it no longer, her eyes closed
> in spite of herself and she forgot where she was and fell
> among the *poppies* fast asleep. "If we leave her here, she
> will die," said the Cowardly Lion. "Let us make a chair
> with our hands and carry her," said the Scarecrow.

"The Deadly Poppy Field," that chapter is called.

Opium—the juice of the *Poppy* and its most important narcotic principal morphine.

If we leave her here, she will die.

Isn't it incredible, staggering, unbelievable, how there is never any way to separate Judy from Dorothy of Oz? As you will know her for all time.

And out of nowhere into the here comes Van Johnson's awed voice saying, "Boy, have you seen the new dressing bungalow the Boss has fixed up for Judy Garland?"

The drawing room was a lovely French gray, gilt chairs with petit-point backs and seats, white bearskin rugs and enough flowers in gold and crystal vases to fill a shop. I adored a rose-pink azalea and I mention it here because of what happened later. This elegant room was connected with spacious wardrobes, dressing rooms, bathroom with walls and ceilings of mirrors, a royal bedroom in radiant pink and everywhere subdued magical lighting. Oh, she had everything, this big MGM star.

When I arrived by appointment a girl from the publicity department, skinny and hostile, was there. I had my first suspicion of her because nobody from Howard Strickling's publicity department should be hostile to me. She kept watching Judy all the time and somehow that reporter sense was making me alert, watchful, where this girl was concerned. Also she was too familiar with Miss Garland—after all, the girl was a fairly minor member of publicity and I wondered what she was doing there instead of Dorothy Blanchard, a charming and kindly woman who was the unit director for Garland's publicity. This girl was too—too skinny for comfort.

I saw myself in a mirror—you couldn't help but see yourself in a mirror—and I was too skinny too, and it seemed to me I'd been wearing that blue tailored suit or one just like it for *years*. The truth is I was paralyzed with terror. Why *me*? What was I doing here? I must be cast for the Cowardly Lion. Oh sure, Judy and I were friends, but not that close, like Colleen and I. But then I couldn't think of any close woman friend Judy had. The only one really close was Mickey Rooney and I supposed this was a woman's job.

If we leave her here . . .

That's who the girl from the publicity department reminds me of—the Wicked Witch of the West.

And it is Mr. Mayer who is the Cowardly Lion, he doesn't want to leave her here to die, but after all he is the Head of Production and all the money men in New York—*the New York Office*, as we called it, Nick Schenck and Bob Rubin and those boys—they keep at him all the time! This too I'd pinned down before I came to my meeting with Judy.

If you remember what Louis B. Mayer looked like, as I do, it is the face of an old-line Jewish prophet, always with a worried frown, meditating perhaps on the Lost Tribes, and you will find that you can put it on Bert Lahr's Cowardly Lion. So he gets more worried and more cowardly all the time, but keeps right on going. Chased as he now was by the New York Office, which was always impatient with delays, upsets, temperaments, star scandals so costly in making movies, he understood what it took to keep *Stars* working, able to work, willing to and confident in their work.

Millions and months of Garland had had to be scrapped.

On one picture she couldn't finish, the loss sounded like the national debt. The production of *Annie Get Your Gun*, in which she was scheduled to star, was held up on her account for years (literally) while writers, directors, casts, cameramen were on salary. Finally they gave up on Judy and made it with Betty Hutton, who couldn't possibly get back at the box office what had been invested. *Summer Stock* took four times its budget. Once, I remember, Judy kept Fred Astaire, whose salary was not peanuts, waiting four weeks for a rehearsal. Fred was among those who tried hardest to help Judy both because he was fond of her and because, as I have said, he regarded her as a genius. Judy—like that other genius, Mabel Normand—had real magic. If you can handle it, no price is too high.

But the great, the incomparable Judy Garland is becoming a liability instead of an asset. The New York Office thinks only in terms of liability and asset. Judy is holding up production on pictures now sometimes to the tune of millions. No star can do that! Sitting in that gilt chair looking at Judy I realized that, no matter how much Mr. Mayer tried, how much he loved her, they'd force his hand if this went on.

Me, I guess I am the queen of the Field Mice that got Dorothy out of the Deadly Poppy Field.

I told the publicity girl I'd come to do an interview and she left, finally, and Judy and I exchanged a few harmless remarks. Judy's dialogue was different! B-Picture Noel Coward. What was all this? The simplicity was gone, she was being sophisticated. This was the kind of thing Joan Crawford did well in *Our Modern Maidens*. I began to cry like a field mouse, and Judy came and put her arms around me and then I was shaking her shoulders, I heard myself crying out, "Judy, you've got to wake up. If you stay here you will die—" and she gave me a push and went to look out the window into a silly little garden and a studio street with sets on both sides. The California sunshine was merciless. Dorothy of Oz was—a woman? Not Little Girl Lost any more— a woman, a woman who looked almost her twenty-seven years, a woman with haggard cheeks and—the flame in her dust was low, it was almost out, a sick and miserable woman and of course nobody ever visualized Dorothy as a *woman* at all.

After a while she said harshly, "I thought you were a live-and-let-live gal, then why don't you?"

"Live and let die—" I said, and she broke in, "All right, live and let die, but it's my life and my business and why don't you mind your own?"

"You're one of a kind, Judy," I said. "Everybody knows that about you. Do you realize that at this moment more people *love* you than have ever loved any girl in the world? You give out so much love to them and they give it back! Doesn't that mean anything to you?"

She began to laugh, she began to say, "You're still a sob sister" —and hysteria showed in flashes like lightning, but I thought No no—Judy Garland doesn't play Tragedy and this is sheer stark tragedy—no no, why am I here? This is like an inquisition— Dorothy with the Winged Monkeys isn't here any more—Judy had begun to talk and it was like slow lava coming over the sides of a volcano—all the Garland *power* was there, it had been kept in now too long, I saw that, we were too late all of us—

"I love him," she said, and the famous familiar throb was there like a—like a dreadful burlesque of itself—"Do you know anything about loving a man? It isn't anything that has anything to do with anything else. Can't you understand that? Maybe it only happens to you once in your life and it's neither good nor bad nor anything, it's all life and breath and everything. He loves me. With all his experiences with girls, all the beautiful sophisticated women he's known all around the world, he loves *me* and it's the first time he's ever really been in love—and if I can—I have to learn to be—I'm so stupid and awkward and inexperienced and I don't know *anything*—"

And all this came from the great actress, the star, the girl who could move millions, and it was beamed on me, and I was buffeted by it until I felt dizzy and—useless—and helpless—

I suppose it is a simple-enough, oft-repeated story.

You've read about Don Juan and the Marquis de Sade and Louis the Sun King—how they were entranced by Innocence and the temptation of their lives was to debauch it. I remember well a great tale by Elizabeth Robins called "My Little Sister" about a rich and powerful man who had to be fed virgins and innocents. It was—has been through the centuries—a well-known, twisted and perverted and sophisticated form of sex indulgence—I forget what the psychiatrists call it. I suppose in this era we have changed it around to *Lolita,* who is the one who does the debauching, but for many centuries, as I say, it had been the other way around. The temptation of a great and shining Movie Star who was literally as factually innocent as a child, who had always worked and lived inside a small town called a Movie Lot, who'd never had anyone really to advise her, no one in whom she could confide, the temptation to laugh and say with the Wicked Witch, "I can make her my slave for she does not know how to use her power for good" must—to give this man a modicum of attempted understanding—yes, the temptation must have been very grave indeed.

To Sophisticate; to pervert; rob of simplicity—

I'm glad now to remember that in the middle of Judy's impassioned speech—*he loves me and it's the first time he's ever been*

*in love—if I can learn to be—*in the middle of this I exploded.
There flowed from me all the hell I knew and had seen. I told her
something *about* drug addiction and the great minds and careers
it had destroyed. I told her a few plain truths about "sophistica-
tion" and its dangers. I told her what I'd never told anyone before,
about my father and how he'd come to use a drug, and how he'd
said If I can't be Earl Rogers I'd rather be dead and so I had lost
him too soon, and I said, It'll be like that with you, Judy, You'll
say if I can't be Judy Garland and sing for them I'd rather be
dead—Papa died at fifty—

As it turned out, she beat him by three years. Judy was only
forty-seven.

I have an echo in my brain, a memory echo, my own voice
saying, "If this low bastard loves you, would he play these kinds of
games with you? Circuses and French post cards and drugs to
hallucinate you or make you hear and see things you don't, to
drag you down into the depths—*that's* love? New ways to stimulate and release your emotions! Oh Judy, you know that's a pack
of lies. That's calling evil good and *that's* the sin against the Holy
Ghost, the one for which there is no forgiveness. He isn't a man,
Judy, he's a mangy coyote with rabies and you are Judy Garland
the one of a kind who—when you sing our hearts fly over the
rainbow and the blue bird of happiness comes and if that's *corny*
I can't help it."

We held each other a long moment.

And she wiped the tears from my face.

She handed me a couple of fake prescriptions and we—oh yes—
we tore them up. But—it didn't do any good.

That day until I got back to Howard's office, I managed to
hold my rage and pain and determination to *Do something* within
myself. But Howard says now that when I arrived there I had
only one intention, to murder that girl from his department
whom nobody had ever suspected of being a drug addict and
pusher, to earn her own had-to-have shots, and if I could get my
hands on the man I— But he had gone back to New York.

I often wonder what it could be like to be an older man, as he
is now, and *remember* things like that. I think that when occasionally I see him, or used to, in a New York restaurant. But

I suppose if you can do those things in the first place, the memory
of them doesn't disturb you.

The rose-pink azalea arrived that evening at my home on the
Hill. The card said *I love you, Judy*. When I reported this to
Howard and Mr. Mayer the next morning they said the azalea
showed that since she sent it *after* my challenge, after I'd tried to
reduce her love affair to garbage, she was willing to try.

The fight was on.

At studio expense—or his own maybe—Mr. Mayer sent her to
a famed clinic in Boston. Ida Koverman, Mr. Mayer's right and
left hands, his chief of political activity, his head of staff, his talent
scout and almost everything else that came along, went to Boston
with her. Ida was as fine a woman as I ever knew. She was a
practicing Christian Scientist. I know from her and because of her
how much love and prayer went with Judy and stayed with her
all those months. When they came back, Ida told me that her courage and humor had been beyond belief. "She was always trying
to help others over their tough spots." Since I know a good deal
about withdrawals—it's hell and anguish—when I heard about
this upsurge of Judy's spirit, I knew what that meant.
Well, we won that one.
But—a war is a war is a war. A battle leaves ravaged nerves,
strange fears, and, as Wellington said, Nothing is as bad as a battle
lost except a battle won. Combat soldiers cry out in the night,
children whose mothers refuse to leave on a light in the dark see
goblins and things that go bump in the night, even when the Tin
Woodman and the Scarecrow had carried Dorothy out of the
Deadly Poppy Field . . .

> The Tin Woodman saw a strange beast come bounding
> out of the grass and it was indeed a great yellow wild cat,
> its ears lying low and its mouth wide open showing rows
> of ugly teeth while its red eyes glowed like balls of fire
> . . . so the Woodman raised his axe and as the wild cat
> ran by he cut the beast's head from it body . . .

Judy too was surrounded by help, as though we were trying to
protect that lovely flame, to keep it safe. Mr. Mayer, Howard,

the boys on the narcotics squad, her directors Joe Pasternak and
Norman Taurog, Ida Koverman. Mickey was on call to fill the
hours with chatter and laughter. Van Johnson used to take her
down to the beach and accompany her on all the rides, especially
her favorite the roller coaster—come to think of it, it's amazing
how like a ride on one her life was.

Now the Cowardly Lion had to run fast to save himself.

1949—that was the year Mr. Mayer sent her to the Boston
Clinic. In 1950 along came *Show Boat* as a studio production of
vast expense. Like the Cowardly Lion, Mr. Mayer always had
more courage than he knew he had, he couldn't leave Judy there
helpless, he went back at risk of his own life, running back and
forth, listening to the shrieks of protest from Schenck, Dietz,
Rubin in New York who didn't want to take any more of these
gigantic risks on Judy. They weren't, Bob Rubin said to me,
chances or risk any more, they were sure disaster. But L. B. Lion
dug in his claws and said they had to give her and MGM one more
opportunity.

Nobody, he said, could make *Show Boat* the way she could.

As soon as Judy got back on the lot, Mr. Mayer sent for her to
discuss it.

Now discussing a story with Mr. Mayer was something! An
experience I've never had with anybody else. I was in his office
one day discussing a story when in came Greer Garson. She was
unhappy at being asked to star in *Mrs. Miniver*. She didn't want
to play a woman old enough to be the mother of a war-age son,
even though she *was*. Old enough, I mean. Greer never was in-
discreet enough to get herself a child. That day with Mr. Mayer
she was being younger than springtime, *she* thought, and to show
her the audience appeal of the Miniver part, Mr. Mayer got up
and gave a performance Garson never came anywhere near.

Carlton Alsop, who was present in person when Judy Garland
came in to discuss *Show Boat*, told me Mr. Mayer gave his most
persuasive pitch, to prove to her that this would put her back at
the very top, if she'd settle down and go to work and put the
picture first—and he came around from behind that massive desk
and began to sing

"We could make believe I love you"

And, Carlton said, it ought to have been funny and maybe it was, because he and Judy began to laugh together as they did a duet

"and make believe you love me"

and then of course they began to cry and Judy said, "There there, L.B., don't you cry. I'll do it for you, of course I will—listen—" and the golden voice began to Make Believe and it wasn't Make Believe any longer. Judy's magic made it real. Real love—real joy—Oh, Judy!

So the flame was high.

We all forgot in her magic that the problem that had dogged her since she came on the lot as a little girl was still with her. She was back to her "forty-nine-inch fanny" and in no condition to fight that weight with hunger. Finally with the help of the Pills she'd been told *never* to use, she got her behind slim but then she kept collapsing. The man she loved—that only-man-I-ever-loved number that all women do—had left her flat as soon as he got her sophisticated enough to be in real trouble.

JUDY GARLAND ATTEMPTS SUICIDE

Eleven years after she first sang "Over the Rainbow," Mr. Mayer released her from her MGM contract. This wasn't another suspension, a third-fourth-fifth warning. Driven by the New York Office and his own discouraged hopelessness, this was final and irrevocable and Irving Thalberg once told me L.B. cried like a baby when he did it.

It looked as though as a Movie Star Judy Garland had died there in the deadly field of Poppies.

We hadn't gotten her out in time.

About a year later.

Metro-Goldwyn-Mayer terminated Judy Garland's contract in 1950.

Nobody else offered her a dime to make a motion picture.

And it was in the fall of 1951 that I was walking up and down and back and forth and stopping now and again to look out the

window. Down twenty-two stories into Forty-ninth Street, I
could see the lights of Broadway on one side, and the entrance to
Madison Square Garden on the other.

New York. The greatest city in the world.

I'd lived at the Forest Hotel with Damon and Pat Runyon, I
could from there walk to my editors in the Hearst Magazine
Building, it was to see them I was in New York.

Nothing makes the heart heavier than indecision, mine was
doing a Danny Deever drum roll with it and felt as heavy as I
could ever remember. Within hours, Judy Garland was opening
at the Palace, the top vaudeville house in the country at a time
when vaudeville was dear to our hearts. From the day Mr. Mayer
let her go, Judy had seemed to sink without a trace—

> "Come with me," said the Wicked Witch harshly and
> severely. "See that you do everything I tell you, for if
> you do not I will make an end of you." Dorothy's life
> became very sad and she grew to understand it would be
> hard to get *back* and sometimes she would cry for hours.

In pictures, Judy Garland was unemployable. No company
was going to take that chance. Judy Garland had come to Metro
as a child, except for *Pigskin Parade* never worked anywhere else,
never had a manager or an agent, knew no more of Show Business
than a Munchkin. Now she was to open at the Palace. You had
to be somebody to do that. The difference was in the amount of
the risk. If Judy Garland didn't draw at the Palace, if she wasn't
a hit, what did they have to lose? A few thousands, a bad week
maybe, not the millions a movie musical must cost with its chances
of failure.

In New York, newspaper stories and ads were cautious. Could
she still sing? Would she show up? If she did show up would she
collapse? Toughest audiences in the world. The Palace. Regulars,
all critics, they paid hard-earned dough at the Box Office, they
demanded their money's worth. If they thought they weren't
getting it the gallery gods were *rough*. Booo—booo—hiss—hiss—
skedaddle you bum—Get The Hook.

I could hardly bear to think of it.

Nor of what the brilliant and severe New York critics might
say.

You have to Go. That card on the azaleas that day—*I love you,
Judy*. Don't you see it requires you to be there? *Be There*, Papa
always told me. Maybe you can stand up and yell Bravo—Bravo
Judy—the way they do at the Met. You can root—you've always
rooted. *Okay, Bill, let's hit one out of here now—Okay, Dicky,
win this one even if you did just hear your brother Bill has been
killed in the war, he'd expect you to*. Okay, Judy, clang clang
clang—zing zing zing—Bravo Judy.

Be there.

My command decision came from an echo in my head of Fred
Astaire saying One of a Kind—Judy is One of a Kind—she's like
Peter Pan, she's never really grown up, we ought to take better
care of her.

The Press Agent at the Palace knew my name from the old
days on the New York *Journal*, he had a press pass for me. Yes
—Miss Garland was in her dressing room, she—she looked okay,
little bit overweight maybe, after all she wasn't a kid any more,
as far as he knew the rehearsals had been okay. I didn't dare ask
him if she still had her first teeth, like Peter Pan.

Sinatra's opening at the New York Paramount—pandemo-
nium. Carol Channing coming down the stairs singing "Hello,
Dolly" for the first time opening night—Caruso singing Pagliacci
—Mazeroski's ninth inning home run in the seventh game of the
World Series to beat the *Yankees*—Can't-anybody-here-play-this-
game, the *Mets* winning their World Series, Citation taking the
Triple Crown—he ran that one without his feet touching the
ground, Clark Gable arriving in Atlanta for the premiere of *Gone
With the Wind*, standing in the door of the plane while the whole
Confederacy gave rebel yells—All that is to qualify myself as
having heard *ovations*.

Judy Garland's opening night at the Palace.

There has never been anything like it. When she sat down in
and on the footlights—

Somewhere Over the Rainbow—

so they climbed over the foolights and took her in their arms and
cried out There there Little Girl don't you cry, we'll get you the
blue bird bye-n-bye—

She played nineteen weeks at the Palace and the last was like the first.

Yes, Judy has a right to be in such company as I've selected for her.

Of Shelley, whose elegy of Keats, *Adonais*, is one of the world's masterpieces, Louis Untermeyer says, "There were two beings who fought it out in the body of Shelley, one was the uncompromising zealot, the passionate seeker for truth. The other a victim of illusions, a beautiful ineffectual angel beating his luminous wings in vain. Shelly's failures were those of excesses beyond his strength to endure."

So it was with Judy Garland.

She gave in excess of what her bodily and often her spiritual strength could endure.

Love is by far the most important thing of all. Wherever we stand in this awful hour of mankind's history, love is all we have left, as Allen Drury says in Senator Fry's deathless speech in *A Shade of Difference*. Love is the only gateway to Paradise and it makes no difference how deep-seated the trouble, how hopeless the outlook or muddled the tangle, how great the mistakes, a sufficient realization of Love will dissolve them and have that audience at the Palace or the Palladium shouting for joy—Judy, we *love* you—More, Judy, More. The girl who sat there on the footlights for the first time at the Palace, now a dumpy woman in black sequins, looking almost middle-aged—*somewhere* she must have found it, for love our neighbors much less our enemies, this we cannot do without help from LOVE itself.

God has given and gives special blessings to those who are able to communicate love and Judy was able to communicate it, she created waves of it and there were no negative vibrations. That was her magic.

No other woman, not even the saint and martyr, has done more—few as much. Her audiences were able to love her. To *love*.

What more is there to tell about Judy Garland?

Wrap it up now, the city desk used to say. This comes in great dizzy swoops, repetitious yet forever melodramatic with here and there the flame showing through the dust and sometimes the dust putting it out altogether.

Her life, as I've said before, *was* like a roller coaster, which someone had turned up to high speed—too high speed—like you'd see in a Laurel and Hardy movie. It's going too fast! That's why Sid Luft, that third husband she married somewhere along in here, and who did a very fine job as both husband and manager for years, finally couldn't take it any more. Nobody could—but Judy. And she couldn't.

She was twenty-nine that night at the Palace. She'd already lived nine lives. For a while the roller coaster of her life continued to go up—and down. No other I ever saw went so far *up up up* and came so far *down down down* as Judy's. It was a wild ride but every time she swung again to the top, hope was reborn. Judy's hope was irrepressible. She might lose sight of it, but it always broke through, and when it did she somehow managed to pass it along to those of us who loved her.

I heard her once at the Hollywood Bowl and she sang as I never heard her and brought back all my youth when I'd climbed there in the old days with my little brother Bogart. She was on top of the world that night and took us with her. Then I'm remembering a time when I was in Las Vegas at Howard Hughes' invitation to play a little blackjack at the Flamingo. Judy was singing in one of the spots, and this time it was what I'd been afraid of that night at the Palace. She kept holding out her hands in that immemorial gesture, but she looked like—like a cartoon of Judy, and she was crying and she kept saying, "Forgive me, I can't remember the words—Somewhere—somewhere—forgive me—" I went back afterwards, she was in a steam shower and she stared at me through the clouds and said, "I know, you want to write the Short Happy Life of Frances Ethel Gumm Luft Macomber Garland and this looks like it might be the moment for me to give you the right ending—I'm in a throat-cutting mood tonight all right."

"I had a half-breed great-grandmother once," I said, "back in Onondaga, New York, who cut her throat and then changed her mind and sewed it up herself with a darning needle."

"Whoopee!" Judy said. "Trouble is, I'd never be able to find my needle in this haystack."

My all-time high, Judy called this one when she told me about it. *Judy Garland?* Everybody said, you must be some sort of nut or saint, or both. Six or seven years since Judy had faced a camera, she'd never faced it without music, and here was Stanley Kramer proposing to cast her in a straight role that would test the technique of Helen Hayes or Bette Davis. A drab, little German hausfrau, come back to testify. And with such super-actors as Spencer Tracy, Richard Widmark, Burt Lancaster and Maximilian Schell.

Action! said Stanley Kramer. And she began her triumph as the little German hausfrau in *Judgment at Nuremberg*, a smash success, in which Judy scored the critical and artistic acclaim of her life. Without one song!

Now we do a big swing, violently.

We swing into total darkness, the unbelievable darkness where Mr. James Aubrey, neither saint nor nut but a combination of Golliwog and Hammer-Head, put out the light. With one witty (?) remark, with one Nero-esque gesture, he destroyed this rebirth and for all of us the potential of "the greatest entertainer of all time," Judy Garland, as an all-time joy on Television where she is so badly needed. For who would have cared if Judy Garland grew older, as Marie Dressler did, or as plump as Sophie Tucker?

The Judy Garland Show hadn't quite found its "format"— whatever that omnipresent TV word means—but we all saw it was shaping and we saw how good Judy was. (All except Mr. Aubrey.) I attended some rehearsals and once the show itself. Judy was in rare form, eager, excited, working well and as near as I could see the entire company of the show that was to present the great star entertainer to TV audiences adored her, was helping her. Hope was high, laughter was present, hard work the order of the set. Judy Garland was a top pro with years of tough experience, give her a little time and success was sure.

"One thing she has that no one else ever has had," the one-of-a-kind-herself Peggy Lee said as we watched the show together one night at her home in Beverly Hills. "Remember how they begin to applaud and shout *before* they can see her? The mere announcement, the news of her approach, fires them with enthusiasm and she gets such a welcome as no one else in our profession ever has. They'll do the same on Television."

We never got a chance, not really. Not even the President of the United States who said it was his favorite show.

Ah well, it wasn't Mr. Aubrey's, so JFK was robbed of that joy in his last days. In one of those "offbeat" moments for which Dr. Frank Stanton finally relieved Mr. Aubrey of his duties as head of CBS programming, Mr. Aubrey said that it wasn't worth while to develop a Judy Garland show. Judy Garland? Who she? And Aubrey gave forth with that ever-classic imbecility, "Judy Garland will have to adjust to television. Television is certainly not going to attempt to adjust to Judy Garland." And for this, after Stanton fired him, he was made head of what was left of MGM, so naturally less and less was left every day.

London, England.

She sang to eight thousand people one night and you could hear them sob with love and laugh for joy so that it sounded like the wind in the willows.

She got married again in London—I don't even remember his name—and this time she wanted a big wedding—an elegant wedding breakfast, the most ornamental cake, an orchestra to play "Here Comes the Bride." She invited everybody she knew on both sides of the Atlantic.

Nobody came.

Literally nobody. Mickey didn't know in time to get there.

A swing from 8,000 to 0—that's something.

A short time later Judy Garland died. You wouldn't have thought she could come back from that one. But she did.

Mozart had a third-class funeral at the cost of 8 fl., 36 kr. The hearse cost an extra 3 fl.

Judy had a very fine funeral indeed at Campbell's in New York and this time a lot of people came. Frank Sinatra somehow looked *grim*, he said to nobody in particular, She will have a mystic survival, she was the greatest, the rest of us will be forgotten, never Judy. Looking down the row at Lauren Bacall's face

that day I remember understanding with the impact of a blow
why Humphrey Bogart loved her as few women have been loved.
Such *compassion*—real deep true. Little June Allyson was weeping bitterly the entire time and Cary Grant kept his eyes shut.
At most funerals there is sorrow, and sometimes, of course, bitter
regrets, and often a sense of beautiful remembrance. But there
was something *all wrong*—yes, we were in grief—but here there
was a tense cloud of *guilt*. At Dwight Eisenhower's memorial
services in the Rotunda of the Capitol Richard Nixon said, "We
mourn his death but we are grateful for his life." That day in
Campbell's we weren't yet able to be grateful for Judy's *life*. It
had ended too soon and we knew it. It hadn't fulfilled her destiny
and somehow we were and knew we were responsible.

Someone spoke, a prayer, a eulogy. The words were meaningless. I kept wondering who was going to *sing*.

At Judy Garland's funeral?

Ask anyone who was there. We all heard it. I suppose we shall
all hear it the rest of our lives.

> Somewhere . . . over the rainbow way up high
> There's a land that I heard of once in
>   a lullaby.
> Somewhere . . . over the rainbow . . . skies
>   are blue
> And the dreams that you dare to dream
> Really do come true.
> Somewhere . . . over the rainbow blue birds
>   fly
> Birds fly over the rainbow
> Why then—oh why—can't I?
> If happy little blue birds fly
> Beyond the rainbow
> Why oh why can't I?

Somebody, loud and clear and strong, said You can now, Judy,
you can now—

I think it was Frank Sinatra.

Once I heard someone ask Liza Minnelli to sing "Over the
Rainbow."

Oh no, Liza said, that's already been sung.

Chapter Five

If it took me half a lifetime to know that Mother Cabrini was a saint my old friend John Cuneo was a good deal quicker. One of her three hospitals in Chicago is named after John's father, Frank Cuneo, who founded the great Cuneo Press. *He* said they all knew Mother Cabrini was a saint. They could, said John, recognize a real estate miracle when they saw one.

In her enchanting *Saint-Watching*, Phyllis McGinley writes: "America's own Mother Cabrini seems to have been canonized as much for her business acumen as for her holiness."

Business acumen is highly valued in America but right here it is necessary to begin to keep in mind that all Mother's was Missionary. For her nuns to have Missions, hospitals and schools where none grew before, to find places to erect her orphanages so she could feed, clothe and care for the Italian children who at that time swarmed New York's streets, hungry and homeless by the thousands. Or to find situations for schools for the poor negroes of the South.

> I did not accept the plantation I spoke about. I am looking for the best one before making a choice. No matter where we open a mission we shall have negroes, they come in large numbers. If we had a hundred sisters we could open at least twelve missions among them here. So plan spiritual exercises for laywomen that you may have a good number of vocations. We need workers.*

* This and other excerpts in this chapter are from *Letters of Saint Frances Xavier Cabrini*, translated from the Italian by Sister Ursula Infanta, M.S.C. Printed with

Often, she managed to get in ahead of Big Business and real estate operators, as when she gobbled up Chicago's old North Shore Hotel. The cops on the beat, her good friends always, helped her to make some exact measurements so that she could come with papers all prepared for the corner she wanted. Again with a little police protection and assistance, by the time anyone else got ready to make an offer she had every bed filled with helpless elderly patients who could not be moved without damage or danger.

Upkeep was, of course, another matter. But Mother Cabrini devised other methods for that. When *bills* came she was known to stamp them PAID and send them back. Everyone accepted this, no one ever complained, and Mother Cabrini explained gently that she knew they really wished to contribute to God's work which was her work and she was saving them a lot of time and trouble. So this was a blessing to all.

Would it be according to protocol to invite a saint to a tavern?
This saint, yes.

After reading Mother Cabrini's own letters I wouldn't have a qualm. She was a great letter writer. She had to be because she was referred to by her nuns as Miss Perpetual Motion, thus letters were her only means of keeping in touch. And she once wrote back to her Mother House in Codogno, Italy, which she had founded—

> Just prepare a little place for me at the foot of the
> Cordilleras, they must constantly remind me of the
> sublime heights of perfection.

—so she would be willing, in true humility, to sit at the foot of our table. She went wherever she was wanted. The prisoners at Sing Sing once sent her a letter of thanks for her many visits signed by every inmate, so she was well acquainted with crime and punishment. A lot of her Houses were for wayward girls, she was a friend to those who had fallen and wanted to help them up onto their feet and give them another chance. She went to the gallows with a young negro down in New Orleans and held his hand until the drop fell, always re-

Ecclesiastical Approbation, Archdiocese of Chicago, Office of the Archbishop, August 7, 1970. Published in Italian by Ancora in Milan, 1968.

minding him that God had infinite mercy and would give him another chance. One of the first things she did in New York, where she arrived in 1889, was to beg food for the orphans along Mulberry Street which was then considered the toughest neighborhood on Manhattan Island.

The proud always do damage because the grace of heaven cannot fall on them.

For the record. The plaque on the wall at the Statue of Liberty reads:

Immigration has enriched the American Way of Life. These are but a handful of the outstanding Immigrants who have contributed an unlimited wealth of creative ideas.

The first name on this list, now an immortal part of America's proudest symbol, is

MOTHER FRANCES CABRINI

Following we find

IGOR SIKORSKY

JOHN JACOB ASTOR

WERNHER VON BRAUN

DAVID SARNOFF

JOHN ROEBLING

ADMIRAL HYMAN RICKOVER

ALBERT EINSTEIN

CHARLES STEINMETZ

Whether Mother Cabrini leads off because of that old-fashioned courtesy *Ladies First*, which vanished when women began insisting they *aren't either* any better than men, or for achievement, worthiness or importance, I cannot discover. It was put there before she was canonized so it could only have been to a gallant immigrant woman who refused to be turned back, who enriched the American Way of life as she moved on the westward tide with her nuns.

What was Mother Cabrini's "creative idea" that placed her at the head of such a company in the sacred precincts of the Statue of Liberty?

Einstein's creative idea was the theory of relativity. David Sarnoff was the father of television, Sikorsky flew the first multimotored planes, John Roebling designed the suspension bridge and built one from New York to Brooklyn, Steinmetz gave us electrical inventions of incredible worth.

Could it be that Mother Cabrini proved for all to see the Power of Prayer to keep lifting you up no matter how often life, people and circumstance kept knocking you down? Certainly nothing—*nothing*—ever made her think small!

> The house is already full of children, the bishop is
> enthusiastic and I believe this will be one of the nicest
> missions. Work hard for true vocations so I can be
> spared to go to the Philippines where they want me. Also
> to Central America. Accompany me with your prayers.

Steinmetz might agree with her creative idea for he once remarked in an interview in his famed laboratory that unless the *last* half of the twentieth century, where you and I now are, returned to the inventions of the Spirit and its presence in our ways and days we would wish that none of the inventions of the first half had ever *been invented*.

And of course it was Einstein who said *In Christianity, as Jesus taught it, without its later additions, subtractions and multiplications, is the solution to all humanity's problems*. He and Mother Cabrini saw eye to eye in this.

> So do not be dismayed or lose courage if someone should
> throw a bucket of cold water on you; in return try to
> enkindle the fires of love of the Sacred Heart in them.
> The illness I felt during the voyage across has
> disappeared and I have arrived with such a florid aspect
> as my nuns don't know what to make of it. I am white,
> pink and fat.

The white and pink I will try to accept, though when I knew her she was brown and gold except for the blue blue eyes. But *fat?* Never. *The size of her* was what people always said when they first met the Mother General of the widespread Missionary Sisters of the Sacred Heart. Why, they said, as they watched her get up off the floor and prepare for the next round, she's no bigger than a pint of milk.

Just who was Mother Cabrini and how did she come to attain this rank in her own order and among the noted immigrants,

from William Penn and Lord Baltimore to David Sarnoff and
Albert Einstein, who built the United States of America?

Miss Perpetual Motion.

What kind of a nickname is this for a nun, much less a saint?

Well to realize at once that Mother Cabrini was a Missionary—
a person sent to work for the propagation of his religious faith in
a heathen land—and little Francesca Cabrini had wanted to go to
China—to convert the heathen Chinese, but the Pope decided that
New York was heathener and most of those who had become
heathens had started as Italians. Mother Cabrini was the first
Missionary *Sister* in history. A pioneer in woman's place, for up
till then all missionaries had been men. Francesca Cabrini had to
create her own order of nuns to get into one at all, and also to
travel the world—nothing else, she said flatly, was big enough for
her.

> The devil is evil and wise but you will be wiser than he
> as a missionary when you have learned humility. A
> missionary should certainly know more than the devil
> in order to free souls as she journeys.

As we accompany her on a few of these travels and view her
achievements in North, South and Central America—it took *continents* to give her room for her irrepressible spirit—as we add
up the accomplishments and daring feats that would have been
hair-raising for a strong man in track pants much less a frail little
woman in a cumbersome black wool habit and a tight-fitted coif,
we come shortly to agree that Miss Perpetual Motion was her
way of life. This at the end of the nineteenth century and the
beginning of the twentieth.

> I am indeed preparing women in general for their new
> role in society by training but also by example.

Bill Bolitho wrote a book called *Twelve Against the Gods*, by
which Bill meant those gods of custom and civilization which
often impede human progress. He had endless difficulty finding
women to include among adventurers like Alexander the Great,
Mahomet, Woodrow Wilson and Christopher Columbus, whom
Mother Cabrini always referred to with a wide grin as the first
Italian Immigrant. Bill chose Lola Montez, who couldn't mean

less, and Isadora Duncan, whom you'll meet in these pages later on, but he evidently never looked at the Calendar of Saints where he would have found such battling adventurers as Joan of Arc, Elizabeth of Hungary, Theresa of Avila and Francesca Cabrini of the World.

And it's always a bonus dramatically if the star part is played by a very tiny lady like Mother Cabrini with her four feet eleven inches and not always a hundred pounds from first to last, rather like a kitten defying the Hound of the Baskervilles. She took on everything with that irrepressible spirit that knows not danger or defeat. Revolutions, yellow fever, hostile authorities, race riots, extreme poverty, debt, disease, disaster and doubts never gave her a shadow of despair, for when she wrote—

> Faith will move mountains out of my way

—she meant not only spiritual obstacles such as despair but the Alps, the Andes and the Appalachians and she surmounted all of them in her time.

> I have just been up the highest mountain in the United States. Pike's Peak it is called though why I cannot say. It was awe-inspiring. I felt a little breathless but I am quite well today.

Note that after climbing *up* Pike's Peak she also climbed *down* into the Colorado coal mines to bring her faith in God's love for them to the Italian miners in the hell holes below. And hell holes they were. I once covered a mine disaster where miners were trapped by the collapse of criminally inadequate tunnels—which was why I thought John L. Lewis, who forced the owners to spend money on safety, was a great man. I remind myself that Mother Cabrini not only went down to them to pray, she did it not in boots, slacks and sun glasses, but in that same full-skirted habit with its starched gimp and headdress. And the square-toed shoes I saw her wear when I went to interview her in Los Angeles.

For in 1916 when I was a cub reporter on the Los Angeles *Evening Herald* my city editor, the fearsome J. B. T. Campbell, sent me quite casually to talk to one Francesca Cabrini, the Mother Superior of the order of Missionary Sisters of the Sacred Heart of

Jesus. These nuns had far-flung schools, some that were of interest to the people of communities where our paper had circulation. "I hear the top woman of the Cabrini High School is in town," Campbell said. "That's the one out in Burbank. She's the big shot for all of them. They tell me she's usually traveling but she's here for a visit and she's quite a character—might be a feature of some kind in it, why don't you go out and take a look?"

Before I started for Burbank, I checked the morgue to see if we had anything on her. Our file Cabrini, F. listed more than sixty Houses in the United States belonging to her Order and important holdings and hospitals and schools in most of the big cities—New York, Chicago, Denver, New Orleans, Seattle among them. She had become an important educator. Her title as the big shot was Mother General. Francesca Cabrini was an Italian and kept going back to Italy to see the Pope, who was a great friend and admirer of hers. But she was by now an American citizen.

Last week I went to lecture to a journalism class at Cal Poly on interviewing and I remember that the first thing I stressed with them was the importance of doing your home work ahead of time. To know the background, the childhood, the interest and achievements and hobbies and friendships and political beliefs and religious ties if any. The reasons why this person is worth interviewing and should be important and worth the readers' time, and on what. Do your Home Work, I said.

Well, I'd tried. What I found in the *Herald* morgue was all very well in its way but it was pretty skimpy. How I wish I'd had *then* the rare volume of *Letters of Saint Frances Xavier Cabrini* which Johnny Cuneo sent me when he knew I was including her in my book. As it was when I met Mother General there in the charming California-Spanish high school and convent she wasn't at all what I expected.

My initial reaction was *The size of her!*

And the second, her eyes. What does she see that makes them look so joyous.

> If they who serve the Lord are not
> glad and joyful, who should be?

When she was eight years old Francesca, whose pet name was Cecchina, informed her older sister Rosa that she intended to become a missionary to China. "To convert those poor heathen who do not know our Lord," she said.

Born on a farm in a far northern province of Italy, Maria Francesca was the youngest of thirteen children whose parents died when she was only two years old, so she was brought up entirely by Rosa, who said, "You a missionary! You are too small and sickly and weak to be a nun and who ever heard of a *woman* missionary?"

True, nobody ever had. There were a good many things nobody had ever heard of in the life of this frail Italian farm girl as she did grow up, in spite of all predictions and expectations to the contrary.

There was money enough left by her father to send her away to school to the nuns at Arluno. At the end of her education, she wanted to stay and *enter*, but she was refused. *She is spitting blood again*, the nuns wrote to Rosa. Her health will never permit her to become a nun, and so indeed it seemed, for though she now had her teaching credentials none of the orders to whom she applied would have her.

After teaching for two or three years in public schools, Cecchina practically backed into a semi-official teaching order called the Home of Providence. Monsignor Serrati asked the twenty-four-year-old Francesca Cabrini to see if she could do anything about *reforming* this weird sisterhood, run by a rich Italian woman named Toldini whom the priest described as a raving lunatic. And here at last Cecchina put on a *habit*, and took *vows*, though they were regarded, as was the whole Home of Providence setup, as without merit.

Soon thereafter Monsignor Serrati made Francesca Superior of the Institute and thus she became Mother Cabrini at twenty-four.

For six years, she did her best to reform and reorganize the Home of Providence and gathered about her a group of six or seven nuns as dedicated as she was herself. But in 1880, when she was thirty, the Bishop of Lodi decided that the Home of Providence was a hopeless task and dissolved it as a Church institution and it would seem that Mother Cabrini was right back where she started from with no place to go.

The Bishop received her and her little band of devoted sisters at his residence and rather casually and even inadvertently spoke the words that were to send the undaunted Mother Cabrini on her true career.

"I've heard you tell people you wish to be a missionary," he said with a twinkle in his eye, looking at the tiny frail figure in the now discredited habit, "but you see there is no such thing as an order of women missionaries." Then—I somehow feel sure, I saw her do it myself—Mother Cabrini raised those incredibly bright, incredibly blue eyes to him, filled with fire and with pleading and with—oh, something else, something I suppose we may call faith, or a sense of destiny, or an irrepressible spirit, and the Bishop said slowly, "It appears to me, Mother Cabrini, that if you wish to belong to an order of missionary sisters you will have to start one yourself."

And the always practical Mother Cabrini said, "I will begin looking for a house."

And she said this from Yucatán to Victoria, B.C., from Manila to Manhattan—I will begin looking for a house!

She always found one.

The first was in Codogno.

When at last, in 1887, she went to Rome to plead with the Pope, he refused to send her to China.

Not China, His Holiness said on their first meeting, saying to himself I am sure *The size of her!*

New York, Pope Leo said. That is where you are needed.

> We must thank God for our sea voyage.
> Other vessels encountered icebergs
> as we did but there were polar bears
> who sought to devour passengers.
> Thank God we did not have to face
> this threat.

But from that day forth we have Rome in July, Paris in August, London in October, Rio in January, New York again in March, the Canary Islands, Málaga, Buenos Aires, Granada, Rosario de Sante Fe, Valparaiso, New Santos, Manila, with more than thirty trips back to Rome to consult her patron and adviser, Leo XIII, and to the mother house at Codogno to recruit vocations for her staffs everywhere.

Making deals.

The miracles accepted by the Devil's Advocate for her canonization are listed as restoration of sight to a child born blind, power to walk for a crippled boy, deathbed recovery of a woman with cancer—these are indeed miraculous. But they do not differ from the other spiritual healers, including Mary Baker Eddy. These two unconquerable women accomplished miracles of another kind which are equally impressive as American affairs of life, if not as heart-warming. To me, Mrs. Eddy's greatest miracle was the founding of the *Christian Science Monitor*, the first national newspaper, under circumstances which as a member of the newspaper profession for many years I know to be impossible. There was in Mother Cabrini's experience of miracles the man upon whose valuable property she inadvertently (?) built a big hospital. A *much-needed* hospital and how she got *permits* and labor crews while ignoring all the red tape that drives most of us up the wall —anyway there it was and she filled it immediately with the aged, the destitute, and homeless crippled children. "Must I move off?" Mother Cabrini asked of the man who owned it. "I—what shall I do with my patients?" And the man said, "No no, of course not," and thereupon did what Mother Cabrini and God, no doubt, had hoped and intended he should all the time. He donated the land to the hospital already on it, thus storing up for himself much good where neither moth nor rust can corrupt, and let me say in all fairness he could well afford the gift, as Mother Cabrini knew before she turned the first spade—and she may even have known that he needed points in heaven.

Recovery of sight, enabling a boy to walk again, these are most endearing miracles, but for me good hospitals for those who need them and really trustworthy newspapers are also priceless possessions.

In an encounter between Mother Cabrini and polar bears I find I would be inclined to back Mother Cabrini.

Don't criticize, murmur or think evil, keep your weapons for battle. Against whom will you fight? Enemies perhaps? No! Against the devil? No! Against the most formidable enemy, our ego—our self-love—which can spoil and impede even the most holy thing.

There should be something unbearably heartbreaking about the arrival of Mother Frances Cabrini in the vast city of New York on a chill dark and stormy night in March 1889. There are among women few concatenations of circumstances so unpredictable and calamitous as those seemingly gathered together in battle array to send Mother Cabrini back to Codogno and checkmate forever any good she might desire to do for her countrymen in this new country.

Not only the weather, which was as foul as March can get on Ellis Island, and the late landing, but there was nobody to welcome her, no roof ready to shelter her in this strange land—

> I shall cross the ocean to go not only to New York but also to Central America. Tell Mother Bonaventura that Jesus does not want half measures. So Mother Michelina must continue with her English at all times, we must learn to speak all the languages in the world. Who knows where we shall be called upon to go in the name of the Sacred Heart?

—and she herself could not speak a word of English.

A letter telling the Pope not to send her at all had crossed her ship in mid-ocean and thus no one on the American shore expected her or was in any way prepared for her arrival.

There she is within a few days of her fortieth birthday, still weighing less than a hundred pounds soaking wet—and soaking wet she was!—staggering with the fatigue of a bad Atlantic crossing on a small ship. The five Missionary sisters who accompanied her had been extinguished all the way by seasickness, and attempting to control those suffering from *seasickness,* or even to recommend *prayer,* is a hopeless task.

> . . . "Give me your tired, your poor,
> Your huddled masses yearning to breathe free,
> The wretched refuse of your teeming shore.
> Send these, the homeless, tempest-tost, to me,
> I lift my lamp beside the golden door!"

In those dark days when Emma Lazarus wrote these words now inscribed within the pedestal of the Statue of Liberty, she certainly was not thinking of a woman like Mother Cabrini and her five nuns. But just the same none of the millions of Italians who had preceded her through the golden door had been tireder, more tempest-tossed or wretched than they were. After failing to find "their house" or anyone to guide them, they spent their first night in two bare rooms in a basement in Chinatown. And yet Mother Cabrini, as she knelt to her prayers on the damp floor, said—so one sister wrote home—with a small smile, "This seems to be as near as I am to get to *China!*"

Still the Orient remained often in her mind.

> There is a territory formerly part of the Orient and now a possession of the United States calling us. Italians are there as well as Eskimos, whom we could evangelize.

But worse than the Chinatown basement was in store on her arrival in America.

For when, on the following day, they did find the Archbishop he greeted them with cold amazement. And with an uncompromising order.

"You are to go back to Italy at once," he said. "We sent many letters to say you were not to come. There is no place for you. This is the only solution—return to Italy—"

Whether or not Mother Cabrini, who had been studying English at every opportunity, understood his words there could be no mistaking his gestures, expression and the tone of his voice. The other nuns began under their pressure to take small steps backward in the direction of the docks and return ship to Rome. Only Mother Cabrini, though her face had gone very white within the frame of its veil, moved instantly *forward*.

"No, no," she said, "no no—" and began bringing letters from the voluminous folds of her habit and waving them at the indignant prelate. Letters from the Vatican, from Propaganda and the powers that had arranged Mother Cabrini's voyage to the new world where so many hundreds of thousands of her people had preceded her. It was not the letters, nor the whispered words in broken English that brought light breaking through the dark clouds on the Archbishop's fine old Irish face. Probably he had no idea he was speaking to a future Saint, he did know he was dealing with a woman of courage and strength and a nun of dedicated faith. In a few moments he had changed his attitude

completely and perhaps drew a deep sigh of relief for this help
—for he badly needed help.

The condition of the Italians in New York, in the United
States actually, at that time was deplorable. It's difficult today to
imagine it. With unemployment and hunger at an all-time high
in their own country, Italians of every class and kind but especially the uneducated—most helpless brand of all—had flooded
into the United States, led by a dream of a country where gold
lay in the streets, hunger was unknown and work was to be
had by all. This wasn't, of course, true then any more than it is
now and the Italians either worked in the mines under labor conditions we would no longer permit or were desperate and idle in
the cities—and without means of any kind to look after their
swarming starving children.

Soon after the arrival of Mother Cabrini and her nuns a New
York newspaper published:

> We have been seeing some dark-skinned women in our
> midst, Sisters of some Italian Order. They climb narrow
> staircases, descend into filthy basements and enter some
> dives where a policeman would be afraid to go alone.
> They are all little, slender, delicate women and their
> mode of dress is a bit different from what we are
> accustomed to seeing. They only speak a few words of
> English. They belong to an Institution that looks after
> orphans and all the poor Italians. These five or six sisters
> newly arrived in our city are breaking ground for the
> work of their sisterhood in the United States. Mother
> Frances Cabrini is their leader, a woman with big blue
> eyes and an attractive smile. She can't speak English but
> her spirit makes itself understood.

And not many years later the same newspaper said:

> The sudden appearance of this small, black-clad blue-
> eyed figure, Mother Cabrini, often dismays bankers,
> bishops, politicians and philanthropists.

By the time she got to Burbank, California, via points east,
west, north and south including Alaska and I was sent to interview
her at one of her schools and got to walk up the hill to her

chapel with her, she was within a year of her death but, as you
will see, as gallant as ever!

In re-creating Mother Cabrini or Margaret Mitchell or the
Follies Girls of the Twenties, who certainly make a startling
impression when compared with the Playboy Bunnies of today, or
Elsie Parrish, it becomes necessary from time to time to re-create
me. Whoever and whatever I was at the time. Over our years we
are such different people and we see those we meet at some special
time when *we* are in that particular incarnation of ourselves, we
saw and heard that woman as we, a woman, were *then*. Not as we
may be now. Sometimes it is more difficult to get at how I thought,
what my own values were, what company I kept and how much
influence their thinking had on me, what was going on in the
world socially, politically and economically and how high or low
my standards—and theirs—were at the moment.

I remember so well a day when I went downtown in New York
to interview Helen Keller at the Lighthouse. I had only a few
days before had word that my son Bill had been killed as an RAF
pilot. And I know that my sorrow was what made me see all
the courage and gallantry of this woman who could neither see
nor hear as she floated toward me in some glory of spiritual light
and love.

I know my visions of little Julia Morgan, who was the architect
of the Hearst Ranch and all its beauties, are influenced by the
fact that I was then spending a lot of my time at the Ranch,
working with William Randolph Hearst, that I regarded it as
next door to Paradise. Therefore, when I know that when she
attended the Paris École des Beaux Arts and the authorities explained to her that she could not be given a degree because she
was a *woman* and she asked just to be allowed to attend the classes
and then repeatedly won all the competitions so that at last they
had to give her the first degree granted a woman at the École,
I *know* I see her as the presiding spirit of the Castle where we
were and which so impressed me.

At the time I was sent to do a piece on Mother Cabrini and
walked with her up the hill to her chapel, I was a know-it-all,

rash, reckless, opinionated young woman, trying to drink up all the gin in Los Angeles and San Francisco and having some success.

I have tried to find a copy of my story about this. But I was an unknown young reporter and Mother Cabrini, growing old and long absent from California wasn't of much interest except to those who sent their children to her school. Probably Campbell put it on the back page of the second section and in the merging of papers since, the *Herald-Examiner* now, the files were weeded out to save space. Because nowhere have I found my little interview with the nun who turned out to be a saint.

So I must rely on memory.

But oh—it is so clear! Mother Cabrini always made very very clear memories for people to keep of her forever.

I have to tell you now that my memory of my walk up the steep little hill to her chapel back of the Villa Cabrini High School in Burbank in December 1916 is clearer than most things. As a memory it is as clear or clearer than the one I took just recently. I can see, hear and smell most poignantly that day which may be long ago in time but in my heart is yesterday. Today?

The Villa Cabrini High School was on a knoll just below the foothills of Burbank and stood in the most beautiful olive grove I have ever seen. As we walked among these silver-gray-green flowing trees, bending in a desert wind, it was impossible not to think of another Mount of Olives, and wonder if a young man from Galilee saw them much as they looked to me now. I have no idea how many acres surrounded the fine adobe-and-brick buildings that made up the school and convent where the nuns lived, but it seemed to me spacious and the gardens were beautiful with roses and fragrant heliotrope against the walls and gay beds of nasturtiums and marigolds. There were high walls and fences all around it as there are today and the convent building itself, badly shaken in the 1971 California earthquake and now condemned, was at the end nearest the gate as I entered.

Soon Mother Cabrini came to me in one of those parlors common to all convents, and I had a most difficult and deadly feeling of stiffness come over me. After that first impact of her diminutive size and her blue eyes, I felt awkward and stupid, I felt that we had no common tongue though I'd been told her English by now was perfect. The one place with which, for reasons not clear to me, I could at that moment associate her was *Denver*. But I couldn't just burst out and say How are things in Denver, Mother Cabrini, could I?

She had known a good many young women and was—must be—a fine judge of them, to head a big order around the globe. And to select those who were to be sent to certain specific fields—

> In the meantime, we must prepare ourselves, for now even Brazil wants us and it would be a mission pleasing to God. They say that serpents abound there and I was thinking of sending you, for you could handle them very well I think. Meanwhile endeavor to control the spiritual serpents of pride and uncharitableness in the novices etc.

I felt sure that she sensed I was restless and felt for some reason quite uncomfortable. I figured out later that it was because I hadn't been in that convent school atmosphere since Sister Mary Regis used to stand no nonsense from me 'or anybody else, and so it was welcome when a few moments after we sat down Mother Cabrini suggested we get up again and go and look at her new chapel. We set out across the grounds where I could see girls in uniform and sisters in their familiar black habits that had always both authority and sanctity and without which it always seems to me a sister is just another dame. Or doll.

I had on this walk a sudden teeth-rattling shift in time and place and me. For as we went across a dusty bit of road and approached the narrow overgrown rough and rocky trail that led up to a small white chapel atop the steep little hill, I was transported back into my so-few school days at the Convent of Notre Dame in San Jose, when this school occupied a square block in the heart of that small California city not far from the St. Frances Cabrini Church where I went to Mass a few weeks ago in 1973. The grounds there, too, were beautiful, had some redwood trees of majestic proportions, and a whole building for the music Conservatory.

As Mother Cabrini and I and two other nuns began the perpendicular climb to the small building, she turned and I saw the exquisite bone structure of her face, the tender mouth and the

startling bright rose flush under the thin aging skin. I didn't recognize it as a fever. But as she held out a hand to guide me and I
took it in mine I knew that she was burning up with it—and
indeed she was and within a year she did. I realized she must be
quite old, for she had little wrinkles around her eyes and nuns as
a rule never have wrinkles. As we took the first few steps, she
glanced back and I met her twinkling eyes and heard her say,
"Always have a special place in which to pray if you can, my
daughter, however small it may be. Of course when Our Lord
told us to go into our closet and shut the door when you pray
he did not mean only a physical place, he meant the closet of
your heart and soul, to shut out fear above all, to put your trust
and faith in God. But I have found it well, found it a joy to have
a little prayer closet if I can. That is why I wanted this chapel
where any of us can go at any time to ask the Sacred Heart for
courage and faith as we follow His footsteps."

The chapel was of thick cement, covered over with white
plaster. At the end opposite the door by which we entered was
a small altar with candles and some branches of olive and above
it a reproduction of the Sacred Heart of Jesus. I do not know how
big it was—is—for it was filled with light, though outside it was
a gray day. And as we knelt I did not know how to kneel as
Mother Cabrini did, even at her age; she melted down with the
grace of a dancer, but somehow I did get to my kness. Nor do I
know how long we stayed there, but my heart was racing and
whether with joy or terror or protest at all this I do not know.
Even now I imagine it to have been a combination of all three.

It was near Christmas, I do remember, and as we went down
the rocky dusty path to return to the school grounds we admired
the Southern California flowers and she spoke quietly of the fact
that she had been here some time for prayer and retreat and
meditation. And perhaps a little comfort? She had had so little
of that in her life.

> Are you making mattresses? I hope you are using ex-
> celsior instead of moss, for the latter is too expensive.
> The mattresses I have are all stuffed with excelsior or
> something even less soft . . . keep going with courage.
> . . . for that mission among the Eskimos we need sisters
> who are unselfish because we will have to endure

privations including intense cold. Who among you would like to go? I am awaiting applications.

As we had climbed the hill, walked through the grounds, she did not suggest that age or ill-health had halted her round of world travels. I had not the slightest idea that death had already touched her. We talked gaily about the Rose Parade, to come on New Year's Day, and in those days we all had to grow our own flowers in our own gardens and make our own floats, since the original idea was to display to our less fortunate neighbors back to the Atlantic Seaboard what sunny California was like in January when they were shoveling snow. And she spoke in a voice warm with love and admiration of some of the Missionary Sisters of that order she herself had founded who at that exact moment were serving in cold and heat and loneliness "though I did not send them to the leper colony," she said. "There were too few lepers, a sister would not have sufficient to keep her busy and that is always wrong." She became thoughtful for a moment and then said, "Perhaps *I* am wrong. How many lepers did Christ heal? Ten—I must find out whether there are ten lepers in this colony they have asked us to undertake." As we talked I became aware that she had herself established all the missions of the Sacred Heart. When a mission, convent, hospital school or orphanage was in working operation, a working staff of Sisters had been installed, she herself moved on to start a new one somewhere else. And that staff was chosen as a great general might choose a staff on the battlefield.

> For example, you will not win a French nun by contradicting her. You must realize that the French character is different from ours and a little more fiery. Soon I will accept a German candidate who is proficient in German, English and French but she too will have a diverse character. We must learn to get along with all and our Italian sisters should learn to adapt themselves. Otherwise we shall not be able to go to foreign missions. Americans, for example, are very forward. How will we treat them if we have not sufficient virtue to bear with them?

Which would bring us of course to her first American convent and school at West Park, New York, where a large piece of property along the Hudson came on the market at a very low price because, it was rumored, there was no *water*. But Mother Cabrini here revealed one more hidden talent. Or produced another real estate miracle? Tucking up the skirt of her habit and taking a twig in her hand, she moved from one border to another in the role of a dowser—one who can search for and find subterranean supplies of water with a divining rod. And of course Mother Cabrini found water—and bought West Park. Immediately thereafter she took off for Rome, in a season of typhoons, icebergs and fog, to bring back seven more sisters to take over this new project. It seemed none of them would venture upon this voyage into a new country across so many miles of ocean unless Mother Cabrini was with them.

It was the house at Dobbs Ferry that she offered the Pope as a residence when it looked in 1914 as though Italy would enter the First World War.

> I have room for all of you here. I feel like preparing a place for the Holy Father also. Tell him I offer him our house, especially the one at Dobbs Ferry. There would be a little more worthy of his presence for as the apostolic delegate said when he came on July 4, "But this is a vatican." It really is very nice.

Somehow I find most moving of all her victory in Seattle, which had always been a place that challenged her. It was not a city with a population strong in either Italians or Catholics, and when Mother Cabrini wished to buy a large old hotel there and turn it into—as usual—a hospital for the old and the very young, she ran into a definite agreement between the banks and bankers and loan companies of the entire area not to lend her any money. It would, said the real estate men and many organizations, bring down property values everywhere if there was to be a Catholic orphanage, hospital, school, etc., etc. within the better residential section where this hotel was located.

If, they agreed, we do not lend her any money she cannot complete the purchase, and so the little nun was turned back and down everywhere she went.

One day on entering a Catholic church she found herself facing a beautiful marble reproduction of Saint Anne reading from Holy

Scriptures to the Blessed Virgin as a child at her knee. Mother Cabrini knelt to pray and when she rose noted that the pages of the book from which St. Anne was reading were blank. From one of her capacious pockets, Mother Cabrini produced an old-fashioned fountain pen—and with careful hand wrote upon the page.

$26,472.

"And what does that mean?" said a sister who was with her.

Gently, almost apologetically, Mother Cabrini said, "I just wanted to be sure she knew how much it is I need in order to buy that hotel."

Two days later one of the bankers cracked. Looking into the bright blue pleading eyes of the little nun, he could no longer find it possible to say No.

Perhaps that was why Mother Cabrini chose Seattle in which to ask for her papers to become a naturalized American citizen.

Mother Cabrini was, indeed, a world traveler. The other great woman religious leader of that time, Mary Baker Eddy, seldom left her native New England. Their paths crossed only once.

In 1903 Mrs. Eddy wrote:

> The sad sudden announcement of the decease of Pope Leo XIII touches the heart and will move the pen of millions. The intellectual, moral and religious energy of this illustrious pontiff have animated the Church of Rome for one quarter of a century. The august ruler of two hundred and fifty million human beings has now passed through the shadow of death into the great forever. He is the loved and lost of many million. I sympathize with those who mourn but rejoice in knowing our dear God comforts such with the blessed assurance that life is not lost. Its influence remains in the minds of men and Divine Love holds its substance safe in the certainty of immortality. In Him was life; and the life was the light of men.

Her sympathy certainly went to Mother Cabrini, even though indirectly. For the Pope had been Mother's close friend, supporter and adviser; the reason for her many long trips back to

Rome was to ask for his wisdom in her affairs and his blessing upon her work as it spread around the world.

Four days later Mother Cabrini wrote from Chicago:

> May God's will be done. If he protected us on earth he will do more than that from heaven. The holy old man had worked enough and was called home in the middle of the battle. Blessed is he who was prepared and fortunate are we to have such a powerful patron. Pray fervently for him and you will be repaid. I felt his death very keenly but a calmness settled over me upon realizing that we have a new patron in heaven. He was pure and holy and very dear to God.

I did not, as I say, have any idea when I walked up the hill to the chapel with her that she herself was mortally ill. True, she seemed so frail that a good strong Santana wind from the Mojave desert around the corner might blow her away. Later that day walking through the gardens of the Villa Cabrini in Burbank, Mother Cabrini told me she meant to stay there for some time. Where, she said, with her joyous smile, it is so warm and pleasant, and I can go each day to my chapel to pray.

Very shortly after I saw her there, she made a sudden and seemingly inexplicable move and returned to her beloved Frank Cuneo hospital in Chicago. Evidently she had had a warning—for there she died quietly and without pain, when she was sixty-five years old.

I can find no woman in American history who packed more irrepressible spirit, more gallantry of operation, more service to God and to mankind into any number of years than little Cecchina, who became first Mother Francesca Cabrini and in time Saint Frances Cabrini.

The thing about Saint Cabrini is that she is such a well-rounded character; she speaks to our condition now as surely as she did in that long-ago before World War I.

She began working with, and as part of what we presently call, a Minority group.

Italians had been very unpopular in New York when she arrived there in 1889. When I lived and worked there Fiorello LaGuardia was its most beloved mayor. There can be no question that the little dark sister the newspaper spoke of seeing with the Italian children on the sidewalk of New York had much to do with this.

Nothing stopped her. Women have been responsible for much of the philanthropy that has kept us the land of the free. Here Francesca Cabrini, an Italian peasant, mind, *not* a financier or the wife of a financier, was a superstar. Throughout her sojourn as a missionary she continued to build, expand and run a great and costly charitable empire, including vast real estate holdings, without government assistance.

> Tell the Commission I have purchased the ground next to our hospital in order to enlarge it because the existing structure is too old. I shall need $200,000 to construct it.

And $200,000 in 1909 was more than it is today.

Of course she got it.

Hers was no easy path to sainthood. Challenged, knocked down and trampled on often, frail from birth to death, her spirit and her faith were *evidenced* in her actions. Somehow I find that I see her best on a train, an old-fashioned snorting train pulling across the vast plains of Texas.

> On the second night of the trip, a short distance from Dallas, at about 10:30 P.M. enemies of the railroad fired three shots at the train. One came in the direction of my head. It was a long, large bullet which could have pierced my head, but by order of the Sacred Heart who was the protector of the present trip the bullet went down under the cushion. All the train personel came to assure themselves that I had not been hurt, much to their wonder. Every moment they came to tell me, "You must have someone who watched over you and even if they shot in your face you could not be harmed." I told them it was the Sacred Heart of Jesus. Being Protestants they did not quite understand but remained with an indefinable sentiment. Tell Brother Bonaventure that Jesus never wants half measure.

In the voluminous correspondence which she somehow found time to carry on (two hundred and eighty-one letters of record), she gives us her own recipe for sanctity.

If you wish to become a saint, what a joy it would be to me if someone should exclaim Oh Mother, the Holy Spirit has really come to me and has taken away all my miseries. Deprived of self-love, my soul feels light. May Jesus sanctify you.

Saint Frances Cabrini's soul, crossing as it always did denominational barriers, still sheds light on the path today for women who are willing to accept it. For by her life she did, indeed, validate her "creative idea," the Power of Prayer to keep strengthening us, lifting us, no matter how often we are knocked down.

I am so grateful she chose to become an American woman.

And thus have her name on the plaque at the Statue of Liberty for all women, as she proved.

Chapter Six

A woman wrote what Abraham Lincoln called the little book that started a great war. Harriet Beecher Stowe—*Uncle Tom's Cabin*.

Frank Sinatra once said Julia Ward Howe's "Battle Hymn of the Republic" should be our national anthem instead of a song like "The Star-Spangled Banner," which only the leading tenor at the Metropolitan Opera can sing.

A woman wrote the book which started our war for survival. And another president, this time John F. Kennedy, said of it, "Since Miss Carson's little book, we are examining the matter." *We* was the Government of the United States and the matter he was speaking about was the danger line of Pollution in the very air we breathe. Rachel Carson—*Silent Spring*.

No American poet has written anything to surpass, in my mind to equal, *Renascence* by Edna St. Vincent Millay.

And while she didn't write it, Barbara Fritchie certainly spoke memorable words John Greenleaf Whittier made part of our heritage:

> "Shoot, if you must, this old gray head,
>   But spare your country's flag," she said.

Oh, we've been in there pitching.
But—one woman writer?
There was one Judy Garland.
One Amelia Earhart.
One American woman saint.

I wonder if I can actually select one woman writer of the many good ones—the few great ones—we've had in America? This is my own profession. Looking over the field I can say that *all* successful writers have to have a touch of the irrepressible spirit whether they know it or not. If they didn't, they'd be doing something else. Which indeed is what I once heard Edna Ferber say to a group of would-be writers at Columbia. "If you *can* do something else, *do* it." For it's a lonely and desperately demanding and precarious profession. Lure, rewards, deep satisfactions, of course. They come after the work has been done. And there many of the clichés are true, which clichés have to because otherwise they wouldn't have had a chance to become clichés. For instance, Hell is paved with sheets of blank white paper. Isn't it just! 10% inspiration, 90% perspiration. Dorothy Canfield says somewhere that sitting down to work is like starting down a ski slope. In a brilliant introduction to Joel Goldsmith's *The Infinite Way*, the monumentally successful playwright John Van Druten says he was always amazed by "the essential mystery of my profession as a writer—the mystery of whence they would be coming, those words that I was going to put down . . . causing me to ask where they have *all* come from, all those many thousands of words and thoughts that I have in the past put down on paper."

They tell me *we* are mysterious.
Writers, I mean. Especially women writers.
If this be true, there's nobody to whom we are more mysterious than ourselves. Just yesterday, as we waited in a cold sweat in the Green Room, to appear on the "Merv Griffin Show," Jacqueline Susann and I agreed that day by day in every way we grow mysteriouser and mysteriouser to *us*, until some days we disappear altogether.
This is an age when there is hardly anybody who isn't either writing a book, intending to write a book, or is damn sure some experience they've had, witnessed or know about *from* an eyewitness will make a *great* book.
Since my life, my mail, my telephone and all other media of communications are filled with words of those who are writing or trying to write something, perhaps if I do know anything

it should get as much space here as how to make instant coffee or put together an electric train.

Obviously, even thinking about how to write discomposes me.

How to facts are few and far between. They differ as the dandelion from the orchid, the jet plane from the velocipede. In looking at many women writers, to help me select my candidate for the One American Woman Writer to invite to the Tavern, I find that the irrepressible spirit comes close to the miraculous in my own chosen field. No use trying to separate the writing spirit from the writer; they are indissolubly bound together.

What if the words don't come to me? And many times they haven't.

Each piece that comes with a beginning, a middle and an end, what with deadlines and breadlines, inspiration or lack of it, critics, politics, phony Best Seller lists, interpretations, poetry, prose and potboilers and pornography, each completed piece is a minor miracle to the writer himself, so I have to believe that honest-to-god working writers *in toto* are a gallant band.

Women even more than men. For writing is a career, a job, and in so many cases the woman is still the wife and mother with all that implies of demands upon the spirit, the heart, the thought process.

In my search for the One Woman writer, to myself I begin with the most gallant of them all. The one who struggled with more temptations, wrote with more desire for the spirit, more *seeking*, for the light, then anyone else. And in a close race I am inclined to like *style*. That's why Arnold Palmer has an army—he has style. Mary Roberts Rinehart wrote even of violence with an elegance that kicks my interest and admiration into the upper brackets. Murder on the Circular Staircase in an elegant country house with an elegant old lady of New York aristocracy playing detective carries this out. Faulkner has to have manure or it doesn't count.

Dorothy Parker had a style so individual and new that it changed style for that generation and generations to come and filled *The New Yorker*, then the most imitated of all magazines, with her imitators. In all the widespread brackets of her work Mrs. Parker had style. As book reviewer for *The New Yorker* her style was as witty and radical as George Bernard Shaw's had been for the *Saturday Review* in London when Shaw molded the London stage and all its work. In her short stories its power lay beneath the humor of "The Waltz" and the reality and tragedy of "Big Blonde"—for which she undoubtedly used herself as the human model. Even in her poems, though it amused her to say she was simply limping along after Edna St. Vincent Millay, the style gives her individuality which contradicts that. If I had to define the style of Dorothy Parker I would do it thus—she could say more in fewer words than anyone who wrote then or maybe since. Disciplined prose that never wasted a word and selected the right one. Sculptured verse that had planed away every superfluous flake . . .

Dorothy was born in a little resort town in New Jersey because her father and mother had gone there for a vacation, and the fatigue of making this move from their home in New York had thrown Mrs. Rothschild into premature labor. They took her back to their town house in the Seventies when she was three weeks old, and she stayed there while she was growing up. At all times, she was a *New Yorker*, so that when, after a difficult childhood with a stepmother and a father she feared desperately, her father died leaving her penniless, she took a room in a house on a New York side street and began trying to sell the poems she had written from babyhood. She sold one of these to Frank Crowninshield on *Vogue*, a Condé Nast publication, and when she went to collect her twelve dollars she asked him for a job—and got it at ten dollars a week on *Vogue*. Later, to her great delight, he transferred her to the new *Vanity Fair*, and there she was, on her destined path, in the glitter and high excitement of New York in the postwar Twenties.

Dorothy Parker and I became friends, I am proud to say, because *chiefly* of our shared admiration for, devotion to and endless study of Somerset Maugham and our dismay and disbelief that *all* other writers weren't and didn't likewise. For our sins of omission in the matter of money, Dottie and I were both working in the Movies. This we considered the depth of degradation, the pinnacle of prostitution and the heraldic insignia of failure. It may be true as the brash Moguls of Hollywood claimed that the coming of film was just as important as the coming of the Printing Press but neither Dottie nor I could regard that as anything but blasphemy. We met ducking in and out of the Ladies Room, the ducking being because we hoped to avoid direct confrontation with those terribly bright, endlessly smiling gals called Scenario Writers, who looked down on us as old-fashioned writers who couldn't get anywhere but in print.

One day we drifted into the Commissary for coffee and I told her my experience on that same lot with Somerset Maugham. I so well remembered the one time I met him in America. For some such incredible reason as to do an original for C. B. DeMille, probably spurred by the same curiosity that sent him to the South Seas. Anyhow, as we met on the lot one day he said, "They tell you they want you to get them out of the Rut. But when I so much as put one foot out, they shoot it off." A superlative description of what happens to the naive and trusting writer who goes starry-eyed into a Studio in hope of turning out better pictures.

Maugham's observation enchanted Dottie Parker and we began then hours of what actually I suppose was "shop talk." Sometimes she came to my house—she and her husband, Alan Campbell, were living in an apartment near by, sometimes in a booth at Lucy's across the street from the Studio, or the Brown Derby. We were both in essence New Yorkers at that time, and New York writers meet, talk, and enjoy friendships mostly in restaurants—"21," the Stork Club, Tony's, Lindy's, the Oak Room at the Plaza, Reuben's at dawn, Luchow's, and many many others, for in New York in those days you could eat in almost any nation in the world.

Much of it was about Maugham and the best way to record it is to set down here, mostly for myself, the conclusions we arrived at and a little something of what the Great Master Technician had taught us.

The best book on writing yet written is Somerset Maugham's *The Summing Up*. A short book. It will take any writer, would-be writer or has-been writer the rest of his life to read it.

His technique is the best in the English language, both in two volumes of short stories and in the novels *The Moon and Six-*

pence, Of Human Bondage and my own favorite *The Razor's Edge*. I know one American woman writer who has studied, imitated and tried to learn from him without, perhaps, as much success as the amount of effort warranted—ME. If I could ever once move back and forth in time with a modicum (what a nice word that is!) of his ease and grace and suspense, I'd be much higher in my own estimation as a writer than I am.

Being a short story writer at her best, Mrs. Parker preferred the Note Books to all else. For Maugham kept Note Books. A habit I wish he'd persuaded me to use earlier.

He kept Note Books allright.

Some of his are published. Dottie told me once that she had spent a weekend, when the people who were supposed to take her to the country failed to show up for the reason she discovered later that she'd forgotten to ask them, *so* she spent it moving *from* the Note of something that Maugham saw, heard or experienced *to* the short story or novel that he made out of it. From a Note came what is probably the best known and perhaps the most successful short story ever written. Originally called "Miss Sadie Thompson" the Note described a girl who got onto Maugham's ship at Honolulu bound for the South Seas. He put down her high-buttoned white shoes, her big floppy hat, her raucous voice, her impudence to a cleryman and his wife who were also aboard. When he translated her to fiction, he kept every one of those things and called the clergyman Reverend Davidson, the story's name was changed to *Rain* in plays and movies for many years. Screen and stage stars wanted more than anything else to have *Sadie Thompson* as a performance to their credit. Best I remember Jeanne Eagels on Broadway and Joan Crawford in films.

How *real* she was. Well, of course, as Maugham's notes prove, she *was* real.

I once wrote a short story and three movie stars accused me of having portrayed them as its heroine—who was slightly soiled around the edges. Gloria Swanson, Nita Naldi and Joan Crawford all thought I had in a small measure violated our friendship. As a matter of fact the *real* character from whom I had drawn my fictional star was Mae Murray. But no writer can afford to have any scruples about this—and if friendships topple then topple they must.

Always always always my own aim is to get nearer to my characters. One way or another. To observe distinguishing idiosyncrasies, mannerisms, habits of speech, ways of dress and adornment, which can convey them to my readers if any. To succeed is to wrest from that mysterious "whence" of Mr. Van Druten's words that create people with actual dimensions.

Katharine Brush, who was showing such promise as a novelist when she died much too soon, creates for me two unforgettable characters. *Red-Headed Woman*, whom Jean Harlow was playing on the screen when her husband, Paul Bern, killed himself in one of Hollywood's most shocking scandals, and I have always believed that Jean's portrayal of the Red Head at that time for all to see increased that shock. Jean wasn't like that at all, but the screen character from Katharine Brush's book was realer than she was. *Young Man of Manhattan* was every sports writer Kay Brush ever knew and she knew 'em all, as I did. Whether her Young Man was Westbrook Pegler, Dick Vidmer, Bill Corum, Grantland Rice or Damon Runyon was hard to determine. She had used them in one spectacular sweep it seemed. But about then Corum of the *Journal* was raced to the hospital in an ambulance and there they discovered that there was no bullet hole in his pants seat to match the one in his carcass seat, so we felt he must be quite a man with the ladies and so could be the model for the hero of Kay's novel. Which, when I reread it today, takes me back to the Golden Age of Sports, to see Babe Ruth mincing to the plate on his toothpick legs, to watch Bobby Jones hit one of those long sailing shots, to see Dempsey coming out of his corner in the famous crouch and Big Bill Tilden moving with the grace and speed of Nijinsky on the tennis court.

That's what a great novel should do. Take you *there, then,* whether it is to the Two Cities of Dicken's *Tale* or the press boxes at Yankee Stadium and the Polo Grounds.

Nothing has ever delighted me in my life as do the letters and the people I meet who ask me where they can go to hear Hank Gavin preach!—Hank being a fiction character in a novel I wrote called *Tell No Man*. This gives him all the reality I had hoped for, beyond what I hoped for. And Hank Gavin is a combination

of a young stockbroker in Chicago whom I greatly admire—
come come, there's no reason not to admit proudly that he is
my godson, Buzz Hargrave, *and* then a newspaperman I knew
well who became a minister and another young pastor who had
a church in Phoenix.

I know one thing. I have to live with them as I create them.
Nor am I alone in this.

Distinctly indeed do I remember when Paul Gallico was living
chiefly with a big white snow goose. I will not say he talked to
the Snow Goose, but I definitely heard him make some very odd
sounds. He had been at Dunkirk, in his own small boat, helping
to bring off some of the British Army who were trapped there,
some left in the water as their own boats went down, and the
Snow Goose was there too. Paul saw him. As the representative,
the symbol, of the Spirit of Christ, who also came to rescue
these brave men. Later Paul wrote it into one of the best and
best-loved of all short stories. The way I make it out, perhaps
someone else could have written *The Snow Goose*. It took
Gallico to *see* it. It wasn't only that the Blessed Virgin appeared
to Bernadette in the Grotto at Lourdes. Bernadette could *see*
her. The others who were there at the time didn't and couldn't.
There were a lot of first-class writing correspondents at Dunkirk. As far as I know the only one to see the Snow Goose was
Gallico. And even if you see with your imagination that may
be the true gateway to reality. If we can learn to let it off its
leash, it can show many strange and wonderful things.

Techniques can be studied as Dottie Parker and I did Maugham's
or Ring Lardner's or James Thurber's. Methods of making characters *real* can be pondered over and emulated. How each
writer decides to operate and where and when and for how long
has to be individual to him. Somerset Maugham told me that
he worked three to four hours a day, wherever he was, always
in the morning. After that, he said, everything he did had to be
chucked in the wastebasket the next day. He figured that a thousand words a day were all any writer could turn out and have
them of any use to him.

On the other hand, to inject myself in such august company,
I am inclined to keep on writing as long as it will flow at all once

it does start to flow. I'm afraid to quit! Suppose it doesn't
come back? So that sometimes I have stayed before my typewriter from dark to dawn or vice versa. In a sort of panic that I
may never be able to do it again! Other times, all I can do is put
one brick on top of another brick. I hate to admit that the difference between the two is not always apparent to the naked
reader. The last pages of *Tell No Man* were written without
any knowledge or cooperation on my part—I read them with
amazement since that was not the way I had intended to end the
book at all.

If I talk about Gallico oftener than other writers it is because
for a time he was my son-in-law and I saw him in my home or
his in operation. He walked the floor day and night when he had
been taken over by a big idea, like Hiram Holiday, then talked
it over with my daughter Elaine, who is now my editor and was
his in those, his fiction-formative years, when he gave up being
sports editor and columnist for the New York *Daily News* and
turned to doing stories for the magazines, chiefly *The Saturday
Evening Post.*

Paul would start to tell a story. Stop. Change it around. Keep at
this for days. He didn't begin to *write* until it was complete in his
head, every word and comma. I couldn't do this. I can't *think*
much. I suppose I might say I am a storyteller. I begin at the beginning, go through to the end and then stop. THEN I go back and
do the rewrite, improvements, cuts and I have learned sometimes
to my dismay that cuts are always improvements. As Dottie Parker
once remarked to me, Since it's a *short* story the shorter the better.
"The Prodigal Son" in the fifteenth chapter of *Luke*, considered
by so many writers as the greatest short story ever written, is in
less than five hundred words.

For Dottie, there was no *going on* until she had each sentence as
perfect as she could make it. She worried every word and phrase,
changed many. This may be one reason we have only that one slim
volume of her short stories, or maybe it was because she demanded
too much of herself. I don't think so. I think myself, from reading
and from the long talks I had with her during our exile in Hollywood, that the vein of gold ran out.

Don't ask why, for I don't know—or maybe I do. Sometimes,
as any of the old boys up in the Mother Lode Country can tell you,

that's all there is, there isn't any more, just that one vein—pocket
—of pure gold and not another flake or nugget anywhere around.

No no.

Her stimulation ran out.

> Oh, seek, my love, your newer way;
> I'll not be left in sorrow.
> So long as I have yesterday,
> Go take your damned to-morrow!

But—it didn't quite work out that way. Her *memories* of Bob
Benchley and of the stimulation of their friendship wasn't *enough*.

As long as they were together that stimulation brought out their
best work, especially Mrs. Parker's. That may be too simple an
explanation. I don't think so.

Let me quote from two authorities on her work so I start off
recording its quality of importance.

Ranked as top critic and reviewer Edmund Wilson said, "She has
put into what she has written a voice, a state of mind, an era, a few
moments of experience that nobody else has conveyed."

The words she would cherish most are those of the writer she
admired most, Somerset Maugham; in an introduction to her stories
and poems in a Portable Edition he said, "In a few short paragraphs
she presents herself to you, to take or to leave, with her pain, her
laughter, her tenderness, her feeling for beauty, her ribaldry and
her common sense."

If you have tenderness, nothing else matters.

If you don't have tenderness, nothing else matters.

This a recent discovery and conviction in my life, I know it to
be true, I know Dorothy Parker *had* tenderness. How often she
got it back—I'm not sure.

All the things Maugham mentions reached their peak in her association with Robert Benchley. A man I know to have been capable of extraordinary tenderness. Those moments Wilson speaks of
were in this friendship of depth, breadth and height. Not a love
affair in today's feeble-minded preoccupation with sex, it was a
friendship-love that began in those days when they were very
young on the staff of *Vanity Fair*, he just out of Harvard, she a
small girl with the most beautiful dark eyes and a wit that was to
become world-renowned. For many years it was the major relationship in their lives. As long as it lasted it gave Dottie what she

needed to bring out those things Maugham says she had and put them down on paper as part of American literature.

Feeling as I do that friendship is the most important thing in life I'm inclined to say that this one in Mrs. Parker's was both the battery that started her motor and the carburetor which added illumination and explosion to whatever she ran on.

Many of these that I've seen have been vital and beneficial to art, industry and government. Producer Irving Thalberg and screen writer Frances Marion did more for the Movies as an Art than anyone I can think of. William Randolph Hearst and Julia Morgan, one of the first women to practice architecture in the United States, produced the famed Hearst Castle and a number of other gems. I have one of my own, without it I am almost sure I wouldn't have made my way through some of the rough seas of my life, and the lives of my children and grandchildren, who all, with reason, call him *Papa Fix*. His real name (or so he says) is John Aloysius Clements from Louisville, Kentucky, and we met as young reporters on the New York *Journal* just after he got back from World War I where he landed with General Duckboard Butler's United States Marines and fought with them at Château Thierry and the Argonne. We covered the Lindbergh kidnapping, the Hauptmann trial, the Roosevelt Administration and a good many others together and for my friend Jack I put on my best clothes mentally, even spiritually. I never make up my mind about anything important and a good many that aren't until I have ascertained his opinion. To this day no news ever breaks that I don't wish to discuss it with him immediately. A bug on *our* telephones would reveal some unorthodox opinions of present-day politicians and pitchers—we both think it might have been better for Nolan Ryan if he'd only pitched one no-hitter and as for this thing about Watergate as two hard-boiled political reporters who covered Jimmy Walker and a good many other elections and administrations it is only fair to say that we are not so much shocked by any corruption as we are appalled by the STUPIDITY of everybody connected with it. Like all reporters we are aware that stupidity is responsible for more crime, heartbreak and disaster than anything else.

In such a friendship, there is an invaluable sense of protection, of assurance and reassurance. This Dottie Parker, supersensitive and self-depreciating artist as she truly was, who insists that all her witticisms were just her effort to be *cute*, needed more than most. She got from Benchley self-confidence, a riddance of her sense of guilt whatever it was about, and thus I claim he was the most powerful influence in her existence. Thank God he was such a great guy—some of the others weren't.

I have more than studying their lives and their work to base this on. First, briefly, comes a night when Dottie came to see me at a house I'd rented in Beverly Hills. I was surprised to see her for we weren't really on "drop in without invitation or announcement" terms, but she knew more about people than any of my close friends, for she had come to be with me in what she alone realized would be a difficult time. I had that day been granted a divorce. A divorce I wanted, one I knew was necessary if I and my children and my work were to survive. My family and friends had been insisting on it; my brother Thornwell acted as my lawyer. *And yet—*

"And yet," said our Mrs. Parker, "every woman of integrity and honor knows divorce is a defeat. An admission of failure to keep the vows you once made in all sincerity and truth. Richer poorer in sickness and health till death do us part—even if you said these in a judge's office they were commitments to a decent partnership. Thus you have failed and down inside is a dream that didn't come true."

Nor could I doubt that Dottie—despite several tragic and well-publicized love affairs that had not ended at the altar—knew whereof she spoke. For she had had those marriage dreams that didn't come true, known these moments of failure. Her first husband, Edwin Pond "Spook" Parker II, she married in 1917 before the young soldier sailed for France. Upon his return, when she found, as have many war brides, that there was no basis for that permanent partnership and they separated, he to return to his native New England, she to remain in her beloved New York, it still took Dottie some years to bring herself to the actuality of that divorce. Alan Campbell she married—divorced—and later remarried. And married they remained until his accidental death from an overdose of sleeping pills.

We spent that whole evening talking, Dottie and I, but she did not speak of either husbands or lovers. Instead it was then she told me that the man who meant most in her life was Bob Benchley.

One of a kind, she kept saying.

The other proof also took place during our Hollywood exile and had a great many witnesses.

A banquet was given, I can't imagine why, for the head man at Paramount who at the moment was a five-foot-four gent whom Mrs. Parker, soon after her arrival at the studio, had referred to as a pony's ass. His name was Cohen. There we were along with a lot of other suffering employees and though as a reporter I had from time to time covered these I did not recall one more sunk in gloom, relieved only a little by the fact that I was at the same table with Dorothy Parker, Leo McCarey and my brother, Bogart, then story editor, which must have been why I was working there. We believed in nepotism. At some point a studio executive named Botsford smoothed down his hair, walked to the dais, unfolded a manuscript and began to read "The Treasurer's Report." This had been written by Robert Benchley at a supreme moment in his career and he himself read it at the Music Box in a show starring Joe Santley and Ivy Sawyer. Supposed to have been written and delivered by some financial bigwig who could neither read nor write nor deliver, it had become a classic and Benchley was called upon for it endlessly. Now here *we* were and good kind capable Mr. Botsford was called upon to read it to those of us gathered to celebrate Mr. Cohen. The occasion, the mutilation of Benchley's manuscript by the honestly amateur Mr. Botsford, stirred all that was passionate, primitive and punitive in little Mrs. Parker, already rebellious at Hollywood. She rose to *her* full four feet eleven inches, picked up a magnum of champagne nearly as big as she was, walked carefully around the table and clunked the reader over the head with it. The sound was horrendous, he went down, as we say, like a poled ox, the diners shuddered with excitement and apprehension and stood up to get a better view of Mrs. Parker, now calmly pouring the contents of her weapon over her prostrate victim. How she got the cork out, unless she'd cracked the bottle on the man's head, I *don't* know. Her satisfaction at saving Benchley from this insult shone and flickered around her.

"It was a desecration," she said.

Why do I always think Dorothy Parker died young?
She was past seventy.
Or was she?

I mean—I am trying to say—how long did it last—her life that I am studying here as I think in terms of the one great American Woman Writer—the Life and Hard Times of Dorothy Parker which offers me one small volume of short stories, and a couple of slim volumes of poetry in which she holds her heart out for you to see?

We had her—for a time.

Strayed from Elfland perhaps, to dwell among mortals and sing us her elfin songs. I've been reading them over, looking for one to set down here for myself that most brings her back to me, my friend whom I loved. There are too many and each with something to say of her so that it doesn't seem fair to have only one. For each seems to come forth as a song of irrepressible spirit and always against such obstacles.

She seems then like one of those green plants with small blue flowers that forces its way up through the pavement itself.

> Razors pain you;
> Rivers are damp;
> Acids stain you;
> And drugs cause cramp.
> Guns aren't lawful;
> Nooses give;
> Gas smells awful;
> You might as well live.

I want to say here what I really think for somehow at this moment I am overcome with her gallantry and courage.

I think one of those times—and there were several when she found that razors pain you and rivers are damp—she didn't come back.

Not the same Dorothy Parker.

Her spirit said to her *You might as well live*, you've still got a lot to learn, to do, to be. So she spent those long later years in a more or less humdrum sort of way, working as consistently as she could at whatever tasks came her way, sitting beside the grave of her genius, remembering yesterday, and her departed friend, Benchley, remembering in cooling blood what she had written when it flowed hot and magnificent within her. Remembering the poems she had once written.

"I never saw a sweeter child—
    The little one, the darling one!—
.I mind, I told her when he smiled
    You'd know he was his mother's son.

"It's queer that I should see them so—
    The time they came to Bethlehem
Was more than thirty years ago;
    I've prayed that all is well with them."

No woman ever showed more *guts* than Dorothy Parker did in the last years. To sit on the sidelines and watch the game in which she had once been the brightest star—no woman was ever a brighter one than Dorothy Parker of the Algonquin Round Table, every word she spoke, and a lot she didn't, was quoted as one of her *bons mots*. Yet as the last of life went on for her, all downhill, she kept her humor and her courage.

Mark Kelly would understand her at our Tavern, he knew all about champions. And Mr. Hearst, sitting with him there, would think only of how she could write. For him, that was the first consideration. Write it! With speed and accuracy, he always said. Dottie had both.

Genius?

Yes, I think so.

Who are we to say otherwise?

And yet—those so slim volumes. So limited sometimes. Such a small output—smaller than Shelley or Keats. And she lived so much longer.

When there are other women writers as I move along on my quest who can—and did—do it all.

Like Edna Ferber.

2

Yes yes.

For the gal who could do it all, did it well prolifically and profitably for over thirty years, I have to see nobody but Miss Edna Ferber of Kalamazoo, Michigan, author of such novels as *So Big*, for which she got the Pulitzer Prize, of *Show Boat*, one of the most successful musicals of all time was made out of that, later of *Cimarron* and most recently *Saratoga Trunk*, the movie starred Gary Cooper and Ingrid Bergman, finally of *Giant* which everyone may recall had the whole state of Texas in an uproar. Of course Texas gets in an uproar often and easily but the one over Edna Ferber's *Giant* was a dilly.

She loved it!

Never having any *personal* life of her own, no husband, no lover, no children, no family except the mother she adored, Edna put it all—all the emotion of her strong, sometimes violent, excitable, high-spirited and even melodramatic nature—into her work and her causes.

There is in a letter once written by George S. Kaufman, that most successful playwright, collaborator and producer of the American Theater when it existed at its magnificent best, a paragraph about Edna Ferber, with whom he collaborated on a number of smash hit plays. I think we might as well start with it—he knew her so well and few of us can compete with Kaufman in delineation of a character:

> I know that Edna does not want to work with me again. We threshed out the whole thing again, with no great bitterness and Edna doing most of the talking. She is so sure that she is right in everything she says—it must be wonderful to be like that. Never is there the possibility in her mind that anything she thinks or says could be less than gospel.

But Edna did of course want to work with him again. For they wrote *Stage Door*, and I believe a couple of others after that. I will always remember the thrill of seeing *Stage Door* with Margaret Sullavan—one of the illumined moments in the theater.

Gospel.

Right. Edna was a fighting liberal and, partly of course because of the power and popularity of her name *as* a writer, she elected a New York Mayor—Fiorello LaGuardia that was—and led the battle against real estate barons and political parties and forces when she broke the tabu on Jews long held by Fifth Avenue and Park Avenue hotels and apartment houses.

Nobody was ever prouder of being a Jew, nor more certain of the gifts of a Jewish heritage, than Edna Ferber.

My impression, however, when we were attending meetings, ringing doorbells, stopping people on street corners to tell them *what*, was that all the time Edna kept the recording machine with which every writer must be equipped going at full blast. Once when Katharine Hepburn came to my house in Beekman Place, New York, there were several newspapermen and writers and an editor or two having a dish of tea or a sup of Scotch and Kate was silent, I saw that she was taking in every movement, every facial expression, every tone of voice. How each one used his hands, the special position of the head as he listened. Edna Ferber, who wasn't really a *listener* by nature, always did the same thing when she did listen. As a reporter I was taught and trained to hear the conversation at three tables around me. Edna, I am sure, got the full significance of every movement, every facial change in everyone around her, and all of it eventually went into, let us say, "The Afternoon of a Faun," one of the top short stories ever written. (Yes, she could do those, too.)

But as definitely as Dottie Parker wrote out of her own life and emotions, Ferber didn't. She didn't have any to write 'em out of. But she was someone who was in on or caused a lot of those that happened to other people, her friends and foes. It was while on one of Edna's political massacres that I was arrested for resisting an officer. I do not usually resist officers or even privates for that matter but that's the kind of fracas my friend Edna got me into.

All these things with her—as with all writers—go into what I suppose the psychiatrist calls your subconscious but which I, for some reason obscure to me at the moment, call the Hopper. *Put it in the Hopper.* My dictionary says a hopper is a funnel-shaped chamber in which materials are stored and later discharged through the bottom; this I take to be my typewriter. I never know I'm doing it, nor am ever sure when or what'll be needed. Once I did a story about a young movie star—this was fiction—who adopted a baby. In such cases, of course, a social worker from the adoption agency made unexpected visits to see that all was well with the child, and it occurred to me that it would be a moving scene if our little adoptive mother was rocking the baby and singing a lullaby at one time when the checker-upper arrived. As I wrote the scene there came to me *in toto* the words of a classical Chinese lullaby, unusual and beautiful, that I'd heard my friend our Chinese cook use when I was a little girl in San Francisco. I had no idea that I'd remembered it, and I don't now, but I did then and it added something quite lovely to my story.

Like many good writers Edna had also had some early training as a reporter—you know they say now that Shakespeare himself wrote some of the bills that were pasted up on London walls as the earliest journals. On the Appleton *Crescent*, in Wisconsin, later on the Milwaukee *Journal* and the Chicago *Tribune* Edna Ferber acquired not only the reporter's instinctive and finally automatic observational response, the ability to keep her eye where the action was, but also the training of memory.

But her actual stories came, so she herself once told me, from her mother.

"My mother always told me stories," she said. "The first stories were told and sung by minstrels. My mother was a minnesinger. She never learned to write them down but she told them to me magnificently, not only in detail as to what everybody wore and ate and said, but with all the drama of the times in which they took place. Often the only times or places in which they could have taken place. I learned to put them down and between us we preserved many things of Americana that I am glad are preserved. She had great tenderness for our country and all that went to make it—and told it with such sympathy that it was easy to write."

I wish I had known Lorraine Hansberry better—and ohohoh I wish she had lived longer.

One night when I went backstage after seeing her great play, *Raisin in the Sun*, she was there for a visit with its star, Sidney Poitier, who is a friend of mine. I wish *I* could write plays but it is a gift far far beyond me. For some day I would do one in which that amazing actor could actually play the real Saint Martin de Porres instead of a version of him such as he gave us in *Lilies of the Field*. We've talked about this and he gave me the statue of Saint Martin which I so treasure to remind me! And Sister Mary Apollonia at the Immaculate Heart Convent out near Paoli, Pennsylvania, once translated a lot of Saint Martin from the Latin and

Spanish for him. If Lorraine Hansberry had lived longer she could have done something magnificent with this—for she herself was black and understood Saint Martin and his life better than anyone. I cherish that one time I met this playwright—I am dazzled by playwrights always, I don't see how they *do* it.

Ferber did that well, too. Mostly in collaborations, chiefly with George Kaufman.

Two other bits about Edna Ferber.
First, the dedication in one of her books.

> To my mother
> who thinks it doesn't
> interrupt if she whispers

Another when she said to me of Millay's *Renascence*, "Once in a while God sings through. It's as though something came whole, direct, without interference, without sweat. I hear that clear note in *Renascence*," and I had to be reminded as she said it that Edna St. Vincent Millay had once said to me, "I am so tired of hearing about *Renascence* I could *die*. It was my first poem and I've written several books since. Sometimes it seems discouraging that almost everybody remembers my first one, written when I was so very very young, better than any I've done since."

I said, "Yes—but if that came through you can always be hopeful as you read it—or hear how much it meant to people—that it might happen again."

I've had somewhat the same experience in a minor way, for nothing about prose, of course, can ever be the same as poetry.

But . . .

Early in my short story career I wrote one called "Never Again." One night at a party on Long Island a girl of whom I was fond got herself blind drunk—by no means a habit with her, in fact I'd never seen her drink too much before—and this produced the old vicious alcoholic circle. She drank too much because she thought her husband, a famed cartoonist, was making eyes at another woman and she thought her husband was making eyes at another woman because she'd had one drink too many. I got her out of there and drove her home and all the way she kept saying that when he came home, if he did, she was going to kill him. *I'm going to kill him*, she kept saying, *humiliating me like that before everybody*. Of course cartoonists always are *too much* one way or the other—Charlie Schulz who does *Peanuts* is my idea of a modern saint. I said to this wife that night, Don't talk like that, you'd be right sorry in the morning when you woke up in jail and they told you you'd killed your husband.

Well, the next morning I went around to their house to see how things were and all she had done was bopped him over the head with a golf club and he had a black eye, when she came to the door she was shaking like Jello in a high wind and she kept saying, Never again, Never again never again—so that's where that story and title came from and like Vincent with *Renascence* I am sometimes so tired of hearing about it I am dearly dead with it. My short story after its magazine debut was published in pamphlets. Used as a text from literally hundreds of pulpits. Circularized by the WCTU. Incorporated in college curriculums as both a short story and as sociological fiction, whatever that means. Naturally, I was proud the first time round, and touched even the second and third. As the years went by I began to wish, like Miss Millay, that they didn't go so far back, that they'd mention one in a current issue of *Ladies' Home Journal* or *Collier's* or *The Saturday Evening Post*. Or in the *Cosmopolitan* of that day, which was then a magazine of distinction and published not only the first short stories of Somerset Maugham but some by F. Scott Fitzgerald, Edna Ferber, Fannie Hurst and Rebecca West. Finally "Wedding Night" ran in *Good Housekeeping* and for a long time held the highest reader check—maybe it still does for all I know. I find a good many people saved copies and that always *heartens* a writer.

3

I love to remember the last words John Steinbeck, an old friend from the Monterey days who wrote *Grapes of Wrath*, said to me. I met him walking along Fifth Avenue on a bright sunny day. He gave me a limp wave of the hand and said—

"I can't get the damn thing to jell and I'm not fit company for man nor beast"

—and went on without stopping.

Writers get like that.

Why then, with all this blood, sweat and tears, do writers write? This is a legitimate question that all writers are asked. Why, when and how did they become writers?

Let's look for a moment at our present best-selling champ (this is the morning of August 6, 1973), Jacqueline Susann, whose work I admire. This is absolutely first-class top-drawer trash, which the reading public requires, always has required, insists upon and righteously adores. They demanded it of Dickens, of Kathleen Norris who wrote two great novels—*Certain People of Importance* and *Little Ships*—and two hundred others that weren't great, they were pure trash. Kipling wrote *The Light that Failed*—and it sure did! He also wrote *Kim* and *The Jungle Book* and I wouldn't want to try to live without them. Even Shakespeare must have thought he had to do it and did it—or what did he mean by AS *YOU* LIKE IT, you silly bastards, all about a girl in boy's clothes and other inanities.

Jackie Susann couldn't help writing and she has become what she should be, the darling and most-bought of the public. I'm with her. She's brought them intense interest at a time when books had not commanded the interest of the public that follows her like a Pied Piper, she brought them sound judgment and good will and a fine observational eye for backgrounds and states of the country. Here's a girl who just plain couldn't help it. She was an actress of some success and apparently began to *think* and be spurred into writing when she did a television show for her husband, Irving Mansfield, called "This Is Show Business." It was an outstanding success and on camera the beautiful Susann would place herself between Clifton Fadiman and George S. Kaufman if she could. She wanted to *write*. Her husband told me that she was always more impressed and interested in any writers who came on the show than in other stars however famous they might be.

At a chance meeting in the Doubleday Book Shop on Fifth Avenue one day when her first book, *Not Tonight, Josephine*, had just come out she told me, "Everyone tells me I'm a little mad, they tell me I am a success in my profession as an actress, what makes me think I can write books when I'm not a writer. But *I* say what *is* a writer but someone who writes books, I write books, I'm going to keep on writing books therefore I am a writer so maybe I'm crazy but I'm not stupid."

People come to me and talk about the books they want to write though they're not really writers. But they don't write 'em. Jackie did—and Jackie does.

Which reminds me of a classic remark once made by the mother of our American humorist, George Ade. His *Fables in Slang*, his stories of Siwash College were startlingly successful and his play, *The College Widow*, ran for years. "Anybody," said George Ade's mother, "can write as well as George does. But George does."

Helen Keller, the lady who had more handicaps than any aching back or an allergy to smog, in that she was also deaf, dumb and blind, says that her *How* was to keep the fibers of her writing consciousness connected with that which was autobiographical. With that which she has known and felt herself. The Little Flower of Jesus, Saint Thérèse de Lisieux, patroness and darling of the American Armies during their sojourns in France, says obedience to the Inner Flame is essential. I suppose all of us do have an inner flame even if sometimes it's no bigger than a wet match. Her own *L'Histoire d'une Âme* is a spiritual autobiography. Some of the history of our souls must be there to make any kind of a great book. As for the actual *writing* of the Little Flower, she proves that if you have a lot to say you will find a way to say it, and this how to say it was given to her *a toute outrance*.

The most important thing for a writer or would-be writer (or as far as I am concerned almost anybody else anywhere any time) is *reading*. I tell this to my classes at the University of Missouri, School of Journalism (the best in the world) and UCLA Pepperdine and Cal Poly.

Read! Read! Read! Read!

If you can't and can't learn then you have no more right to wish to be a writer than a kid who can't watch the White Sox or the Cardinals has to want to play baseball.

Gets you a bad reputation if you refuse invitations because you have to stay home with a book. But what is a writer without a bad reputation of some kind? When to a would-be hostess I gave this excuse, she said, "What book?" and I said, "David Cecil's *Melbourne*," and she said, "But you've already read that, I'm sure," and I said, "That's why I know it's worth staying home to read again," and I was too polite to add, "And who do you think you're going to have at your dinner table to compete with the company of this great mind and a great writer writing about him? To say nothing of the young Queen Victoria and later Victoria at her most Victorian and Caroline Lamb and Lord Byron?"

Don't ask *me* what a writer should read. Or what *you* should read.

Anything—big or little, important or trivial—that makes one shout Hallelujah they invented the printing press. It's a wonderful world where you wake up every morning and know they're still there—the Books. You can go to your shelves, or the book stores, or the libraries, bless them all, and find every kind of entertainment, laughter, tears, adventures, people, tragedy comedy melodrama from the first day when we *read* "God said, Let there be light" right up to the assuaging absorbent comfort of Agatha Christie and Miss Marple or Hercule Poirot, for which I am forever grateful.

I never read anything that bores me. Never have.

At any age.

I don't care who told me how great it was or how intellectual it has been made to seem. I'm not an intellectual and I don't care, for *if* the writer isn't good enough not to bore you, then he isn't good enough for you to read. As the first requisite of a candidate is that he be electable, so the first requisite of a book is that it must be entertaining.

Once upon a time I found a journalism class reading a heavy tome of useless information written in time to Chopin's funeral march. They looked ready for that last narrow bed, but I'd brought along my Xeroxed copies of Damon Runyon's lead stories on and at the Hauptmann trial—those shook 'em up allright. When I gave them an assignment with a fast deadline after that, they sprained their ankles and their imaginations to go and write it for me. Out of that class I got two good writers and one that landed a job in an advertising firm.

A suggestion. For myself to remember.

When I am working on something that requires a kind or style of writing it's well to read whatever author did that best. On short biographies I sink myself in Lytton Strachey, who in *Eminent Victorians* created a new style and tempo in this field. I can quote

by heart—and enjoy it always—the opening paragraph of his
Florence Nightingale. He brought the Lady with the Lamp out of
misty sanctification into our lives. I remember how much it helped
me when I was asked to write the story at the time Clark Gable
died. I thought—oh no, no, I can't. I am in too much sorrow myself. Then I thought, Oh yes you can! This is your chance to build
a memorial to your friend. Not of stone or marble. *Of words.* As
Strachey did for his Lady. I cannot do it as well but by keeping
that model before me I can *do* it.

So—I tried.

That's about all I ever do. *Try.* If some time you're very pleased
with it, chuck it in the wastebasket. It's illegitimate, for always a
writer's reach must exceed his grasp.

4

Sometimes our language, in spite of my constant companionship with Roget's Thesaurus, cultivated assiduously along with all
other writers, is woefully inadequate.

My purpose here is to select the best—topmost—successfulest
American woman writer of our times, the one who best exemplifies
the spirit of the American woman as it has existed to the glory and
benefit of her—and our—country. Let me say now that the Batting
Titles right now today are held by women, no possible question
about this. No man writing today can challenge them. Nor can I
think of any woman writer shoddy enough or hungry enough to
say, as a man writer did recently, that a book he had signed is
sloppy and not his best, is prostitution of his talent because he needs
the money! No man of today is a champion if I think in terms of
James Thurber, Ring Lardner and Jack London.

Now as for women I have narrowed it down some and wish to
consider two—and these as different in style and content as it is
possible to be.

Anne Morrow Lindbergh and Rebecca West.

At once I grant that Rebecca West is a native of Ireland who
lives in England when she stays home, which is seldom. But she is
such a best seller, so beloved, in the United States and she does
write in English so I would like to include her *in*, as that wonderful
man, Sam Goldwyn, used to say in the early days of Hollywood.

For she *is* a woman writer in our language, much read by our country, and so far in a class by herself that to think of including her *out* gives me what my grandsons call a pain in my gut.

They were born, 'tis true, only fifteen years apart yet it stretches into real difference when I note that they were in different centuries, those events. Rebecca West in *1892* and Anne Morrow-to-become-Lindbergh in *1907*.

Anne was the first to sail a new sea.

Rebecca West has had the monumental courage to write prose as though it was poetry and once on a third reading I got over a hundred new words for colors out of a book of hers. She is a Dame of the British Empire and began by writing novels none of which are extraordinary. *The Return of the Soldier* and *The Judge* are at best top trash, and that's all that can be said for the last ones, of which I have forgotten the names and it's not worth while looking them up.

Along in those early days she became noted—notorious—for a passionate extracurricular association with H. G. Wells, who put it in a glass bowl called *Ann Veronica*, a novel, for all to read. Writers do this, I kid you not. Nothing is sacred to them and nothing should be. Writing—the story—must always come first and I am holding only two things back myself. One a letter written by Franklin Delano Roosevelt about the Third Term and the other a dramatic tragedy involving members of my family and a lot of good *that's* done me! They just plain resent the fact that I *know* about it—or come to think of it for the first time this minute maybe they feel *slighted* because I haven't used it. People are always seeing themselves as the characters in your books when, God help me, most of them are too pallid and commonplace to make much copy.

Fortunately Rebecca soon took to reporting. And this is a word I use instead of non-fiction (I dislike Nons) and by it I mean covering real events. History in the making or in the recently made as *news*.

Nobody has ever done this as well as Rebecca West, not even Thomas Babington Macaulay, on whom my father raised me so that, while I never really got out of grammar school, I am historically pretty sound. Rebecca West made a seamless robe out of the past, the present and the future and, if you put it on with her, you live for a time at least in three dimensions. She is the top writer who can take you with her on her travels and keep you entertained every moment. I am a bad traveler, and so I know that if she can do that to me she can do it with anybody.

How clearly I remember, how utterly I can relive, my first encounter with the greatest of her books.

BLACK LAMB AND GREY FALCON

Now what, I said to myself the first time I encountered these strange words, does that mean?

I was staying with Cissy Patterson, the owner and publisher of the Washington *Times-Herald,* and working out of its city room for INS. Her mansion—and mansion it was and used sometimes as the White House when that center of the Universe was having trouble with the plumbing or the roof about to fall in—her mansion in Dupont Circle was filled with all Cissy's kindness and she had the time, money and taste to provide her guests with the books she thought they wanted to read most. On this occasion apparently she thought I wanted to read—or needed to read?— *Black Lamb and Grey Falcon* by Rebecca West, enormous black books marked I and II. When I opened the cover, inside I found that these dealt with A Journey Through Yugoslavia in 1937.

Yugoslavia? I thought. Now what?

The dedication read:

> To my Friends in Yugoslavia who are
> now all dead or enslaved.

> Grant to them the Fatherland of their
> Desire and make them again citizens
> of Paradise.

Things began to fall into some kind of pattern for me.

Yugoslavia was in the Balkans. The Balkan States, on the Balkan Peninsula, were Romania, Bulgaria, Albania, Greece—and I could remember that when I was a very young girl and even after I went to work as a reporter there was always Trouble in the Balkans. So much so that it became rather like the cry of Wolf! Wolf! when there was no wolf, and then one day in the city of Sarajevo somebody assassinated an Archduke, Francis Ferdinand of Austria, and *that,* children, was the external event that en-

gulfed Europe in the First World War which we finally had to
enter to make it come out right for the good guys—so there had
indeed been trouble in the Balkans.

This is all history now but once in my cub days on the paper it
was news.

Just the same I said to myself, Maybe this is more than I want
to know about the Balkans, as Anatole France once remarked about
Penguins.

On the other hand—*Rebecca West*.

No one, then or now, could be a more avid *fana*tic about
Rebecca West and any of her works that were reporting. I look
up to her as the best of our profession. Sometimes the word
Journalism—or journalistic writing—is thrown at me in reviews by
critics who certainly couldn't have lasted two editions on any
journal I ever had to do with including the New York *Times* and
the Chicago *Tribune* and the St. Louis *Dispatch*. And I wonder
why it is used with opprobrium. I suppose one way to deal with
what you can't do yourself is to belittle anyone who can. If you
can't make it as a reporter, become a critic or a columnist. How
about that? To say it may show more courage than sense but once
in a while you have to counterpunch.

Before I met her I considered Rebecca West the top woman
reporter who ever lived and about this, since Mr. Hearst and
Walter Howey considered me pretty good in that field, I feel my
opinion is expert. Her coverage of the trial of the arch traitor
William Joyce, who broadcast during World War II from Ger-
many as Lord Haw Haw, and which later appeared as a book
called *The Meaning of Treason*, is so good it rules out any jealousy
or envy as even Simon and Garfunkel must feel when they hear
Chopin and Schubert. It is the Supreme.

With my granddaughters Kristen and Kathy and Tracey I had
been visiting Paul Gallico at his villa in Antibes and when I departed for London he wrote his good friend Rebecca West and
told her to look me up. This she kindly did and asked me to come
down to her country estate for a visit. I could hardly wait but
while I was packing, Rebecca on the phone was explaining that
something had happened to the *drains*. She would come to London
instead, could I lunch with her the next day at the Savoy Grill and

Must I bring any of my granddaughters because, said Rebecca, in that case I will have to ask mine and it takes her so long to get untidy enough to come out. Besides her husband has just divorced her, she married a negro, you know, and he said he was tired of being her social conscience. It was not, he had told her, a good atmosphere in which to attempt a happy marriage. At this point I interrupted because my clock showed me an approaching appointment with a Beaverbrook editor, and said their father had flown over to take his two daughters home and Kris had a lunch date with Graham Greene, Jr., and he has promised to buy her a *savory*. She says she has read about them in English novels for years and doesn't know what one really is because it seems the English eat them at both ends of the meal—which it turned out simply means that the English eat what we call canapés or toast spread with anchovies or caviar or cheese for dessert if they feel like it.

Rebecca came to London and stayed at her Club, which fascinated me since it is something women in America do not have, and I saw London with her—from the room where Dickens held his little sister-in-law in his arms as she died, to the lowest step at the entrance to the Tower of London where Princess Elizabeth set her foot on her way, she thought, to the block where her mother, Anne Boleyn, had lost her head, to the illustrious graves in Westminster Abbey.

I saw then in this great lady of the literary world that the women of England had always accepted Wordsworth's definition:

> The reason firm, the temperate will,
> Endurance, foresight, strength and skill;
> A perfect woman, nobly planned,
> To warn, to comfort and command.

In my workroom today is a memento of that visit to London, filled with enchantment by Rebecca West. When I left for America it seemed a small if courteous gesture, no measure of my thanks, to send her a few dozen roses. By that time Kris and I were flat broke anyhow, though we had been Conrad Hilton's guests in his own suite at the London Hilton. So a few pounds hither and thither scraping the very bottom made small difference. The memento I treasure is a picture of Rebecca West with a bowl full

of those roses and a note to say Thank you, "I just wanted you
to see how lovely the roses are."

Who else would have thought of that?

Have you ever had your picture taken with the roses—or dande-
lions or anything else—someone sent you?

Neither have I.

Though I did have one in a ski cap Win Rockefeller brought
me from Peru. He said it cost him ten cents and I had to be reminded of Dorothy Parker's

> Why is it no one ever sent me yet
> One perfect limousine, do you suppose?
> Ah no, it's always just my luck to get . . .

One perfect *ski cap?** And that's hardly fair either because as I
said in *The Honeycomb* Rudy Vallee did once give me a perfect
Cadillac. Of course my training that a *lady* can accept only flowers,
books or a handkerchief from a gentleman—

However—

I hadn't met Rebecca West and fallen victim to her personal
warm humor and bright blue eyes when Cissy Patterson came up
to my room with *Black Lamb and Grey Falcon* as my reading
matter for the visit. Behind me lay a morning of White House
Press Conference with FDR who *really* knew how to conduct
one, *and* an afternoon in the Press Box at the Senate. I was ready
for a new Dorothy L. Sayers or an adventure with Nero Wolfe
to make me forget the growing tension of the controversy
around our entry into World War II. However, said I to myself,
what you need most is sleep. So don't fuss.

I can only remember that far from putting me to *sleep*, I had
been in Croatia, Dalmatia, Herzegovina and Bosnia and just
arrived in Belgrade where I was reading:

> It is said that Belgrade is the center of the European
> Spy System and it may be that some of these people
> were spies. One about whom such a doubt might be
> harbored came up to me while we were eating our
> chicken liver risotto, an Italian whom I had last seen in
> a night club in Vienna. I remembered our meeting be-

* The original, of course, was "One perfect rose."

cause of his answer to my inquiry as to what he was doing in Austria. "I come from Spain," he said, "but I have never good fortune. I hoped to bring a bull to fight, but the bull, he will not come."

This, I now find, is on page 473 and I read it by the dawn's early light coming in at Cissy's guest room window.

The Meaning of Treason—The New Meaning of Treason— these are examples of the finest reporting ever done by any woman, or any man for that matter. She has all the hard-hitting, news-worthy, I-was-there quality of Damon Runyon, plus the editorial sagacity of a William Randolph Hearst, with a dash of the emotion of a good reportorial sob sister like Ernie Pyle.

If we finally do inaugurate a Women's Hall of Fame and I am on the Entrance Committee, which I feel I should be, having been around practically longer than anybody, I shall nominate at once as the first figure to be placed there Anne Morrow Lindbergh.

No one can drive three mules.

This is the Irish proverb. Referring to the Liberated Woman and her inability to really handle a husband, children *and* a career—it is wrong. Anne Morrow Lindbergh can, did and does. She has located the *source* of woman's irrepressible spirit, which of course can drive anything. And so she handles her three mules by what she herself calls Grace.

Married to Charles Augustus Lindbergh, most famous of aviators, and, between us, not a man I would wish to try to make a happy home and marriage with from what, as a member of the Press, I know about him. We the Press (for the People) found the Lone Eagle extraordinarily difficult to deal with. And Anne's marriage has lasted almost half a century. As a mother, she survived the kidnapping and death of her first son when he was not yet two years old and has had the courage and spirit to continue a fine family, kept out of all spotlights, naturally, but one of her sons today ranks very high in the engineering field at a great university. And I regard *Gift from the Sea* as the best written, most illumined and illustrious book of our century.

She is a new dimension among women.

I must go into my own coverage of the trial of Bruno Richard Hauptmann for the kidnapping and murder of Charles Augustus Lindbergh, Jr., to show you something of her life story, and of why, perhaps, *Gift from the Sea* is a gift she has made to every woman in the world.

> The witnesses never to be forgotten by me;
> Anne Morrow Lindbergh
> Charles Lindbergh
> Betty Gow
> Dr. Jafsie Condon
> etc., etc., etc.

For me Anne Morrow Lindbergh came first—not only me, for every member of the Press in that Flemington, New Jersey, courtroom.

THE BIG MOMENTS

We who sit in this courtroom have seen something we will never forget. When Anne Lindbergh sat on the witness stand we saw a slim young thing in black who will never be entirely happy again but who, a great woman and a great lady, was gallant in grief.

Anne Lindbergh didn't break, she didn't faint. None of the things movie actresses do in big scenes.

I would rather have seen her break than to behold that brave smile. I would rather have seen her faint than watch those pauses when her face grew whiter and whiter and it took every drop of her courage to speak at last . . .

The new dimension she gave us was spiritual leadership, the irrepressible light of true gallantry under fire. This gently reared daughter of a fine family, as we used to call such people dedicated to principle, integrity and honorable conduct, knew the joys of a quiet and cultured home, the felicity of a united family where father and mother both put home and family ahead of everything else, even though Dwight Morrow was a banker and an ambassador of note. Like Kate Hepburn—and it has always seemed to me they have the same kind of beauty, the beauty of bone structure, more that of sculpture than painting—*principles* and rules of conduct were ingrained from her cradle. Anne Morrow's years at Smith, the woman's college that it seems to me has avoided so many of the mistakes made by some others, were rewarded by academic distinction. And when the world's hero—the most shining one we've ever had—Lindbergh came to visit the American ambassador to Mexico on a friendship flight it wasn't the beauty of the family, oldest daughter Constance, or the youngest, as the fairy tale always has it for the Prince, but the middle one, Anne, whom he carried away with him. He was then, of course, the catch of the century. And yet—when I pick up a volume of *Gift from the Sea*—and there seems to be one in every room in the house—I find that here is humility of the kind a candle shows when shining alone in the dark. There is a lot of dark but the candle knows it has been given light that no darkness can stand against. And between the rich gentle home life and the cultured education, this woman writer of all others has produced an utter *simplicity*, a purity of style and plainness of speech, a value of content that is outstanding. It had to come from that Higher Source.

I find all my copies underlined to such an extent that I hardly know where to begin to select a few quotes.

> Woman must be the pioneer in this turning inward for strength.

> Why have we been seduced into abandoning this timeless inner strength of woman for the temporal outer strength of man?

> Moon shell, you will remind me that unless I keep the island-quality intact somewhere within me, I will have little to give my husband, my children, my friends or the world at large.

> For it is the spirit of woman that is going dry, not the mechanics that are wanting.

> We throw ourselves indiscriminately into committees and causes, not knowing how to feed the spirit, we try to muffle its demands with distractions.

> Mechanically, we have gained in the last generation but spiritually we have unwittingly lost.

Speaking of woman as the mainstay of the church, she says:

> Here no one could intrude with a careless call of Mother, Wife, Mistress of the Household. Here finally and more deeply, woman was whole, not split into a thousand functions. She was able to give herself in that hour of worship, in prayer, in communication, and be completely accepted. And in that giving and acceptance she was renewed; the springs were refilled.

So here for Anne Morrow Lindbergh, as it can be for all of us, was that Grace which made it possible to drive the team—any team—however few or many.

Besides *Gift from the Sea*, she has written what are to me the best books on flying. *North to the Orient* and *Listen, the Wind* usher us into that new world where man *flies*. She presents it to us with a wonder, a strength, a fearlessness that means much to and in this new world, committed to the air element of the Universe. So this is another thing that, for me, makes Anne Morrow Lindbergh a great woman writer to be considered as maybe the One. For here she has also the sociological aspect that adds importance and scope—certainly travel by air today is a sociological problem and she deals with it as no one else ever has.

I have here to make an apology to myself.

Our most distinguished American woman novelist is beyond question Pearl Buck. No other American woman writer has won the Nobel Prize for Literature. Of course, also, the Pulitzer Prize, for *Good Earth*.

Personally, I couldn't like and admire anyone more than I did Pearl Buck.

When I was going down almost weekly to do the Mike Douglas TV Show in Philadelphia, she was kindness and courtesy itself to me. She often asked me to lunch and we sat in a corner of the Warwick Grill. Or she invited me to her home on a beautiful Pennsylvania farm, than which there is none more beautiful in the world, where she lived with all her adopted children. It was indeed a haven for children in need, and she spoke to and of them with eloquence fired by a passion of caring—and her Chinese garden there was what I hope heaven will be if I ever get there. Only a spirit of irrepressible gallantry could have planned, planted and made to grow that garden. For no one has more enemies to fight than a gardener. Even if she had a green thumb, as I'm sure she did, there are the endless hours of weeding and digging and watering and praying over. The result was a gem I'm grateful to have spent some hours in with this great woman.

I *know* that her works merited the Nobel Prize and the lesser Pulitzer. I am sure she was as happy and proud and content with such recognition as no other woman writer has ever had. It will not, I am sure, trouble her in the least therefore that I cannot read her books.

Here I am, a stray, forlorn minority of one who cannot read Pearl Buck . . .

Someone is going to ask me about Willa Cather.

Bound to. Just as when I eulogized Tom Mix as the great American cowboy who created the art of the Western, people always asked me about William S. Hart—who was a Shakespearean actor of the third class and afraid of horses.

Willa Cather was a fine—maybe our finest—American woman novelist.

She was a horrid, harsh, repellent woman and a lousy unscrupulous reporter. Truth is the one perfect defense for libel, so I'm going to let that stand no matter what my lawyers or those of my publisher say about it.

I once followed her trail when I hoped to write a life story of that great American woman—*and* writer—Mary Baker Eddy. Probably the greatest all around American woman of all time. Think about her a moment. She is the only woman who ever started a major religion, which Christian Science most certainly is. Her book *Science and Health with Key to the Scriptures* is an all-time top best-seller. The Mother Church in Boston, built by and for her by her millions of followers, now takes in with its Publishing House as much ground as the Vatican. She affected *all* Christian religions with her insistence that Jesus actually meant what he said when it came to casting out devils and healing the sick. Mrs. Eddy did more for copyright and copyright laws in the years she spent in Washington on this project than anyone else has ever done for us. And when she started her great newspaper, the

Christian Science Monitor—started it with a brief letter instructing them to begin to publish it at once—she was in her eighty-eighth year. I do not include her as a writer, though no American woman has written a more successful book, because writing was secondary to her propaganda purpose—a good one, of course. And if I find it fascinating because she had to invent practically a new vocabulary for her teaching, she did it to such height that it has now become part of ours.

As I followed Mrs. Eddy's life through New England—she is, by the way, the only woman whose journey through life is put forward in an automobile club road map pamphlet showing each of her homes and the places where important events happened—on the trail I also followed Willa Cather. Out of it, to my amazement, I found Willa Cather had stirred with grim fancy the most vicious and inaccurate of all the attacks on Mrs. Eddy. This contributed to a magazine serial and later a book by Georgine Milmine. Fortunately Mrs. Eddy was the most successful counter-puncher in the feminine history of our country so instead of Miss Cather doing her harm, these attacks were used by Mrs. Eddy to spread her teaching and the truth about herself.

5

A serious mistake, to say Edna Ferber could do it all.

To me, poetry is another world.

There are times, there is work, I have met people, where I feel sure there is a line, a beam, a channel open to the Source. We know this about the greatest teacher of all, whatever our spiritual or religious beliefs may be. Jesus of Nazareth taught us from the Source of all wisdom and love. No other explanation for the infallible provable truth of his teachings. Mozart invented music so far beyond any human conception up to his moment of truth that we know it came from the Light itself. Shakespeare—Titian when he painted the Entombment—

I feel this way about poetry. Real poetry, I mean. Keats, and Shelley, and Whitman and Emily Dickinson and, in our twentieth century, Edna St. Vincent Millay.

One day I was walking through the lobby of the Plaza and met face to face a short, square-built woman in a brown coat with the wrong kind of fur collar carrying a paper shopping bag. It was around noon so I persuaded Edna Ferber to come into the Edwardian Room for lunch. I say persuaded because she was, as usual, steaming along and didn't wish to stop for food or conversation. After we had ordered, I suddenly had to ask myself a direct question. Can she really do it all? So I asked her one.

"Edna, my love," I said, "have you ever tried to write poetry?"

"I wouldn't dare," she said simply.

From Miss Ferber, who had jolly well dared to tell George S. Kaufman how to write plays and Fiorello LaGuardia how to run the City of New York.

"Have you?" she asked back.

"Me?" I said. "Heaven forbid. And that was why I was furious with *The New Yorker!* It made me look so silly."

"What did *The New Yorker* do?" Edna said.

So I explained that once upon a time in one of its more impish moments—or probably on a day when James Thurber was on vacation—they had published a poem under the heading

EDNA ST. VINCENT MILLAY

and

ADELA ROGERS ST. JOHNS

I had been horrified then, told Edna Ferber how horrified I was, and find I am horrified still. Truly and honestly, I regard myself and did then as a first-class newspaperwoman, a fair-to-middling short story writer, with two real good stories to my credit though "Never Again" and "Wedding Night" are still not to be mentioned in the same breath with Ring Lardner. *A great artist*, Dorothy Parker called Lardner in her book reviews when a collection of his stories was published; she titled this review *Hero Worship* and I'd like to join that society.

But the very idea of having my name joined with that of a great *Poet* who has to be some kind of seraph among writers has me back chewing my fingernails, a practice I abandoned when I was three.

Remember, from the day she won a poetry contest with *Renascence*, Millay was in some measure our Poet Laureate. Crowned thus and expected to give us Poetry to celebrate our victories, to show us our guilt and outline the heartbreak we should have for it, to speak to us in winged words to show us the way, as poets should.

There was *Justice Denied in Massachusetts* at the time she walked with others around the Governor's Mansion demanding that justice for Sacco and Vanzetti. (I think I forgot to tell you that Dorothy Parker and Robert Benchley were also there, walking hand in hand.)

Edna St. Vincent Millay thought Sacco and Vanzetti innocent. As I did.

There were poems written for *The Saturday Evening Post* on order to recall the true meaning of the Fourth of July. And there is "Memory of England":

> I am glad, I think, my happy mother died
> Before the German airplanes over the English
> countryside
> Dropped bombs into the peaceful hamlets we
> used to know—

Or:

> Say we saw Spain die. O Splendid bull,
> how well you fought!

Or "To the Maid of Orleans":

> Joan, Joan, can you be
> Tending sheep in Domrémy?
> Have no voices spoken plain:
> France has need of you again?

ending:

> Martyred many times must be
> Who would keep his country free.

Oh yes, she said in ringing and sometimes terrible words what our hearts used to feel—I wish we had her now—or do our hearts no longer feel as we did then?

Distressed as I was over that *New Yorker* headline good came of it for me. Miss Millay was amused and, she said, pleased by it, she was kind enough to say she liked some of my prose very much. And so I was then invited to Steepletop. This was the farm and its farmhouse in upper New York State that Edna and her husband, Eugen Boissevain had searched for, found, bought and

reconditioned years before. Boissevain was the ideal partner in this
happy and extraordinarily productive marriage. He protected her,
her time, her inspirations and gave her at Steepletop the ideal
place for her to live and he made it possible for her to live there
in the big reconditioned house by taking both the running of the
farm itself and the household off her shoulders. Two souvenirs of
that visit are treasured in my Memory Chest and *that* is something
there isn't enough money or time in the world to buy. What
would I be, what could I do or think, without my memories? One
of those I brought back from Steepletop was the man-woman husband-wife love I saw existing for everyday needs between Edna
and *U*gen as she called him. It is difficult, by the way, to know
what he or anybody else called Edna St. Vincent Millay Boissevain. Or what she called herself. In the book of her Letters, which
is one of my prized possessions, she signs herself variously—on
December 5, 1912, to Mr. and Mrs. Arthur Davison Ficke:

Edna St. Vincent Millay

All her early letters to her mother are signed:

Vincent

A list of her school courses to a teacher is:

Vincent Millay

In 1921 one to Norma is:
Your big sister
Vincent

And on the same day to Edmund Wilson a letter is signed *Edna*.
Then variously:

Edna M.

Edna Millay

Yours for a carefree winter
Edna St. Vincent Millay

To a member of her family occasionally her nickname Sefe and
once or twice, a family joke, *Edener.*

I must go back for myself to that husband-wife love I saw at
Steepletop. For everyday needs. This can be? I said to myself. A

man and woman can love each other with romantic and kind devotion over many years? I saw the golden *kindness* in every word and deed surrounding Vincent and Eugen. Oh—writers do need this so! They are so unsure so much of the time. That is why they can fall to such depths as Norman Mailer has done. Kind words—praise of what we *do*—sometimes I suppose it is to wonder why writers should have it more than someone who sells bonds or teaches school or heads a business. All I can say, very humbly, is, that if *we* don't get some of it somewhere *you* don't get any of it from us, anywhere any time. The oil of kindness helps, it seems, to give birth and I have seen this myself over and over and over.

For instance, our hero Ring Lardner wrote most often in the cold horror of a hangover. This is not to indicate that a hangover is a good time to write. For most people, the clear wish to die at once prevents any functioning of whatever sixth or seventh sense has to do with writing. But Ring once told me that the only way he could survive the hangover horrors was to justify his existence by writing something and selling it for his wife and four sons. Let me tell you, his wife Ellis was as much responsible for his greatness as he was, maybe more. She understood all this, and upheld and renewed his confidence. Instead of berating him with reminders of *you weren't really very funny last night*, Ellis gave him silence and solitude and soda water. As a result, we have *The Golden Honeymoon, The Champion* and *You Know Me, Al.* Three stories as different as *Hamlet, Henry V*, and *A Comedy of Errors.*

If poets don't get some measure of this protection they die young as did Keats and Poe. Millay got it at Steepletop.

And the other things I brought away from there were Millay's love of music and her steely sense of self-discipline. This is something I know about—it is called *keeping up your music.* You ought to, they tell you. It's a shame you don't keep up your music so you can at least play for your own satisfaction. Most of us don't. When I find a mature woman who has played the piano very well as a girl and still does, I know I am looking at a self-disciplinarian.

No one has more liberty never to do another stroke of work and starve to death or live off someone else than a writer.

I'm a fan for *Letters.*
In this day of telephone, teletypes, automobiles and telegrams,

the art of letter-writing is being lost. Yet nothing else ever re-
creates times and people with more excitement, heart and truth.
Even ordinary letters from your grandmother when you were
away at school or your granddaughters now that they are. When
they are back and forth between the beautiful English stage star
Ellen Terry and George Bernard Shaw or from Saint Frances
Cabrini to her sisterhood or Jane Addams to raise money for
Hull House, they must be superstars among letters.

In his magnificent play *The Skin of Our Teeth*, Thornton
Wilder sets forth that a new civilization can and must begin after
the last one has been destroyed or destroyed itself *only* by and with
the books that have been saved. If you want an exciting evening
among friends who can read, find out what books they would save.
What books they believe must be there when the glacier melts.
I have already decided on some volumes of letters and of course
among them Mother Cabrini and the *Letters of Edna St. Vincent
Millay*.

Now, oh dear dear dear me! as my grandmother used to say
with her choice of four-letter words for emphasis, I am having a
time here because I want to quote a lot more than space permits.
By no means just for writers, but for all human beings who need
words of comfort or inspiration along about here in this modern
world, and its pressures.

> When I become so exhausted with my own work that I
> can neither think nor see, so twisted and entangled by
> anxieties, either about personal matters or about the
> awful mess the world is in that it seems that if I ever
> extricate myself at all it will be at least a double curva-
> ture of the mind, the only thing that will *straighten
> me out* is to read Latin Poetry . . . when I lay the book
> down I am at the same time serene and exhilarated.

I cannot read Latin Poetry as did Miss Millay, and the chances
are neither can most of the folks I know—or who may read this.
Nevertheless, somehow, somewhere, from somebody or something—what with the goings-on in Washington, the pollution, the
threat of a Silent Spring, the rise in prices, the traffic and the taxes,
the self-centeredness and the lack of kindness to each other around
us—we must find its equivalent for ourselves.

Mine, I tell you flatly and frankly and without embarrassment, is prayer.

Not answered prayer.

How do I know what the answer is?

Maybe as the little boy who didn't get his bicycle told his father the answer is NO.

Just being able to pray in my way. After I've made a fool of myself. When I am *worried* about a child or a grandchild. When I can't *work*.

Prayer that listens. Reaches out. Seeks.

I hope the *seeking* is all.

I pray best for my own straightening out when I walk beside the Pacific Ocean in front of my house, or San Francisco Bay anywhere on its four hundred miles of shore, until I am too exhausted to remember all the mistakes I made last night! To be sure, sometimes this makes you so serene that the exhilaration doesn't come and you go on in this lovely serenity and never write a word. You become a beachcomber. Or a dropout. *But* the only thing that can bring about the triumph of evil is for women who are good, or trying to be, to do or say nothing. I mean, when you try to be a beachcomber you know a dropout isn't permitted you or anyone. Not now. Thus having walked beside the ocean or the bay until anxieties disappear, I take a plane. I don't mind the airplanes, but like everybody else I scream with resentment that somebody stole my trains. Without even asking me. Trains were among the great tranquilizers, weren't they? Every time I'm in an airport where you see humanity with its belly being gnawed by all the little foxes, I long for the tranquility of my trains. But there I take a plane and, after hours of fighting to reclaim my luggage which has slyly gone off to New Orleans, I find a New York hotel room where I can lock myself in and get everything I need from Room Service.

Man wants but little of what he sees here below, nor wants that little long, so they say, but as a writer I can get it *all* in a New York hotel room. Like at the Barclay, where I am safe and sound and never have to go out unless I want to, which I seldom do.

One more warning about writers. To anyone who requires a lot of sleep, unless you can duplicate Somerset Maugham's precise

procedure, I say Don't Try It. Most of us have to be able to stay
awake for long periods of time. *If* a piece starts to flow, God
willing, we have to stay with it. When I first started to write
fiction in my spare time—Ha!—I had a house full of kids and
small brothers and some not so small and *they* were more trouble.
I got to know more than I wanted to know about sunrises. My
real work started when everything was *quiet*. Not that I need
quiet. I grew up in a city room with telephones and shouts from
editors and roaring presses, but when the household is quiet you
do not have to do anything about anyone, like being sure the
children don't fall off the roof when they step in a beehive, or
down the well out on the farm, or die of hunger. Thank God,
with three hours' sleep I was—and am—okay. That gives me
1,825 hours a year (more or less) sleep than usual and it has been
in those odd hours that most of my work got done. My grandmother had another old Irish saying:

> Nature requires five
> Custom seven
> Laziness nine
> And wickedness eleven.

Sarah Orne Jewett says she loved the sunrises in the Country of
the Pointed Firs and you *know* she saw a lot of them. You share
them with her in an uplift of tireless irrepressible spirit.

It was at sunrise—five-thirty in the morning—that Edna St.
Vincent Millay Boissevain wrote her last letter. Some months before that she had written:

> I want to give more than two dollars to the American
> Cancer Society. Here's my cheque for fifty. My own
> sweet wonderful darling died of cancer.

That was in the spring—in the fall—

> Dear Lena:
> The iron is set on high. Don't put it on where it says
> "Linen" or it will scorch the linen. Try it on "Rayon"
> and then; perhaps on "Woolen." And be careful not to
> burn your fingers when you shift from one heat to
> another. It is 5:30 and I have been working all night.
> I am going to bed. Goodmorning—
>   E. St. V. M.

She didn't go to bed. She started up the stairs. They found her halfway, curled against a step, with a smile on her face. I suppose —no no. I'm sure that's the way she would have chosen to go, having worked all night on her beloved poetry. She did love it more than all else in life, and she was a most loving spirit.

6

Having explored, examined, eliminated, I can now select the One Woman to invite to the Tavern at the End of the Road.

Partly, perhaps, I have chosen her because she was in many ways the least likely, the least prepared, to write that long-awaited Great American Novel. Again, one of a kind she was, as the novel itself is one of a kind and her only one. She spun the Great American Novel out of irrepressible spirit alone.

She had none of the long, disciplined inspirational training of Millay and Anne Morrow Lindbergh. Millay wrote *Renascence* when she was a student at Vassar. Mrs. Lindbergh's *Bring Me a Unicorn* is a selection of her diaries and letters while she was still a student at Smith College, I could then predict her future, for she had a talent that shone forth and was getting the training and discipline to use it, to know how to say what she had and wanted to say.

The One Woman I've chosen had no desire to start a holy war or right a great wrong as had Harriet Beecher Stowe.

No spiritual Cause, as had Saint Thérèse or Mary Baker Eddy, whose writing in both cases was a way and method of putting forth a Teaching.

There was in her life none of the literary stimulation that super-charged Dorothy Parker in the company of Robert Benchley and the other brilliant Knights of the Algonquin Round Table.

Nor can I find a taste for fame and fortune. Edna Ferber had this as she sought and used both fame and fortune well to become a leading Citizen as well as a top writer.

No editors clamored for her copy and it didn't pour forth in answer as do Jacqueline Susann's books of the Seventies.

Here is my invitation to Margaret Mitchell, who wrote *Gone With the Wind*.

Here is the American Woman Writer with such an irrepressible spirit that nothing could daunt her. Here indeed is a woman who had something to say, something she must say, something our world needs to have said so that it will *remember* the pains that gave our country birth and this need and desire connected her with the Source of all Good, all genius, all how-to, all blessing. When it's like that nothing—*nothing*—will stop it.

Margaret Mitchell didn't just write *Gone With the Wind*. She lived it onto paper.

With passionate nostalgic love, with an irresistible *yearning* for the time she missed by only a few short years and of which she had heard from her cradle, she loved and lived this book into being.

And *being* what is I am sure the Great American Novel.

In the last part of the last century and the first part of this one of today, this book was much discussed, hoped for, seriously expected.

When this expectation becomes a living force it produces masterpieces as it did with *David Copperfield*, and Allen Drury's *Advise and Consent*.

Margaret Mitchell was a Southern Lady.

I capitalize that because they usually did. And meant it.

When I saw her at the opening of her picture, *Gone With the Wind*, starring Clark Gable, Vivien Leigh, Leslie Howard and Olivia de Havilland, she was denying with fire—she was a little sprite of fire and air—that until she was ten years old she thought the south won the War Between the States. "My grandmother and my mother saw Sherman march through Georgia," she said haughtily, "but it is natural that we recall Chancellorsville better than Gettysburg and remember Robert E. Lee better than Ulysses S. Grant. They say losers remember the longest but we had much glory and many great men to remember."

And there was, let us be honest about it, a steel edge of bitterness in the lovely Southern voice.

I had met Margaret Mitchell some years before, before *Gone With the Wind* was published to make her famous. I have always been glad of that, for it showed me the frail young woman who couldn't possibly have written the dynamic historical magnificence of this stupendous novel. But who had the irrepressible spirit to do it nevertheless. Not the battered unhappy middle-aged woman, suffering so desperately from the results of that fame and fortune and the demands it brought to disrupt her peaceful contented Southern life.

I've always thought it must have been prettty awful if the fox found out that the grapes *were* sour when he got 'em, and for Margaret Mitchell who didn't want the damn grapes in the first place it was worse.

My own newspaper service, INS, had sent me as far south as Atlanta, one of those times no doubt when somebody noticed what they were paying me and figured I ought to be doing something more than lunching at "21" to earn it. I was to find out if Southern belles were still the most beautiful and alluring women in the United States and above all how they were reacting to the new hair styles. Girls used to put their hair up—a signal that they were now women and ripe for love, as differentiated from little girls. Today hair changes but little from the cradle to the grave and that may be the reason for the astonishing discontent and dismay and emotional dysentery of the middle-aged woman whose place is not in the home. She hasn't put her hair up yet and there she is. It's like the baseball players blowing bubble gum, you expect them to show up for tomorrow's game in their rompers. The boy's joy and excitement and first acceptance of responsibility when he put on his first long pants has disintegrated because he keeps on his little-boy pants most of his life at least part of the time. Thus manhood—now there's an obsolete word for you! Manhood. *And* womanhood. Womanhood?

What have we here?

Once in the deep South of Atlanta, I went naturally to the Atlanta *Journal* and there met a slim little Southern girl, extraordinarily pretty but without any of what Up North we'd call personality plus. Soft brown curls, a small heart-shaped face, they called her Peggy but above a piece of hers I read in the *Journal*'s Sunday Supplement it said *Margaret Mitchell*. A name nobody outside of Atlanta had ever heard. She came of several good old Atlanta families—there's no need of a family tree here, just accept that her mother's maiden name was Stephens, that the brother

who was to play a startling role in her life was thus Stephens
Mitchell, and that they were aristocrats of Irish descent. Those
Irish ancestors were to be those of her Scarlett O'Hara, now ac-
cepted as the second most famed beloved fictional character in
English literature. If you remember that Sherlock Holmes *is* a
fictional character—and so is James Bond. I found almost at once
that around the office and everywhere in the town she was called
Peggy—Peggy Marsh. The Peggy of course as a diminutive of
Margaret, and Marsh since she was married to John R. Marsh, an
Atlantan of equally ancient and honorable lineage who was at
this time, and for all the time of his marriage to Peggy, first a
clerk and then a minor executive in the Gas Company.

Undoubtedly it is because I now know that in those grubby
cardboard boxes (the kind your husband's shirts used to come
back from the laundry in) and those time-worn frazzled gray
envelopes, sticking out of drawers and spilling from overhead
cupboard, was the manuscript of the Great American Novel
that in retrospect I think my visit to the Marshes' home was
outstanding and dramatic. Poor writers used to be pictured as toil-
ing over their masterpieces in garrets and attics. This two-room
apartment was the reverse. Not a cellar exactly, but you did have
to go down a couple of steps.

No wonder its occupants, Mr. and Mrs. Marsh, called it the
Dump. And in the Dump little Peggy Marsh was *writing* something. She had given up her newspaper employment and was only
doing those occasional interviews and features, as she called them,
for the Sunday Magazine Section. That choice, many of her friends
decided, was partly dictated by growing frail health—Peggy never
had been *strong*—and of course the deterioration was partly the
result of her innumerable accidents. Today we should certainly
describe Margaret Mitchell as accident-prone. If there was anything to fall off of, under, or over, *from a child* Peggy managed it.
Her slight but noticeable lameness came when she fell off a horse
in one of those Paper Chases, meant in that locality to simulate a
Fox Hunt. They soon found that this delicacy—*Peggy's always
been delicate*, they told me—wasn't the only reason she had quit
the paper. She was, they discovered, bit by bit, writing a *book*.
What the book was about, they had no idea. Peggy never once

discussed it with anybody. Over the many years when they went to call on her—and they did, they always did and would, whether she lived in a Dump or pitched a tepee or had a mansion—she would remain a Stephens, a Mitchell, and on her husband's side a Marsh. These had been names to conjure with Before the War and had shone in the late Confederacy. Nothing that happened to her now could change her status in Georgia.

When they went to call on her, what did they find?

The picture is clear to me.

A little rickety sewing table. Behind it an ordinary straight kitchen chair. On it, a battered typewriter.

Here they found Peggy often hard at work. Could it be poetry? Ladies often read poetry, it was said that Peggy understood Browning and was thrilled by Lord Byron—still, in the South, considered shocking.

I knew at the time she took me to her home what she was writing, for, as one newspaperwoman to another, and as a stranger simply passing by as it were, she told me. With a dismissive wave of the hand, a deprecatory smile. It wasn't, she said, probably a novel, at least it might turn out to be one, but it was still in pieces, so, she asked me with that shy smile, How could she tell?

"I've had to do such a lot of it over," she said, "for many reasons. I had to do the whole first half over because I had to change the heroine's *name*. Do you ever have trouble with names?"

"Everybody has trouble with names," I said.

It is impossible to be writing about writers and their trouble with names without pausing in this alleged narrative for a moment to quote Dorothy Parker's famous words on the subject:

> So at the end of this last book, Christopher Tietjens is left with Valentine and the child that is to be born to them, to carry on the Tietjens gentleness and courage . . . It has always been a thorn to me that the man should have so difficult a name as Christopher Tietjens; and as for the woman he loved, fine and brave as Ford has made her, I could never let her near my heart because her name was Valentine Wannop. That is quibbling, I know, and of the silliest sort. But that's the way I am. Take me or leave me; or, as is the usual order of things, both.

This is in a review of Ford Madox Ford's book *The Inheritors* and says about all there is to say about *names*.

"I called her Dorothy to begin with," Peggy Marsh said. "Probably from my first love, Dorothy of Oz."

"What have you changed it to?" I said, more out of politeness than any sixth sense that I was to hear for the first time a name to become famous through the known world and eventually on the moon no doubt.

"Well—" said Peggy, "I don't really know. I'm calling her Scarlett with two t's. Do you like it?"

"It's unusual," I said. "People will remember it."

As indeed they have.

I'm sure they wouldn't have remembered Dorothy.

Literally because of Scarlett we know the Civil War, we know the history of our country, its terrible dramatic melodramatic glamorous colorful Civil War, and a civil war *is* the most terrible thing that can come upon a nation. Also the most dramatic. We know our own, what brought it about, the desperate years afterwards more from Margaret Mitchell's fiction than from any facts we've read—at least I feel that most of us do. We not only know Scarlett, Rhett Butler, Melanie and Ashley Wilkes, Mammy and Aunt Pittypat, memorable characters with real dimensions, we know all they lived through. In the book being created in that basement room on a battered typewriter by the frail little Southern Lady who'd never written anything else and was never going to, we come to live, breathe, love, win and lose and feel a sympathy for the South, long gone, that we never do anywhere else. We owe to an American woman writer our heart-knowledge of its tragedy, way of life, place in the history of our country.

You see?

Having something to say, that you can't live without saying. That no working conditions, however poor, inconvenient, uncomfortable or dampening can stop you from saying. If this was ever true, it was of Margaret Mitchell. Her breath and blood stream, memories and emotions, were alive in a sort of deep nostalgia for the Past in which she'd had the misfortune not to live. But all the scenes, action, dialogue, costumes, food were as familiar to her as her own four walls in Atlanta. The Atlanta of today and yesterday were one and the same to her.

Margaret Mitchell, Mrs. John R. Marsh, this is another instance where much was owed to the husband in the case. Very lucky for her, and consequently for us. Although he saw little of what she was doing, since it was, and for so *long*, in bits and pieces, still she could talk to him. His encouragement, his interest, his praise and pleasure, were welcome—they always are. Even more, he was earning that weekly salary on which they could live as comfortably as they wanted to do. A salary that came in every week. For his wife, Peggy, this was being financed, subsidized, as much as Titian was by the Venetian state or Michelangelo by the Pope. She never had to give her time, energy and interest—all of which so often work on a nebulous thread—to stopping just when it seemed to be *going well*—for instance in the great scene where Scarlett met the Union officer at Tara—for the purpose of earning a few bucks with which to pay the rent. Frail as the young writer was I'm sure she couldn't have done the final putting together of her eleven years' work on this novel in her spare time.

Today I realize that what looked to me on the surface like a safe, placid routine sort of life, without anything to give it tension, was lived in an emotional uproar like going over Niagara Falls in a barrel. True, no children to care for. No bill collectors playing wolf at the door. No Causes or civic disturbance ringing telephones and doorbells all day long. *But* about that time Scarlett was putting Melanie into that wagon to try to get her through battle lines to Tara. Or she was trying to borrow money from Rhett Butler. Or falling in love with him too late for him to give a damn.

If you don't believe that Peggy Marsh Margaret Mitchell was living those things, I've written this chapter in vain.

I remember my small son Dick coming into my workroom one day and upon finding me weeping real and bitter tears into *my* battered Remington came rushing over crying, "Ma—what's the matter?" and I said *She's just found out it isn't a hospital, it's a jail.*

In those days young Dicky having lived in the house with it all his life knew about writers and writing and was sympathetic to

them and it, so all he said was, "What are you going to do with
her now?"

So that Peggy Marsh in her *eleven years* of writing *Gone With
the Wind* did live in tension beyond ordinary belief. She tried to
live through all that came after the smashing, spectacular, unprecedented and unequaled success of it all. So totally unexpected
that there was not time to adjust or prepare or work out her
defense.

She was always, as I've said, walking or falling into accidents.
(Most writers are unbalanced one way or another.) In the end she
walked into one that killed her before her fiftieth birthday.

As in modern picture technique, I would like to change focus,
cast, setting and dialogue with one big swerve of the camera and
no explanation except that I believe it will bring Peggy to you
more clearly.

We were in a flower-filled drawing room on Cumberland Terrace in London, this along in the Thirties. Tanis Guinness Mon-
tagu was giving a tea for me to meet some of her friends and I
daresay for them to meet me.

There was a pause, breathless with suspense, and then someone
said, "Oh no no. She didn't." To this Lady Colfax said firmly,
"Of course she didn't. It's just one of those things people say
about the King. They love to gossip about His Majesty now as
much or more than they did when he was Prince of Wales. I sometimes feel he is *too* democratic. Now see what it gets him into.
This American woman!"

"But," said another voice, "I saw it. I was there, at the Garden
Party and I saw it. She was a friend of Lady Furness and she
did. She dropped her handkerchief and waited for His Majesty
to pick it up. I think she did it on purpose, I really do."

"You mean—this *Mrs. Simpson*—surely that isn't possible even
for an American."

All eyes turned upon me. As it happened, I was the only American woman there. Tanis and I had come over on the *Berengaria*
with Douglas Fairbanks, Jr. I was supposed to be going to do a
motion picture with him, this was actually a cover for me to find
out what was going on between His Majesty King Edward VIII

and an American woman named Wallis Warfield Simpson. I had
confessed this to young Doug who had friends in the Royal Family and was sure the whole idea was absurd. The look I was getting
from Tanis' assembled guests wasn't exactly an accusation, but it
certainly conveyed disbelief. Also curiosity. For English Society
—even the select group admitted to the King's innermost circle at
Fort Belvedere—didn't know as much about this growing alliance
as we did in America. *We* were sure the King was in love with
Mrs. Simpson, might even marry her and try to make her Queen.
In England there were rules about what could or could not be
printed if it involved His Majesty. The idea of the King marrying
an American woman was too far out to be believed.

I said, "But you see, she isn't an American woman."

"Don't be absurd," said a tall, elegant dowager. "The one thing
we do know is that she's an American woman."

"Not really," I said.

"Then what is she?" Tanis said.

"She's a Southern Lady," I said, "and though Edward VIII
may be King of England, Emperor of India and Defender of the
Faith, he's a *man*." They waited, watching me suspiciously. I said,
"A Southern Lady always expects a *man* to pick up her handkerchief. That's why she drops it."

Time was soon to prove that Edward VIII was not only willing
to pick up the lady's handkerchief, he was willing to lay down
his Crown so they could become the Duke and Duchess of Windsor
in the most headlined romance of our century. That is the effect
Southern Ladies have had for years and always expect to have. As
did Scarlett O'Hara in *Gone With the Wind*.

I look back and examine all this carefully because this is about
the woman who wrote the all-time best-seller from which the
continuing all-time movie was made and I still don't believe it.
Obviously, the irrepressible spirit carried her through the long,
tough, harrassing, desperate job of work—this frail, slightly lame
young woman, under five feet, in a one-piece sack dress so commonplace I don't even remember what color it was. Still—I remembered from some bits of history I'd read that these Southern
Ladies, with fan in hand and dangling keys and followed by faithful
retainers, ran enormous plantations, controlled a staff of hun-

dreds of field and house slaves, brought up their families and were famous for their banquets and barbecues without even breaking into a sweat, for no Southern Lady ever broke into a sweat.

No way to put Margaret Mitchell's accent on paper. Take any Southern accent you've heard, triple it, add honey and spice and the lower notes of a guitar and you're listening to Peggy Mitchell as I did that first day. It sure does something to you, that accent. If at first it seemed a little *too much*, I know now it covered a tough cookie. Takes a tough cookie to spend eleven years writing a book—or eleven months for that matter.

It takes a tough cookie.
Mostly you do it alone. Usually nobody cares or somebody cares too much and starts shouting for copy. Mostly they wonder why the hell it takes you so long and since you don't know you can't tell them.

"I write whatever chapters are in my head," Peggy told me apologetically, pushing aside the decrepit sewing table and its battered burden.

I was right sure she'd never finish it. And if she did, she'd never submit it to a publisher. She wasn't *interested* in getting it published. Few Southern Ladies had ever had anything *published*. In Boston, maybe. New England, perhaps. But not in Atlanta, Georgia.

Destiny took it out of her hands with a series of coincidences only destiny could have arranged. Lois Cole, a girl from Atlanta who'd gone to New York, worked for a publisher, came home on a visit, and brother Stephens gave her the manuscript and in spite of frantic wires from Peggy she refused to return it and Macmillan decided to bring it out.

Sometimes now I wonder if Peggy didn't foresee that anything like this would bring a change in her life with which she knew she couldn't cope. With care, with a planned routine, she had strength to handle her daily existence. None to spare. To add one extra thing would destroy that balance and send her crashing into darkness. A change she didn't want would come to be dealt with.

"And that change," her brother Stephens told me recently, "I believe that change killed her."

Because we're talking about writers, I'd like to tell you what I believe.

Peggy Mitchell had been living in the world she created. The world you and I live in when we read *Gone With the Wind*. This happens. I *know* that sometimes when I have been writing a dense rainstorm, with thick black clouds and flashes of lightning, I've been shocked to find my windows framing a day of sunshine. Minor—but to a writer of the frail intensity of Peggy Mitchell, I think she not only lived her story onto paper but lived *in* it. Into this crashed not only the world of her own today, but another world, one she didn't want to know, and it brought her fame and fortune and all the violence, all the demands, the publicity, the people, the notoriety which she hated bitterly.

On the night of the big opening of the Movie in Atlanta, with the Governor, the Mayor, all the stars of the cast present, she said to me in a voice hard and brittle with resentment, "I wish I'd never written it."

But—writers cannot help writing what they have to write. Failure or success has little to do with it then. *David Copperfield* had to be written, though there were times when it nearly killed Dickens. Then they expose the writer—who to some extent may be a sensitive, imaginative, temperamental *oaf*—artist—idiot—scatterbrained nitwit—genius—jinni—prodigy—*I* don't know, take your pick—the writer is now exposed to a harsh world of either exaggerated approval or disapproval.

Look at this picture of Peggy Marsh.

It has never left me.

An American woman in her early thirties, pleasantly happy in an affectionate marriage with common interests and familiar jests. A social life among old friends with accepted customs, manners and above all a shared background of *values*. A way of life in which she was always at ease. She might call her home the Dump but it was a place to which her friends came and where she made the best coffee in Atlanta. No surprises, shocks, change of pace, no intruders from those unknown races to which the Enemy still belonged. Losers remember longest and Sherman was not going to march through Peggy's Georgia under any name whatsoever. Her mother, her grandmother, had suffered all those upheavals; she was of a postwar generation. Any of this might drag her out of the hard-won peace of defeat. Edith Wharton, writing in *Age of Innocence* of a time which began only a few years after Appomattox can tell her story without ever mentioning the War. Apparently none of the people she knew had been involved. With Peggy Marsh it was different. And now all she wanted was to attend church, read books from the library, have the companionship of her husband, her brother, to set up her sewing table and live again in memories she had been given from birth.

Never to leave Atlanta.

She'd tried leaving it. She'd been persuaded to attend a Northern College. And she'd been so homesick she'd ended in the hospital. They had to send her home to save her life. This very love of her own land, her own state and city, her own woods and garden plots however small, this was the fire that warmed, the light that shone in her book.

Love. It's the thing we all want—long for—need.

Love of something, someone, it not only makes the world go round, it makes the typewriter go round, and nothing else ever equals it. So there Peggy could be forever, in the land she loved past, present and future.

Word came from Lois Cole up North.

Macmillan wants to publish your book.

A genie spoke. An angel waved a wand. The world and everything in it changed for little Peggy Marsh. She became forever Margaret Mitchell.

If you remember another sensationally successful book by a woman writer we come upon *Little Women*. Louisa May Alcott. Now we move North, but just the same in the last of that beloved trilogy, *Jo's Boys*, we come upon a chapter in which Aunt Jo, having written a successful book, is so besieged by reporters, fans, women's clubs and those who wish her autograph that she pretends to be her own maid when she is caught in her own hall.

"I'm sure," Margaret Mitchell wrote, "that Scarlett never suffered more during the siege of Atlanta than I have during the siege that has been on since publication day."

Within months—weeks—days—*Gone With the Wind* had achieved a success that no other novel in world history has known. Within weeks, Peggy Marsh's book had rushed into millions of copies. Came the sale of the movie rights, headlines as to the casting, the long search for a Scarlett O'Hara, found at last in an English actress named Vivien Leigh.

Privacy vanished totally from the life of Mrs. John R. Marsh of Georgia. Margaret Mitchell became a national, international figure, demands were an avalanche, they came in triplicate.

Private life?

What private life? You must be *crazy*.

[39]Miss Mitchell Declined

This footnote is the common factor about Margaret Mitchell in David Selznick's Memoirs as he tells the detailed story of his production of the world's favorite picture from the best-selling novel of all time.

That footnote follows everything whatsoever that he asked her to do.

Thus Miss Mitchell declined to

Confirm that only Clark Gable should be allowed to play Rhett Butler.

Work with Mr. Selznick as he began to map the production.

Work with Mr. Selznick on a preliminary outline of a script.

Suggest an actress to play Scarlett O'Hara.

Help find an actress ditto.

Give her approval or disapproval of those Mr. Selznick wished to consider for the role.

Work with a script writer.

Suggest any script writer with whom she would work.

Have consultations with Mr. Selznick about casting, directing, script writing. *Or* Cast, Director, Script Writer.

Have consultations with the script writer.

Read the script.

Read scenes from the script.

Look at tests of actresses who wanted to play Scarlett O'Hara which included Paulette Goddard, Katharine

Hepburn and Shirley Temple. *And* all other actresses
between 6 and 60.
Look at the locations being selected.
Look at the drawings made by Menzies of *Tara*.
Do some super-duper publicity with Mr. Selznick as
suggested by Hollywood's most famed press agent,
Russell Birdwell.
Have her picture taken with any of the cast, Clark
Gable, Leslie Howard, Vivien Leigh, Olivia de Havilland.

All these Miss Mitchell *declined*.
In fact declining became with her almost a way of life.
But there was one thing she didn't—couldn't—have declined and
that was to write *Gone With the Wind* in the first place.

Again and again and again I say it, nobody in the world can stop
a writer. Not even himself.

James Thurber, one of our truly greats if only for *The Secret
Life of Walter Mitty*, was going slowly blind. He just went on
writing and drawing with bigger crayons. Edgar Allan Poe wrote
"The Bells" and "Annabel Lee" in times between desperate ill-
nesses before he died at forty. And time itself offers no real ob-
stacle. It didn't take me eleven years to write my own novel,
Tell No Man, but it took me all my life to know what's in it about
God and man.

What's in it is that man cannot live without God and that, as
Toynbee has shown us, neither can nations or civilizations.

The last line of my book says:
Tell no man.
But I have.
I *had* to.

If not, well—maybe all of us would say along with Huckle-
berry Finn and Mark Twain, greatest of all American writers
male *or* female, If I'd a' known what a trouble it was to make a
book I wouldn't a' tackled it, and I ain't a-going to no more.

Chapter Seven

This is to be the one story I wanted to tell most. One I felt I must bring from the great American women of the past to the confused and considerably less great American women of today. The one which illustrates for me the high-spirited courage, the love of others beyond and before self, the smile that comforts and shares faith even when it covers a breaking heart and a tortured body.

Hearts do break, you know.

Through the centuries it has been woman's part to prove that the spirit has wings, to rise above broken bodies and broken hearts, to warn, to comfort and command good instead of evil.

From the first word of this book, which has kept me awake so many nights, from the first day when I looked into my Tavern at the End of the Road and saw who sat there. My son Bill, and my father; William Randolph Hearst, the greatest newspaperman who ever lived; Mark Kelly and Clark Gable and Damon Runyon—*men*. Men I'd lived with and worked with, whose love and loyalty and bravery were breath of my being. And discovered that there was not a single woman. From the moment my friend, Colleen Moore, she of the social graces who knows exactly how to arrange a table so that it has the maximum of gaiety and the minimum of social goofs, and the exchange of worthwhile thoughts, began to help me to repair this unbelievable oversight, I have known where for me was the best—the *best*—of all the stories of the gallantry of woman's unconquerable spirit.

Do unto others far more than you expect them to do unto you.

Do it whether you like it or not. Whether you *can* or not. To get up off the floor when you can't, a definition given me by Jack Dempsey, himself the Champ, as part of being a champion.

Out of all the women who made me talk about them in this book—

Just the other day at a Teachers Conference in the Ojai Valley Inn, I had the good fortune to meet Dr. Karl Menninger and his wife. He is one of the few psychiatrists in whom I really have faith because he has faith in God. When we spoke of his book—for when writers get together they talk shop—*Whatever Became of Sin* and I told him about my own Great American Women he shook a finger at me and shouted, "Don't you dare leave out Rachel Carson. You wouldn't do that, would you?" and I said, "Of course not, she's one of the greatest."

Then the other day at a class I was helping, I hope, at Pepperdine University in Malibu, a girl with long straight blond hair said, "Do you have Isadora Duncan? I found out when I was in Paris that she is the *only* American woman who is really taken seriously as great in Europe. You aren't leaving her out, are you?" And to myself I thought of how little chance I'd have to do *that*, since my friend Robert Thom regards her as the greatest woman of all time, and can talk about her for hours without repeating himself.

So I said, It isn't possible to overlook Isadora. She left San Francisco while I was still in my crib, but I knew people who'd known her there and she became the first American woman to be considered an *artiste* in Europe they all told stories about her. Later Mr. Hearst sent me to Boston when the Law closed her dance presentation there. Of course Boston was Boston, and at one point did an equally good job of crucifying Mary Baker Eddy, whose church and publishing house bring thousands of pilgrims to that same city today.

All the time, from the very beginning, I've known what my story of great gallantry had to be. Of the wings of the spirit lifting a woman higher and higher.

But—I said to myself said I—

A Follies Girl?

Surely not. With saints and patriots and scientists and heroic adventurers?

For you who were unfortunately born too late or being born in their time never got to New York City when it was the most brilliant and exciting city in the world as well as the biggest when they reigned there supreme among womenkind—for you I must identify

The Follies Girls.

Who were they and how and why and when?

Have they an inalienable right to fame and immortality among American women and not just because one of them is the heroine of my finest story of gallantry and kindness and courage?

With saints like Mother Cabrini, and geniuses like Judy Garland and Margaret Mitchell, heroines of adventure like Amelia Earhart and friends of the human race like Miriam Van Waters and Margaret Sanger—you're going to tell the great story of woman's gallant spirit about a Follies Girl?

In a way I am pleased about this, the men in my Tavern at the End of the Road are sure to send up a cheer when I send in a Follies Girl, for they were lovely to look at and delightful to know. The strange thing, however, is that women, too, were wildly enthusiastic about them. A Matinee at the Ziegfeld Theater was like a matinee for Katharine Cornell or Helen Hayes or Ethel Barrymore. And of course Fanny Brice and Marilyn Miller and Anna Held were stars of the Follies in their day.

Perhaps this is the greatest secret and the shrewdest showmanship of Florenz Ziegfeld, who invented them and showed them as the Ziegfeld Girls. They were not beauties. They were not girls who spring like Aphrodite from the waves as goddesses already. From the first time he began to select them they weren't picked to be *rara avis*.

Somerset Maugham in *The Summing Up* says, "One of the most curious things that has forced itself on my notice is that there is no permanence in the judgment of beauty. The only conclusion is that beauty is relative to the particular needs of a particular generation and that to examine the things we consider beautiful for qualities of absolute beauty is futile."

I am quite sure that Mr. Ziegfeld never read this, but he understood it perfectly.

The sign above the Ziegfeld Theater was in four words a masterpiece:

GLORIFYING THE AMERICAN GIRL

Think of it a moment.

Is there any girl among us, any girl you know today, who cannot be glorified? As I write this, the most popular woman star of this day is Barbra Streisand. By some magic of voice, of glowing personality, of interest in her audience she has been glorified to stardom in spite of being in actuality as homely—not to go so far as to say ugly—a young woman as it has been our whim and will to promote to such heights.

This was the supreme proof of Ziegfeld's showmanship. It not only kept his theaters filled with women as well as men, it affected whole generations of American girls and women who began to glorify themselves and it actually motivated and gave impetus to industry in the form of perfume and cosmetics as though a magic wand had been waved.

About the time I first interviewed Emily Post, when her name became a synonym for etiquette and proper behavior and all the possible graces of well-conducted woman and girlhood, the Follies Girls were at the heights of their fame and influence and nothing —I would like to reiterate and underline that—*nothing* I ever saw one of them do on the stage violated Mrs. Post's rules of conduct. Not even what they wore. Personally, I always thought this enriched and heightened their appeal—for I do not myself think a diamond looks as well in the gutter as it does in a ring on the fair hand of a woman.

Mrs. Post's rules were designed to provide that setting, not to take the fun out of life.

I may not be one of a kind about many things but I honestly believe I am one of a kind about having seen *Emily Post* dunk. Or should it read Emily Post *dunk?* We lived in the same apartment building at the corner of Seventy-ninth and Madison Avenue, I in a sublet on the fourth floor and Emily with the whole top floor and a roof garden around it. And one afternoon she asked me to come up for tea! I admit I was a leetle mite nervous. My grandmother taught me good table manners, no doubt about that.

But in the meantime I'd been a reporter eating wherever and however for a good many years—and one thing about the elegance of the Hearst ranch, the lunch was buffet even for the Queen of Romania and informality prevailed even at dinner. So I had a moment or two of trepidation as I took the elevator up to tea—always sounds elegant to begin with—tea—as the guest of the lady whose name was synonymous then and still is with grace, culture, and caviar.

The garden was exquisite. The tea came on a delicate little table with Wedgwood cups and plates and Staffordshire silver, and the fragrance of the tea was instantly recognizable as something rare and wonderful from China. And on one of the lovely silver-bordered plates were some fresh sugar-coated doughnuts!

One of these Emily Post picked up between the thumb and forefinger and *dunked*. Unmistakably, without hesitation, and in a manner that *if* it had been anybody *else* I would have considered anti-Emily Post enough to be almost vulgar!

I never had more fun in my life than dunking doughnuts with Emily.

And the Follies, in the long years of their smash hits on Broadway, provided another dimension to that graceful setting for the American girl. Of course the Follies was a Revue—one of the first and certainly the best I ever saw. The stars were many and brilliant. Most of us recall the advent of a shy young man named Will Rogers, who came out before a curtain with a rope in his hand and while he spun and wove it in fantastic patterns told us what he had read in the papers. Nora Bayes came onto a softly lit stage to sing "Shine On, Harvest Moon," W. C. Fields and Bert Williams did their show-stopping acts, and a lanky Jewish girl named Fanny Brice sang a song—a single this was—called "My Man." Marilyn Miller—delicate as a rosebud at dawn—did numbers as a prima ballerina, and Anna Held, just imported from her sensational success at the Moulin Rouge in Paris, sang "I Jus' Can't Make My Eyes Be-ave" to about a thousand encores it seemed to me. And always between acts, behind acts of this sparkling review, and the real stars of it, were the Follies Girls in magnificent, exciting, glorious costumes. The Chorus!

These Follies Girls I want now to introduce into the ranks of fascinating American women aren't just window dressing for the men waiting in that Tavern at the End of the Road. No no.

In my days on our New York papers, the *Journal* and the *American*, I knew a number of them. Later of course some of them came to Hollywood—and success in the Movies. They had—what was it they had? They were all sizes, shapes, colors, nationalities and backgrounds—and at first glimpse seemed no different to speak of than four of the first ten girls you'll see. They had, I *know*, I am *sure*, they had some special secret about the heart of a man, whether they ever married that man or not.

They spoke to him the language of the heart.

The most successful would have to be Marion Davies, who came from Brooklyn where her father was a municipal court judge. She became the permanent and powerful and endlessly enchanting mistress of William Randolph Hearst, in the tradition of mistresses-en-titre such as Madame la Duchesse de Pompadour to Louis XIV, whom she is said to have completely controlled politically, or as Nell Gwynne to Charles II of England, and several in the United States whom we are not supposed to name. Though some who covered Washington during Woodrow Wilson's term in the White House were sufficiently aware of Mrs. Peck to refer to the Princeton professor as Peck's Bad Boy.

Marion Davies was the mistress of the newspaper king of the world, William Randolph Hearst. For the many years when I went regularly to what is now called the Hearst Castle at San Simeon, now open to millions each year as a State Monument, Marion Davies was the hostess and the mistress of the Castle. When President and Mrs. Calvin Coolidge visited there it was former Follies Girl Marion Davies who greeted them, saw to their comforts and entertainment and bid them come again when they left. I have, partly in the course of my profession, visited a good many of the great houses of this country, of England, Ireland, and France. And I was once received at a Garden Party by Queen Mother Mary and I also stayed at Government House with the Duke and Duchess of Windsor. I have never seen a more gracious, charming and kind—oh yes, always so *kind*—hostess than Marion Davies was when she was mistress for so many, many years at San Simeon. She made those comfortable who were perhaps not accustomed to the grandeur and magnificence; she encouraged

those who were shy, and many were; she found something for
everybody to do and sparked conversation and inspired both interest and laughter. Whether the guests at what we called the
Hearst Ranch were Douglas Fairbanks and Mary Pickford, one-
time king and queen of the Movies, or Queen Maria of Romania in
person, the social hostess with the mostest, Evalyn Walsh McLean
of Washington, or a new Hollywood starlet, a first-hit writer, a
Jewish producer who spoke with an accent that made him difficult to understand—I don't know how she did it and that's a fact
but if the Follies taught Marion Davies the kindness and per-
ception she showed me for so many years I wish we had them for
a few of our present-day careless, shoddy, so-informal-you-are-
uncomfortable-most-of-the-time gals I see around today.

As a movie star, which she was, with great all-star casts and
fine stories, Marion was handicapped always by the fact that Mr.
Hearst insisted on producing her picture. True, he paid for them,
but that too was a handicap she never overcame. She was a great
comedienne, might have been as great as Mabel Normand or
Carole Lombard or Beatrice Lillie. I will remember till I die, and
I hope thereafter, the day she came down to lunch in the stately
perfect dining room at the Ranch from a speech lesson in the
library. The Talkies had turned Hollywood upside down and made
changes as devastating to it as the Civil War had been to the South.
Stars were falling like disconnected comets, stage directors were
being brought in from New York to supervise dialogue and, since
they didn't know one end of a camera from the other, a good deal
of chaos was going on.

Mr. Hearst was determined that his silent star Marion Davies
should learn to *talk*. This was doubly complicated by the fact
that Marion stuttered. While even with her Brooklyn-Irish accent
this was somehow endearing in person—we had all felt it was part
of her charm—in a candidate for continued stardom in the Talkies it was totally impossible. Mr. Hearst imported a New York
stage director and the great Shakespearean coach to whom Jack
Barrymore had gone for years. And Marion spent half of every
day up in the library wrestling with the immortal lines of the
Bard of Avon.

One day she came in late for lunch, we were all seated at the
long table, Clark Gable, Charlie Chaplin, Randolph Churchill,

Edgar Selwyn and his wife, Sam Goldwyn, Gertrude Atherton, Rupert Hughes and a dozen others. Marion didn't hesitate, she came to a full stop behind her chair, made a wide gesture with her hand and stood staring at it. Then the famed lines began—

"*Out*, d-damned sss-s-ss-pot! out, I sss-say! . . . all the perfumes of Arabia will n-not s-ss-ssweeten this little hand . . ."

If you have never heard Lady Macbeth played with a stutter, try it yourself sometime. I had to leave the Shakespeare Theater in Stratford-on-Avon when the star began to walk forward with her hand outstretched.

Mr. Hearst had first seen Marion in the Follies, and once on the night of his birthday—we celebrated those birthdays with parties and with anything we could think up which might amuse him— Marion decided to reproduce the number she was doing when this historic moment occurred. She had the costumes as she remembered them made at MGM and gathered around her five ex-Follies Girls—Billie Dove, Eileen Percy, who had married the famed song-writer Harry Ruby, Dorothy Mackaill, Nita Naldi, Ivy Sawyer Santley—and they tripped out on the stage constructed in the ballroom at the Beach House singing "The Girl on the Magazine Cover." A lovely coincidence, which as a fiction writer I wouldn't dare to use, that Mr. Hearst who owned *Cosmopolitan, Good Housekeeping*, and a dozen others should have seen the woman he was to love the rest of his life as a Girl on a Magazine Cover.

More often than almost any question, I am asked why Mrs. Hearst didn't get a divorce and then Mr. Hearst could have married his Follies Girl. Many who claim to know insist that Marion did want him to get a divorce and either he or Mrs. Hearst refused. I have told the exact truth about this in a book I wrote called *The Honeycomb* and because it still keeps coming up I'm going to quote it here—

Why did William Randolph Hearst not get a divorce to marry Marion Davies? By then, so many people did get divorced.

This is not as complicated as it appears.
Two good reasons.
Millicent Wilson Hearst.
Marion Douras Davies.
Magnificent and amazing that the two women in his life always

seem to have thought about *him*—what was best for him. They gave him some trouble now and then, to be sure, but they always seemed in the end to *act* as they thought best for him.

Once upon a time Clare Boothe was a guest at the Hearst Ranch at San Simeon. By then Clare Boothe was married to Henry Luce, founder of *Time, Life,* and *Fortune,* one of the most creative publishers of all time. Marion Davies, who was not married to anybody, seemed to us to take Mrs. Luce with a slight twinkle. The following conversation between these two ladies was reported to me by Eileen Percy, Dorothy Mackaill, and Bebe Daniels, Marion's best friends. This is what they told me:

Clare Boothe Luce said to M.D., "Marion, dear, you know my play *The Women* was a great success with no help from anyone. I valued my artistic independence and integrity so after I married Harry Luce I still wanted to be judged on merit, without fear or favor. When my next play, *Kiss the Boys Goodbye,* was presented, I asked Harry to order his publications *Life* and *Time* to deal with it fearlessly—forgetting that the playwright was the wife of the owner of those publications. None of the reviews of the play was favorable. Those in the Luce magazines were vitriolic. Now I must do something about this. I wondered, dear Marion, what exactly are your arrangements with Mr. Hearst about reviews of your pictures?"

Said Marion Davies to Mrs. Luce, "Dear C-CCC-Clare, it c-cccouldn't come up, ccccccould it? You see, Mr. Hearst l-l-lloves me."

We all loved her.

We loved her because she never once used her enormous power for anything but good. In the last days of Mr. Hearst's life she ran the Hearst Empire. At one time, she was officially Vice President. This blond ex-Follies girl movie star was in charge of the most powerful press organization in the world as Madame Pompadour once ruled France. All orders—preceded on the phone by "Mmmister Hearst says"—came from and through her. I sat beside her once or twice while she transmitted them.

The answer to the controversy as to why no divorce is fully known to me and I think now it not only could but should be told. Few knew it, some who did had no reason to speak. Now time has passed, the main characters are part of that past rather than the present.

The first reason there never was a divorce and that Mrs. Hearst still wore her wedding ring by right when she was eighty-six was—Mrs. Hearst.

To know Millicent Hearst even somewhat, as I have for over fifty years, is to be sure beyond doubt that she would never hold a husband against his will. A beauty herself, she grew more and more important in the social life of New York and Europe. I vision her in those years wrapped in chinchilla at the opening of the Met or in a box at Madison Square Garden for one of the big fights staged under her patronage for the Milk Fund by the sports staff of the New York *Journal-American*.

All Mr. Hearst ever had to do was ask for a divorce. That's all. He never did.

A couple of times some sort of property division was discussed. Nothing came of it. Once when a Spanish grandee with a historic title became a Penelope suitor of Millicent's, there was talk that *she* might want to be free. Nothing came of that, either.

The final choice about the divorce was Marion's.

I went over this once with Eileen Percy Ruby, Dorothy Mackaill, Bebe Daniels, Connie Talmadge—her best-loved circle. They confirmed that she had said to them several times in the thirty years she lived with Mr. Hearst what I myself heard her say once in my own house on the Whittier ranch when she and Mr. Hearst came to dinner.

I had been telling him about the new old-brick English house I'd built on the only running water I could find in Southern California and he said politely that he'd like to see it. To my amazement, he agreed to come to dinner. He *never* went anywhere to dinner.

The only other guests I had were Tom and Vicky Mix, Buster Collier and Constance Talmadge, and a banker he was fond of, Irving Hellman, and his wife. I was wild with excitement, I can tell you.

After dinner we wandered about looking at my redwood library and the fireplace big enough to stand in, and the stables, and as we walked back Mr. Hearst and Marion fell behind. She had been

on him all evening, something to do as usual with young Jack, the
third Hearst son. He was about sixteen then and always in trouble.
Marion was saying that he needed a *firmer* hand. People, Marion
said, who are divorced are always too soft with their kids, they
have a guilty conscience.

"But," Mr. Hearst said, "I am not divorced and I do not have a
guilty conscience."

It was the only time I ever saw Marion cry.

She said, "Sometimes I don't know what to do. You know you
can't live without me."

"I would prefer not to," Mr. Hearst said gently.

"I won't let you get a divorce," she said. "I've told you before
and I tell you again. You're a great man, a great power in our
country. You must have dignity. They can attack your politics and
throw dirt and all, but you mustn't ever give them anything that
could—could make you lose your dignity. It is all right—it's
sound historically, or traditionally, and dramatically, if it *is* wicked
—for you to have a Follies girl and blond movie star as your
mistress. Look at Louis XIV and Charles II and Herod! If you
divorce your wife, the mother of your five sons, to *marry* her, a
girl younger by twenty years, they can make you look like an old
fool. You can live down being thought old-fashioned and even
immoral but no man, you say it yourself, has ever lived down
being ridiculous. I'd rather take our chances this way.

"But you cannot pretend we are a good example for the boys,
though they seem fond of me. You need to keep a firmer hand
on young Jack. He's the most like you—he's brilliant, you know."

So when we went inside Mr. Hearst asked to use the telephone
in my library and he called the city desk at the *Examiner* and said
to Harry Morgan, the night city editor, "Perhaps it would be
wise to let Jack stay in jail overnight. We must be firm with
these young fellows, Mr. Morgan. Some wise man has said that
the ultimate result of shielding men from the results of their
folly is to fill the world with fools. We must not be guilty of such
indulgence."

Not long after that young Jack married a Los Angeles debutante
of good family as the first of several wives and at the wedding I
saw Mrs. Hearst again and there was no way to know whether

she knew how much her son owed to Marion—as her grandsons did later.

Marion sent a beautiful wedding gift, she was always an advocate of marriage, was Miss Davies. One unmarried couple were having an affair in Hollywood and, visiting the Ranch, continued the romance there. They were told by Miss Davies that they'd either get married or go down the Hill. The girl, a young movie star, had the temerity to say, "Look who's talking," to which M.D. replied, "Mr. Hearst and I can't get married. You and Harry can." What's more they did.

There is a story about the return to America of Charles Augustus Lindbergh just after he flew the Atlantic and of how he came to Hollywood that shows something of Mr. Hearst's respect and care for his mistress-en-titre, how in the smallest matters of courtesy he protected her.

Overnight—this time truly overnight—the Lone Eagle had become the greatest hero the United States has ever had. On his arrival in our film capital a short time after the ticker parade of the century in New York, Mr. Hearst entertained for Lindbergh at a beautiful *thé dansant* at the Ambassador. The guests included every star in the firmament plus all the brass in any field and their wives. Lindy, tall, slim, very quiet—looking back, I am sure he was still in a state of shock from all that had happened—sat at the head table between Mary Pickford and his hostess, Marion Davies. We were fond of *thés dansants* in those days and it had many advantages over the later cocktail party in that soon everyone was *seated* at the flower-laden head table and all the smaller ones around the shining dance floor, and Guy Lombardo's music began.

A moment of silence prolonged into tension.

If Lindbergh had ever drunk tea before it had undoubtedly been in a Harvey Eating House and he had no idea he was supposed to open the ball. We saw then that there was also involved a Social Predicament.

If he takes Mary Pickford will this be adjudged an insult to Marion Davies? If he chooses Marion, will this violate protocol that nobody must step on the floor before an anointed queen? Moreover this is a clean young Galahad, idol of American youth, should he so honor the mistress, no matter how much we love her? Even if *we* didn't print it, everybody else would.

Mr. Hearst needed no advice from his columnist Emily Post.

With elephantine grace he moved. Before we could expel the
breath we were holding he had offered his hand to Marie Dressler,
conducted her regally to Lindbergh, and presented him to her. In
less time than we got a new breath, the Grand Old Lady of the
Movies, the incomparable unequaled and beloved Marie Dressler,
who was also friend and intimate of grand duchesses and society
leaders, and Lindy had taken the floor together. We sat watching
them. Gloria Swanson and I were reminiscing about this the other
day as one of our shining memories. Recalling how we burst into
applause and then cheers as the tall blond hero and the stately old
lady moved the length of the floor and back alone in a waltz. Then
Mr. Hearst indicated and Douglas Fairbanks, the Prince Consort,
bowed to Marion and he himself took Mary Pickford out in royal
fashion to join these couples on the dance floor.

You see, Mr. Hearst l-l-lloves me.

I knew a number of other Follies Girls quite well, before I came
to know the one whose name was Lilyan Tashman.

Billie Dove has special interest.
More than any other woman she can—and did to me—explain
the mystery of Howard Hughes and his baffling oft-headlined relationship to and with the Ladies.
I believed then, and looking back with careful memory and re-
construction, I think now, she was the woman he loved. Most
women, even if they have had several husbands and a few other
men in their lives, will tell you that there was One Man. So it is
with men about the One Woman. All of us who heard him will
remember forever the King of England saying, "I have found it
impossible to carry the heavy burden of responsibility and to discharge my duties as King as I would wish to do without the help
and support of *the woman I love.*" I saw the Duke and Duchess of
Windsor often together after he had abdicated his throne to marry
her—and they believed it had been worth it.
Always there has been mystery around Howard Hughes—mystery about many things and certainly about *women.* He collected
beautiful women, made movie stars of them and never spoke to
them. Paid beautiful girls huge sums of money, gave them beautiful apartments and never went near them. Was twice married—

once to a girl while he was in college. Neither of these seemed to be *in* his life, as it were.

Myself, I am positively sure that the one woman he loved was an ex-Follies Girl named Billie Dove. And she loved him. From her, I came at last to understand something of this young genius from Texas whom we are inclined to forget has done so much for his country.

Howard was a boy I'd known ever since, as a skinny kid, he came up from Texas to visit his uncle, Rupert Hughes. Rupert was then a top best-selling author who had started the so-called *debunking* school of biography—his was about George Washington. At that time, Rupert was much better known and more sought-after than his brother, who had invented some gadget that helped an oil well to produce more oil faster. This was beginning to make millions for the brother and his son, who soon added to its strength and usefulness. But when young teenage Howard came up from Texas to visit his Uncle Rupert it was Uncle Rupert who was the center of attraction. Rupert had a wonderful house in the Hollywood foothills, and there gathered many of the Eminent Authors who were working for Louis B. Mayer and the Movies. Plus Mary Roberts Rinehart, Theodore Dreiser, Gertrude Atherton, Kathleen Norris, James Oliver Curwood and Peter B. Kyne—who composed the Best Sellers list of the times. And there I first met a tall, skinny kid with a shy and enchanting smile, big brown eyes and a shock of dark hair that fell over his forehead. We formed a friendship at the time which has lasted until this moment, in spite of the fact that I once had him grounded for flying too low over Malibu Beach where my children were playing.

I would like to quote here a column I wrote for the Paso Robles *Press* at a time recently when Howard was under senseless and inaccurate attack:

> Do you know what Howard Hughes really wants to do? He wants to fly his own plane again.
>
> He still has his pilot's license, and though he's in his late sixties—gotta be though it seems impossible—he swears he can pass his physicals and he'd like to fly that spruce goose or whatever they call it out of the hangar with his own hands on the controls.

What's more, remembering Howard Hughes as I've known him since he was in his teens, he might just do this.

Somewhere amid all this whirligig and rassamatazz of people nobody ever heard of—people who don't seem to care what they do, say or write, other people so gullible they'd buy the Washington Monument—we seem to have lost the real Howard Hughes whom we once knew pretty well and of whom, along with the kookiness, we'd heard much good.

Two big things have been overlooked as far as I've been able to see in this now-you-see-him-and-now-you-don't three-ring circus generated around the billionaire.

Have you ever thought what it must be like to be so rich that you can't buy the one thing you want most? A little seclusion and privacy in which to do the work that really interests you?

"But," he said to a friend of ours the other day, "every time I try to go into seclusion they say I'm dead or an oddity."

Oddity! Too mild a word for what they say about Mr. Hughes—but it's one of his own words and so was part of the full process of identification for this friend—as were words in a message he sent me from the Bahamas a ways back. I wanted him to see a wonderful woman who had thanks she wanted to give him for saving many, many lives among the poor. He wouldn't see her—he shuns emotion and is afraid of thanks—but he sent me a message that could have come from no one else in the world. A few years back he'd opened a big hotel in Vegas and I was on the guest list for its opening. I ran into him one day, and said I didn't like big new hotels, I loved the simpler friendly warm Flamingo where I could play a little small stake black jack—and the message I got from Howard was "Tell Adela I can't see her friend but any time she wants to go to the Flamingo and play a little small stake black jack to please be my guest."

Please?

But Howard always says please. If he says anything.

Consider for a moment what Howard Hughes has done.

Many young men with that kind of dough do nothing at all. Howard from the beginning has built businesses where vast numbers are employed and has always kept such supervision over them that they are famed as great places to work—and have had less difficulty with labor than others. When Howard Hughes owned TWA it was regarded as a model airline, and he ran it under his personal supervision and introduced many firsts in safety and performance. He sold it when he himself was no longer prepared to keep his eye on every flight.

He has financed hospitals and research and again has invented equipment and operational techniques which have moved things along at the swift pace he approves. There is at least one large hospital I know of myself—and I'm told there are others—where the money and again the help come from Howard Hughes.

He himself has invented not only oil equipment and airplane manufacturing tools and machines but also hospital and research devices. I remember a hospital bed he invented at the time he was bedridden as a result of a crash—the only flying accident of his many millions of miles. He made a round-the-world flight which we followed breathlessly which pioneered a number of vital things and was also at the time a good-will mission for the United States with many nations, and he came home from that one almost as big a hero as Lindbergh.

As Babe Ruth used to say, "One day you're a hero and the next day you're a bum." But I don't want to forget that Howard Hughes has been a hero. And that, I think, is the real Howard Hughes, though he has all the inventor's oddities.

My godson William Wallace Reid, a young architect who lives in Santa Monica, used to be a close friend of Howard's and traveled around with him—just the two of them. Bill Reid thinks Howard Hughes is a great American, but one day on a journey where as usual Howard was flying himself he said to Hughes, "Couldn't you at least buy a little suitcase? That cardboard shirt box you carry around—they won't let us register in a good hotel." And Howard Hughes said, "If I carry this nobody will know who I am—they'll say, too, well if it was Hughes he could at least afford a suitcase!" Bill thought then, as another friend who spoke with Hughes a short time ago insists, that the one thing Hughes really loved was aviation and flying.

Which brings me to the second thing that has been ignored in this recent turmoil and whoop de do.

How many inventors have you known?

With all due apologies to Edison, Marconi and Karl Benz, who set up the first one-cyclinder self-propelled vehicle, inventors are ALL nuts. They are geniuses of a breed that never—or rarely—touched reality. They are like patchwork crazy quilts, with their eye on only one patch ever. They are eccentric. Great wits, Dryden says, are sure to madness near allied. The great brains that have inventive genius are sure to have their own kind of peculiarity or bats or whatever you choose to call it, and Howard is one of them. Add to this the possession of Billions and you have a combination that makes a great man but one who is different from other people if he survives at all.

I flew down with him one time from the Hearst Ranch —where he came quite often and was utterly overawed by William Randolph Hearst, as who wasn't? Mr. Hearst treated him with paternal kindliness, and they spent a lot of time on the architecture and building processes always going on around what is now called the Castle. But when I told Mr. Hearst that I needed to get down to the *Examiner*, then my paper, and Howard was going to let me ride with him Mr. Hearst was perturbed. He said, "Are you quite sure you want to fly with this young man?"

I said, "I thought you liked him."

And Mr. Hearst said, "Of course I like him. No one can help liking him. He must have had a very nice mother, he has such fine manners. But I think him a little erratic."

"Maybe on the ground," I said, "but not in the air— he's a great pilot and he's invented lots of things that make flying better and safer."

He's a billionaire inventor—that's all that there is about Howard Hughes.

Except about the Ladies.

A succession of movie stars were connected with Howard Hughes and his—by this time—many millions. Lana Turner—Jane Russell, whom he starred in a movie—

But I want to come to Billie Dove. *The woman he loved.*

One of the very few Follies Girls who were really beautiful. She wasn't a good actress, and she had less personality than most. I always thought she was timid—and it takes a very brave woman to be beautiful. Beauty gets a woman into all kinds of things—like the Trojan War and the Guillotine—for which she has no desire or fitness or tendency. That's why I think the girls of today have gone in so much for uglification—it gets them in a lot less trouble and drama—and of course less joy and achievement, too. There is a difference between glorification and beauty.

I had often thought of Billie Dove as a lamp of rose and white jade fashioned by a sculptor's hand, but without a light on inside.

The day I met her in New York—years ago now—the light was on! Shining in all the glory of being in love, and falling in love can make a plain woman look glorified. Of Billie Dove it made you understand about Helen of Troy and Cleopatra and women whose beauty changed the map of empires.

We had run into each other shopping on Fifth Avenue and I said, "You look happier than most women ever get. I'm so glad. Can you tell me about it?"

She said, "Yes—it's hard for me not to talk about it. You can come and help me shop for my trousseau! Isn't that marvelous? And we've had the silver monogrammed—"

"Then you and Howard are going to be married?" I said.

"He went back to California today," Billie said and even her voice was *radiant,* "and I'm going to finish up a few things and probably go day after tomorrow—and then— Come and see our silver!"

I saw the silver. It was a fine early English pattern—and it was monogrammed with H.

We went down the Avenue. I saw her fit a rose going-away suit and a hat with seven little tiny pink plumes on it, and—

It has been my fortune, good and bad, to see women in emotional crises. That has been my business as a reporter most of my life. You are always not only where the action is but where the emotion is. In the death cell at Sing Sing—coming down the stairs at the White House for the first time as First Lady—at the altar—and I had to be right, often, to recognize the truth on the witness stand, or the lie, to commit myself and my paper to what I believed women were feeling and whether what they were saying was the truth. I am interested to find that the dictionary recognizes *heartbreak . . . the heart . . . considered as the seat of life, thought, feeling emotion . . . as to die of a broken heart.*

That day on Fifth Avenue I saw Billie Dove in the *rapture* of a loving heart—a requited love. As we added some finishing touches to her wardrobe, she was shining with joy. Joy always seems to me a step beyond happiness—happiness is a sort of atmosphere you can live in sometimes when you're lucky. Joy is a light that fills you with hope and faith and love. Or maybe it's the other way around. When you are filled with hope and faith and love you have *joy*.

I can remember so well that day with Billie Dove in New York. Partly I think that it was the surprise and delight of seeing her so—so animated, so many expressions on a face I had always thought of as expressionless—so vivacious and jubilant. The next day we had lunch together at "21" and the magic was still working. For almost an hour she spoke to me of Howard Hughes.

My recollection here comes down to what I *hear*. Recollection comes from what you see again as you live it over in memory, from what you hear in an echo from the past, sometimes in what you smell. I will almost find my son Bill beside me when I get a whiff of peanut butter, as the grandchildren make sandwiches.

Tenderness.

That's what I hear Billie Dove saying. She admitted that she was shy—and I knew that beautiful women often are. They have coped so long with people enchanted by what my beautiful daughter Elaine used to call *my looks* that they tremble with fear. Elaine, who refused a five-year motion picture contract offered her by Irving Thalberg, then the power at MGM, said with a fury, "Mama he only wants me for *my looks*." She always felt that half the time she never got to *know* people at all.

And it was, Billie told me that day, Howard's *tenderness* that made her feel so safe with him. The word, especially as she said it, surprised me. Always it had been possible to imagine the tall, lanky, good-looking young Texan, with his far-seeing eyes and fighting jaw, as passionately in love, as riding in like young Lochinvar out of the West and carrying off any girl he wanted. But tenderness, that outward expression of inward kindness, hadn't occurred to me. Billie was very sure. She talked a great deal about his future, about how much he wanted to turn his inherited talent for invention to help others. She showed me some of his presents to her, and they were thoughtful and personally oriented, not just what a very, very rich young man would buy for a former Follies Girl now a movie star.

No matter what has happened since, I have always kept in my consciousness the Howard Hughes that Billie Dove, who wasn't the most articulate girl I ever knew, managed to convey to me.

I went out to put her on the plane. People weren't all flying yet but of course Howard Hughes was wedded to aviation and among the very first to see the potential of vast airlines flying across continents and oceans on schedule carrying passengers.

She was flying, I knew, to her wedding.

I waited for news of the wedding—for it belonged and would of course be on the front page. Then, as it didn't appear, I thought of Howard's love of secrecy, of how much he disliked being in the spotlight, of how he hated to be *watched* in everything he did. Might be a secret marriage, an elopement, carried out in Mexico or some small town . . .

Some day a great American novelist, if we ever have another one, will write a book about a man born with the kind of genius or great ability that takes him into the Public Eye, makes him the center of public thought, who is not only totally without any of the know-how in handling the Press which has a *right* to know what he is doing, but hates it with a real passion that makes him misjudge those who work in the cause of that first of all freedoms, a Free Press. Men of outgoing accomplishment shrivel sometimes at what is called Publicity—even when it is to the benefit of themselves and their work. Men of true statesmanship get out of balance and destroy what they might do for humanity. It is to be remembered with gratitude for the blessing that Einstein understood perfectly the right of the Press and was always a favorite with newspapermen everywhere. Howard Hughes, on the other hand—who when he was at ease in private had as delightful and generous a character and personality as I have ever known, and I did know him well—hates the public spot where he had to live much of his life. Many of his years have been tormented by his inability to live with his fame and fortune in the spotlight that has always been turned upon him.

Thus I figured that he might have decided to keep his marriage to Billie Dove secret as long as he could, but came the day when I knew he couldn't have kept it that long. The Press finds out in time, no matter how much money, brains and invention go into deceiving it. It was *news* if the young millionaire had married an ex-Follies Girl movie star, and must be told to the public. When that certain amount of time had passed, I knew there hadn't been any marriage and I wondered some, but it wasn't until years later that Billie herself told me what had happened.

Billie Dove's plane soared over all the miles between New York and the airport used by Hollywood. Her last word with Howard had been that he would meet her. All arrangements, so far as she believed, were made; they would be married as soon as the beautiful house he had bought in the Wilshire District was ready with all the things they'd bought in New York.

He didn't meet her.

Naturally, she thought there had been some mistake.

She never heard from him again.

Remember that Billie Dove was a world-famous beauty, a former Follies Girl, now a movie star. She wasn't some nameless waif and as far as I know she was pretty unforgettable.

But those are the *facts* as Billie told them to me.

What is more, they were told to me again word for word, syllable by syllable, monogrammed silver and house and furnishings and linens and all some years later in an MGM dressing bungalow by another beautiful movie star named Lana Turner. That he was as much in love with Lana Turner as several hundred men in person and several million men in movie theaters were and would continue to be, she herself believed. Lana has always been one of those girls—when a man falls in love with her, that's it, brother. And she had had a good deal of experience. She wasn't the kind to think every man who cast an eye upon her or spoke soft words was head over heels. On the other hand, she had criteria by which to recognize the signs. And as far as she could see and hear, Howard Hughes had 'em.

But he didn't meet that airplane either!

There was some Snow Queen in Lana, and the day in her dressing room at Metro when the whole thing was well in the past and she told me about it her voice and her heart were pretty icy. But I got the feeling that it was as much bewilderment—just not being able to understand what the hell was going on or had gone on—as any heartbreak that rattled Lana.

It was my lovely ex-Follies Girl Billie Dove who gave me the secret of Howard Hughes. We were the only two women at a dinner in Tom Mix's house—Vicky had been called away or something—and we left the men to their brandy and went into Vicky's exquisite French drawing room and somehow something suggested Howard—

"There isn't any mystery about Howard," Billie Dove said. "I loved him, he was so vital and interesting, so alive and so very kind. He could think up kind things to say to you, the ones you wanted to hear most. I remember even now that when I talked to him he always seemed to *listen*, really listen with a lot of interest as though he thought I was brainy and witty and all the time I knew I wasn't. But somehow with him I began to believe I was. You see, it was very sad. I was never angry, how could I be? I was the woman he needed to be his wife. I really didn't want a career. I never did. I got into it because I had to make a living and—everybody said you ought to try for the Follies and so I did, though Mr. Ziegfeld almost didn't take me because he was afraid I didn't have any sense of humor and he said a beautiful girl without a sense of humor was too much trouble. You see, I knew that Howard didn't love me just for the way I looked. He liked being quiet, he liked not having to talk all the time. He liked simple things and going about so nobody noticed you—and I had learned how to do that. He liked going for walks in the park . . .

"Don't you see that whatever he did to me he did it much more to himself? Don't you see that whatever twisted him and made it impossible for him to give himself, that twisted him away from—from being able to love and be loved—somewhere, somehow he'd been hurt or frozen or something and—don't you *see*—"

There sat Billie Dove, the tears on her face pleading with me.

"Don't you see how much he needed me? Much more than I needed him. More than anything in the world he needed to be able to love, to come alive with someone else, but—you know people who can do the things Howard could do—people whose brains and—and blood stream are so violent with creative forces. I'm not saying this very well, but I knew it then. Howard loved me as much as he could love anybody, and if you can't really love all the way then it's heartbreaking to watch." And I knew that her heart had broken much more for the man who couldn't love her than for the girl who had loved him. Billie wiped some tears from her face. She said, "Don't you see it's—it's about Howard I'm so sad? He was the one who was hurt because he never did find it—not the tenderness he needed. He was the one who was hurt most—"

Billie Dove married a fine man who had a beautiful home, lots of money, they lived happily ever after. Which was as it should be.

Just the same I wish she'd married Howard Hughes—somehow.

Ruby de Remer was a Follies Girl who made a sensationally successful marriage.

But there are two extraordinary things that I like about Ruby and Ben Troop.

One was the way he fell in love with her.

He'd seen her in the Follies and she looked exactly like his dream girl, that he'd been dreaming about all his life. And when he finally succeeded in meeting her—being a rich and socially distinguished young man from the West this wasn't too difficult—he was simply and instantly bowled over for life. One of the other girls whom he'd known without interest agreed to take him to call on Ruby, and there she was when they arrived on her knees with a pair of scissors painstakingly changing *price tags*. A nice woolly dressing gown bore a label saying $58.95 and Ruby was carefully removing it and substituting one saved from the past which read $22.50. A small set of place mats and napkins in ivory with big red roses was marked $14.75 by Macy's but the lovely Follies girl with the blond curls down her back was removing the figure 1—so that all they cost was $4.75.

"And," said Ruby de Remer with a quick mischievous smile, "Mama will think *that's* extravagant! In Denver, where Mama lives, they think New York is extravagant all the time. And Mama just can't believe what my salary is as a Follies Girl."

I like a good mother-daughter story and I can still hear with delight Ben Troop telling me of their first trip to Europe after they were married. Ruby, he said, wasn't overawed. In fact, as they beheld a Raphael masterpiece in the Vatican Ruby paid it her highest compliment. "Oh Ben," she said, "wouldn't that look beautiful in Mama's house in Denver?"

"I think," said Ben, "she was sort of disappointed that I couldn't buy it for her."

Apparently it was a joyful thing to take a Follies Girl to Europe on her honeymoon.

I checked my table in the Tavern at the End of the Road. Plainly, *plainly*, I could see a Parade of Follies Girls passing in sparkling review. A whole *dozen* of them wearing feathered silvery headdresses taller than they were—Ziegfeld had a *thing* about *feathers*. Which may have been the source of the fashion in feathered hats ladies wore then. A sort of Ben Ali Haggin tableau, a moving, glittering dance with fifteen or sixteen lovelies carrying bowls of fruit and bottles of wine and a Fashion Salon with originals by Lady Duff-Gordon of London, each girl in a too-elaborate evening gown of her very own. Somebody wore a headdress of candles and a golden candelabra sitting amid her curls, and there were see-through hoop skirts, and sometimes a girl carried a fan in her hand and wore one on her *head*, and Ann Pennington seems in my memory to be totally clad always in fringe. There they were—with hoop skirts swaying, fans waving, headdresses alight, to the melodies of "Tell Me, Little Gypsy," "Second Hand Rose" as Fanny Brice sang it, "Hello, Frisco" danced, it seems to me, by Bert Williams, and a chorus doing an "Up Up Up in My Airoplane"—and a girl named Dolores was clad entirely in peacock feathers!—I told you about feathers, didn't I?—and Kay Lauren, a special glorified number, waving flags—

Then with a sort of bugle call and tallyho or *something* to get my attention—I was thinking of another *man* who had to be waiting there at the Tavern, *had* to be, a little man who was quite literally in a class by himself. The Man who wrote the poem I still have about THE Follies Girl, Lillian Lorraine.

Let me tell you about Harry Ruskin because he is somebody we ought not to forget. I've always been sorry that he decided to die—he said he was tired and would like to try it somewhere else for a while—just when we had started to write a book on *Comedy and Gags I Have Used.* It would, I am sure, have become a textbook in departments of Drama. For Harry had done it all. When I knew him first he was the only writer at Metro-Goldwyn-Mayer who got a salary fifty-two weeks in the year—most of them were laid off for twelve or so. His salary was tops for a writer and he wrote the Dr. Kildare series for Lew Ayres, forerunner of the plethora of series about doctors that swamp the airways, *and* most of the Andy Hardy pictures starring Mickey Rooney.

Harry Ruskin certainly brightened the corner where I was during my time at Metro-Goldwyn-Mayer.

Ask Carey Wilson what time it is, he observed as the famed producer went by my open office door, and he'll tell you how to make a watch.

We were coming out of a projection room where we'd been viewing a Margaret O'Brien picture at Mr. Mayer's request to see what ought to be done to it—"The goddam thing's got leprosy," commented Harry Ruskin, "and he wants me to give it a manicure."

Once he arrived at my house on the Hill for a party carrying under his arm *half* a toilet seat. He felt I should know *why*—and so at this point should my readers.

Some of my editors insist this is not clear and have asked me to explain. The difficulty with this is that I am on principle, and by my grandmother's upbringing, against vulgarity and ever since I heard from these editors I have been trying to find a nice way to say he was carrying half a toilet seat for my half-assed friends and I am having some difficulty therewith, because I can't seem to *think* of the way to expound this simple truth and *not* use a vulgar word.

Harry was always openly grateful that his father had known how to make *shoes.* The guy in Hollywood, he said to me once, who doesn't know what he'd do to *eat* if he lost his job is always the first one who gets fired. Papa made shoes and I'll always *eat.*

For many years Ruskin wrote for Florenz Ziegfeld and the Follies. Short skits, what were called Blackouts, consisting of a brief drama of some kind, and concocted material for W. C. Fields, Fanny Brice, Will Rogers, Bert Williams, Nora Bayes and Jack Norworth, and Marilyn Miller. No one knew Flo Ziegfeld, the Follies, the Follies Girls better than Harry Ruskin and when in the much later years I used to lunch with him at MGM in the famed Commissary where you might see Clark Gable, Jean Harlow and Dressler all lunching on Mr. Mayer's famed chicken soup, and later still when he came often to the Beverly Wilshire where I lived to outline his coming text on *Comedy and Gags,* the one thing he found easy to remember and impossible to forget was Lillian Lorraine.

The Follies Girl.

I'd heard and heard about Lillian Lorraine from *everybody* who ever had to do with the Follies. Or everybody who'd ever seen the Follies. I remembered her very well myself because the first time I ever went to the Follies the man I was with pointed her out at once. And a few minutes later, in a floating gown of pale green chiffon, she walked along with the others—she turned to smile at the audience—she kept right on walking—and walked into the orchestra pit! It scared everybody in the theater senseless, but like Dempsey when Firpo knocked him out of the ring in the first round our Lillian managed with the help of a few musicians to climb back onto the stage and continue to be a Follies Girl.

"What was it," I said to Harry Ruskin, "about Lillian Lorraine?" Without one exception, everyone who ever talks of the Follies mentions her first. I did an interview once with Ziegfeld, in a little coffee shop near the theater where he was holding tryouts for new Follies Girls. And Ziegfeld said, "The epitome of the Follies Girl is, and I am sure always will be, Lillian Lorraine." I knew he had tried hard to get her to marry him and that she was the one girl both his wives, Anna Held and Billie Burke, were always jealous of. So it was natural that I should say to that expert Harry Ruskin— What is all this about Lillian Lorraine?

When I once asked Will Rogers, the least susceptible to feminine wiles of any man I ever met, about Lorraine these were his exact words, "Lillian had it all," and then he said in the famed Oklahoma drawl, "When I was a kid, I once heard a man say if he ever wanted to marry a girl she must have it all—she must be a lady in the draw-

ing room, a cook in the kitchen and something out of the Arabian
Nights in the bedroom."

"Was Lillian Lorraine ever a lady?" I said.

"Oh, sure," Will Rogers said. "I remember real well once when
everybody was pleased because she was being called for every night
at the Stage Door by a johnny named—well, anyhow, he was the
most eligible bachelor in town and we heaved a big sigh and said
Well, at last Lillian's got some sense. Turned out she married the
chauffeur—" and Rogers grinned at me and I hope you're old
enough to remember that shy deep grin. Memory so often holds
that for which you sigh but you're so glad glad glad you have the
memory.

So when I asked Harry Ruskin—on one of those afternoons at
the Beverly Wilshire—What is all this about Lillian Lorraine, Ruskin said, "I wrote a poem."

"A *poem?*" I said, "I didn't know you—"

"I don't," he said, and peered at me over his glasses, "but this
time I did. It's called 'Lillian Lorraine.' "

And here I present it to you:

Lillian Lorraine

She wasn't the most beautiful girl in the world,
You couldn't even call her pretty.
You can see a sexier girl on every street
In almost every city.

She wasn't the smartest girl in the world
She couldn't spell words longer than bee
Addition was a mystery to her
And so was geography

She couldn't cook and she couldn't sew
And she wore the silliest hats,
She never learned to drive a car
And she had a thing about cats.

She was a soft touch for any pal
Even if the story was bad,
She put her lipstick on upside down
And she howled if the movie was sad.

None of that matters as well you know
For she came to you from above
Whether she loves you or whether she won't
Whether you get her or whether you don't
She's forever the one girl you love.

"And that," said Mr. Ruskin, "is as lousy a spur-of-the-moment lyric as I ever heard but it's Lillian Lorraine just the same."

"Harry," I said, "were you in love with her too? Was that why you've never married?"

"That's not why I never married," Harry Ruskin said. "As I've told you before, I wouldn't marry any girl that'd marry me. But of course I was in love with Lillian Lorraine. I've never seen anybody to come anywhere near her—" And that, my children, from a man who had spent years writing on a lot that had Garbo and Joan Crawford and Jean Harlow and Norma Shearer and Marion Davies and another former Follies Girl named Mae Murray.

So there's Lillian Lorraine and now we come to Lilyan Tashman. *The* Follies Girl that I am personally inviting to the Tavern because—well, let me tell you about her.

The Lilyan Tashman story is very short.

As my first city editor once told me, the story of creation is told in fifty words.

At one time, Lilyan Tashman was called the Best-Dressed Woman on the Screen. I think she was. She had the figure for it, and the flair, and she always managed to dominate her clothes. She took the dress to the party, the dress didn't take her. To me, Lil was much more than that. She was indeed and indeed a woman of irrepressible spirit, of loving her neighbor as herself—and more.

I can't be sure that Emily Post—whom I so greatly admired because I still believe everything is more fun if you live by the rules and only run off into melodrama and adventure once in a while—so I'm not sure whether it was Emily Post *or* Dorothy Parker who said that the first dogma of Etiquette is that the *morning after* the party everyone says, "Oh no, darling, you were wonderful. You didn't do a thing! Wearing that lamp shade was a little unexpected but you looked lovely in it." Or "Don't worry about it. Nobody noticed you'd maybe had one over the limit."

I still remember one party at the home of Bill Haines, then top comedy star at MGM. Later he became Hollywood's leading interior decorator and reintroduced those white rooms after the early California style. He started on his own house, one of the most beautiful I ever saw, it was that house which sent so many Hollywood stars to him for advice that he gave up acting altogether. This particular party had gardenias as a theme, they were fragrant and graceful and Bill had them spilling over everywhere. The Guest List was a Who's Who in the Motion Picture Art and Industry and everyone asked was dressed up. A very elegant Hollywood Party.

The next morning I called Lil Tashman. You know, you *always* call somebody. Somebody who was there too. You can't bear the suspense of that lost-from-midnight-on. Tentatively, hopefully, poor dope that you felt in the cold gray dawn of that morning after, you tried to find out *what happened* in that portion of the party and evening of which you'd drawn a total blank.

"Weren't the gardenias *lovely?*" I said.

"They were indeed, " said Lil Tashman in that deep throaty of-the-Tallulah-Bankhead-school voice.

"And—" I started to go on.

As I've said, it is customary at this point to speak what is purely hallucinatory. *You were just fine, darling.* All this, for me, is thirty years ago, but I can still feel the cold dew on my brow as I waited for the consoling lies.

I didn't get any. Nary a one. Tash was fed up with them, apparently. She said, "Yes, it was a great party, Bill's house is beautiful, the gardenias were super, and *you*, my friend, were a mess. And so was I. Let's face it. I remember distinctly talking to you in that sensational upstairs gallery and you had propped yourself against the wall to try to keep upright and, honey, you didn't make it. You went flat on your face and, let me tell you something, I think you're great and I couldn't love you better *but* you are without any exception the lousiest drinking woman I have ever met. Once in a while I think I am—and then again I vote for Louella Parsons—and actually, it's no contest. You take the cake."

I *know* that it was while an ex-Follies Girl named Lilyan Tashman was speaking that I got the Message. I know I wouldn't be alive today if He hadn't used that ex-Follies Girl in that crucial moment, for it was then that I first reluctantly accepted the idea

that some day, somehow I must do something about my drinking—
like stopping. Her words carried a power of conviction. It took
guts to break through that social hidebound tabu—*you were just
fine*.

In addition, I was then writing about movies and movie stars
not only for my Hearst King Features Syndicate and INS, but for
Photoplay, the most powerful publication connected with the
movies, and I had also broken into the field of high-class magazines, called the Slicks, with millions of circulation. The first story
of a movie star ever published in a non-fan magazine was my pro-
file of Greta Garbo in *Liberty* and I was doing some for George
Horace Lorimer of *The Saturday Evening Post* and eventually a
series of life stories of stars for *Collier's*.

This I offer simply as an additional reason why it took guts for
Tashman to tell me the truth. Mostly, I got presents like sets of
silver and diamond bracelets which Mr. Hearst would never let me
accept. Anyhow, it took guts for Lilyan Tashman to speak the
truth in so forthright a manner.

If there was one thing Tashman had, it was guts. As you will see.

Early in her movie career, she had married a young actor-star
named Edmund Lowe.

This brought her rather specially into my life. For Eddie was a
San Francisco boy I'd known since I was a kid. When I was at
Notre Dame Convent in San Jose, he was at Santa Clara College,
only a short piece down the road, a football and track star, with the
same good looks that later made him a leading man and a movie
star, always a favorite with us girls. For every so often, we put on
our black veils and were taken in line by Mother Superior and
Sister Mary Regis over to the beautiful chapel at Santa Clara.

I got to go even oftener, this really is a believe-it-or-not—I was
majoring in music at Notre Dame Conservatory and my instru-
ment was the *harp*. As far as I can remember, this was partly because there never *was* a harp. And it was difficult to bring your
own. In those days before TV or even radio was entertainment, we
filled our evenings with our own music, and very nice it was, too.
Everybody sang, there was always someone who played the piano
or the guitar and the mandolin. Harps, no. There were harps in the
choir loft at Santa Clara. So when we went over there to High

Mass, I was always placed behind one of them in the choir, having been taught the Bach and Handel and Beethoven Masses. Eddie Lowe was in the fine male choir (and glee club) and thus in a position where we could pass each other notes in our prayer books and this we did from time to time. He soon began to call on me in San Francisco, and was one of the many young men who came supposedly to see me and turned out to be a circle of admirers for my father—a lot of them were in Stanford or California Law School.

At the time, Eddie Lowe was figuring on going to Stanford Law when he finished Santa Clara but somehow, partly on account of his looks, he drifted into the theater—into stock companies— finally from those in Los Angeles, the Burbank and the Belasco, into the movies. He was big, handsome, and the Fathers at Santa Clara had sharpened his wits to match and he and Lilyan Tashman fell violently in love *at first sight*. By that time he was a star and she was a Follies Girl who'd become a movie leading lady and character actress. They got married and built a red-and-white house at Malibu, at the far north end of the Malibu Colony, which was then *really* a Colony of Movie Stars including Gloria Swanson, John Gilbert, Constance and Joan Bennett, Bert Wheeler, Buster Keaton, Jack Warner of Warner Brothers, Tom Mix one summer or two, Charles Ruggles and his director brother Wesley, Allan Dwan, one of the top producer-directors, Tod Browning ditto, Buddy DaSylva, famed composer, Robert Leonard and his beautiful wife, Gertrude Olmstead. And on and on.

I saw a good deal of Eddie and Lil. And that was why I suppose I knew of the trip around the world.

The truth about it.

It remains in my overall lifetime tapestry A Great Love Story and my top tale of the irrepressible gallantry of a woman.

Before they sailed, Lil came down to number 106, my weather-beaten Malibu house where I lived with my children.

She wanted to tell me—somebody ought to know in case, she said—that she knew she was dying of cancer.

A cancer of the stomach, inoperable and terminal. She had slipped away to San Francisco and in the Dante Sanitarium had an exploratory examination. It was beyond hope or help.

"But," she said, with a big smile that set everything in the room a-dancing, "I'm not going to tell Eddie! We're going to have this trip—and it's going to be the gayest, the most fun, the most in love, the most beautiful trip since Anthony and Cleopatra. I'm going to be everything he wants me to be in his best dreams and he'll be able to remember it always—when I'm gone. He shan't have anything but happy memories."

It was a couple of days later that Eddie drifted in. There was, I remember, a magnificent sunset going on far out over the blue, blue Pacific.

Lil's doctor, it seemed, had had other ideas about the trip, different from Lil's. He wasn't going to take any such chances—and so he had told Eddie the truth. He said Lil, with her incredible courage and—yes, he said, inspired by love, love for her husband— Lilyan Tashman Lowe might be able to take the trip around the world without betraying that Death was her constant companion. Death—and pain.

"That," said Eddie, so quietly that it made me think of the old days at Santa Clara when he served the priest as altar boy in the Mass, "I'm not going to let her know that I know. She's going to make this the happiest second honeymoon any man ever had—and if she's got that kind of guts at least I can try to live up to it."

They took love, joy and courage along on that voyage.

It was, so Eddie told me later, a dream come true.

Lil had her wish, and never knew that she had inspired Eddie with such love that even in the last days he had cared for and cherished her the more both for her pain that she concealed and her courage.

So that was another Follies Girl.

Eddie and I used to talk about her often. Remember the witty things she said, but remembering too that her wit was never cruel. We'd remember what good company she was. I used to add, in silence, Thank you, Lil dear. From my heart.

You see, it *was* heart language they had, for come to think of it they could speak to the heart of a woman, too.

Chapter Eight

At a Press Conference in the White House I said to Franklin Delano Roosevelt, "Mr. President, you used the words 'a Liberal.' Could you tell us what those words mean to you?"

In that Haavaad accent which we had trouble with in the beginning Mr. Roosevelt said, "A Liberal is a man who builds bridges across the chasms that separate humanity from a better life."

"Also a woman who—?" I asked him.

"I should say that women have built as many, maybe more than men," he said. "We walk across the bridges women have built every day of our lives."

We had a secret, President Roosevelt and I, which I think it is now timely to reveal. With a raised finger, he would sometimes indicate a member of the Press at one of these conferences. This meant, please stay afterwards. When it pointed thus at me, it meant he had a new *Eleanor* story to tell me. I do wish that before Elliott wrote that silly book he'd spoken to any of us who covered the White House when his father was president. We could have straightened him out on that monumental goof about his father having an affair with Missy LeHand, his personal secretary for so many years. Better than any other man or woman, even in Hollywood, F.D.R. knew how to handle the Press. He did it by telling them everything, and then tying their hands with that suave, friendly, presidential *Off the Record*. Please listen, Elliott. He was so newsworthy personally and professionally we never let him out of our sight. If he'd had an *amour* with his secretary surely we would have known and covered it? He was no more capable of committing adultery *in* the White House, *under* his wife's roof, than of infecting it with cholera germs. His romance, with the exquisite beauty Princess Martha of Norway, was known to us all. We also knew he carried the burdens of a World War, of the discovery of Communist infiltration in our State Department which had to be handled with genius or it might bring on another war, of the aftermath of a Depression, of problems of what to do with our excess of little piglets in a world where many were starving. If the Princess gave him joy and release we figured certainly we would not say him nay. Nor did Eleanor, who really loved him and had been the one to persuade him back into politics after his illness. We knew, we saw daily, that he loved, respected, and admired her, all but poor old Westbrook Pegler—he had to have somebody to yap at. We knew the President sent Mrs. Roosevelt on those desperate jobs he couldn't do himself in his wheelchair because, as he once said to me personally, "The only person I can completely trust is Eleanor. She can walk across Niagara on a tight rope and never put a foot wrong." Does anybody here want to believe he would have made her an object of shame or ridicule in her own house? Perhaps Elliott can change this in the next edition of his book, if it ever has one, which seems to be most improbable.

A Liberal then is a woman who goes forth again and again against obstacles to build bridges over worn-out laws, over conditions that separate her from new vision, a better life, greater service to mankind. The four women I've put together here are as different as four women can be—an unknown chambermaid, a firebrand revolutionary, a gentle lady, a Bible quoting Ph.D.—yet each was, in her way, a bridge builder who directly and with impact affects the lives of women today. And each of them will bring something very special to our table at the Tavern.

Bobby Kennedy told me the last time I saw him in a TV studio in Santa Barbara that his brother Jack explored many kinds of greatness, researched many men, before he selected those whose stories are told in *Profiles in Courage*. His subjects were picked from those who couldn't be lookers-on, and no Kennedy ever was a looker-on, they fought in the front ranks, which is why they were so easy to shoot. Bobby quotes from Carlyle one of Jack's texts, *We desire not to have the courage to die decently but to live manfully*.

Or *womanfully*.

With love, with desire to serve, with courage and, I find as I think all will, with dauntless *stick-to-itiveness*.

Like one woman who built a cantilever bridge we still use. What can *I* do—*just one woman?* How can I, all alone, accomplish anything? I may have great thoughts and dreams, but what can I *do?* I saw one woman, Mrs. Elsie Parrish of Illinois, Kansas, Washington State and Anaheim, California, stand alone before Nine Men robed in all the power and glory of the final judgment and accomplish for all women a practical fact of freedom and justice on which we still walk across a chasm that once separated us from equal pay, opportunity and decent working conditions.

> Anyway you look at it, the decision of the United States Supreme Court in this state's minimum wage and hour law for women is destined to rank alongside the famous Dred Scott decision in the shaping of this nation's future.

Fine words those, worth repeating and remembering. From that story on the front page of the Wenatchee *World*, published in the center of the apple-growing country, which is more breath-taking in spring than cherry blossoms along the Potomac.

The decision referred to is that given by the Supreme Court in the case of West Coast Hotel Co. v. Parrish et al. The Parrish being *Elsie Parrish*. Sometimes it is possible to see the plans of Providence working out some gigantic coordination of the Woman and Her Moment in matters that affect our country and everyone in it. But—sometimes it isn't. "Nobody," said Elsie Parrish to me the other day in Anaheim, "so much as noticed me or my decision. They still don't."

Isn't it amazing that the women of Lib and let Lib do not know the name of the woman who won this early big victory for them, bigger than the Vote, which of course was inevitable?

One woman? Not only merely one woman, but a woman of whom in our everyday speech we might say she didn't amount to much in the great scheme of things. No money. No fame. No connections to open doors. No special training. An ordinary middle-western high school education.

Elsie Parrish being called as a
witness on her own behalf
before the Supreme Court—

Washington, the capital of the United States, moves me more
than any city I have ever seen. More than San Francisco by the
Golden Gate, or London where the shades of Shakespeare and
Great Elizabeth and Keats and Dickens still walk.

The White House, that center of world power. History catches
up with you there and shows you Jefferson buying the state of
Louisiana from Napoleon for $15,000,000, Lincoln in that most
terrible of all tragedies, Civil War, Teddy Roosevelt, teeth bared
in that ferocious grin as he declared war on the Trusts, Calvin
Coolidge breaking his usual silence for an immortal line, "There
is no right to strike against the public safety by anybody, anywhere, any time."

The Lincoln Memorial where quite often I met Bobby Kennedy,
his shock of uncombed hair flung back as he looked up *listening*—
yes, he listened—to the man who once said, "Without the assistance
of that Divine Being who ever attended him [Washington], I
cannot succeed. With that assistance I cannot fail." Did that young
man have any premonition that he was to share Lincoln's martyrdom? It wouldn't have stopped Bobby Kennedy if he'd known
it for sure. One day when we met there he told me he gained
strength from the presence of Lincoln. "Presence?" I said. "Come
here," said the Attorney General. "Stand still—*listen*—" and from
somewhere for me unrolled:

As He died to make men holy,
Let us die to make men free.
While God is marching on.

There on the hillside overlooking the marble city, the Tomb of
a Soldier Known but to God.

The tall white monument to the man from whom the city gets
its name, reaching, aspiring, forever pointing upward—a man's
reach must exceed his grasp—

And the Supreme Court. What a word. Supreme.

Who was she? Why was she there—our Mrs. Everybody-No-
body-Somebody-Anybody—such an ordinary figure in such an
extraordinary place?

Elsie Parrish, being called as a witness on her own behalf testified as follows:

I reside in Wenatchee. I have been employed by the West Coast Hotel Company. I was doing general maid service such as making beds, cleaning, dusting, etc. which is generally known as chambermaid work. At the time of my discharge the hotel company owed me $216.19. I had in mind that I should be paid—should have been paid— the state wage and that it would be paid. I took what they gave me because I needed the work so bad and I figured they would pay what was right—the state wage . . .

But they hadn't. Not by some $216.19.

Upon such small things do momentous Causes depend. By such small events are high principles determined.

Four years later, in the Supreme Court of the United States, Elsie Parrish was saying the same thing.

"It wasn't *right*," she still said to me in Anaheim last week.

Anaheim is a beautiful California town in the midst of orange groves and Elsie Parrish's house was surrounded by them and by grandchildren. I had telephoned and she came to the door at once, looking much younger than I had expected, dressed in something pink and fresh-washed and ironed. Her husband came out a moment later and—I won't say hovered—but I was sure it was curiosity *and* protectiveness that held him there. Elsie said she was surprised. "I was surprised when nobody paid much attention at the time, and none of the women running around yelling about Lib and such have paid any since. And so I'm surprised now to have you pay attention. I had to do it," she said quietly, with a ring in her voice. "What they did wasn't *right*."

In simple sequence what happened in the Case of Elsie Parrish is as follows:

Mrs. Parrish worked, as she stated, as a chambermaid for a hotel in Wenatchee, State of Washington . . .

The State of Washington had a Minimum Wage and Hour Law regarding the employment of women in any working capacity . . .

But many employers there—and elsewhere for that matter— refused to obey this law either for the minimum amount of pay or the minimum number of hours. And as is so often the case, nobody had the guts to do anything about it. Women accepted whatever their employers chose to pay them, ignoring the legal provisions completely . . .

Until Elsie Parrish came along . . .

Upon a given day when the hotel company paid her according to its own ideas and *not* according to the law of minimum wages —Mrs. Parrish asked for the amount owed her under that law—and when the hotel refused to abide by it, she found herself a bright young lawyer and brought suit to force the hotel company to obey the minimum wage law.

To this, the West Coast Hotel Company responded with a declaration that a minimum wage law was in itself Illegal, Unconstitutional and probably Immoral.

In the superior court Mrs. Parrish won her case, and thereupon the Hotel Company appealed to the Supreme Court of the State of Washington which upheld the law and the case of Elsie Parrish. Thus defeated in the State Supreme Court the Hotel Company decided to go all the way.

Came that great moment in Washington's omnipotent judiciary.

The Nine Men, high on the Bench, in their black leather chairs, robed in might and majesty.

And before them One Woman. All her legal moves behind her, she had that day as I remember so well an extraordinary dignity. Perhaps she should have been awed and overawed by the great gleaming pillars, the vast roof, the cathedral windows, the Nine Men, but she was not. She was *right* and if a woman—one woman —is *right*, she rides taller than anybody.

It was Chief Justice Hughes who read the decision.

Now it is to be found in Volume 300 U.S.—Number 3

OFFICIAL REPORTS

of

THE SUPREME COURT

Opinions from March 2 and including March 29, 1937. Inside:

West Coast Hotel Co. v. Parrish et al.
(paragraph 3) The State has a special interest in protecting women against employment contracts which through poor working conditions, long hours or scant wages may

leave them inadequately supported and undermine their
health because

1. The health of women is peculiarly related to
   the vigor of the race.
2. Women are especially liable to be
   overreached and exploited by unscrupulous
   employers.
3. A state law for setting minimum wages for
   women is not an arbitrary discrimination.

The blessing and benefit of these decisions by the Supreme
Court are obvious to anyone who reads them.

We owe the fact that we have them as part of the laws of our
country to one woman.

The woman who kept saying It's *right* to have such a law.

And the country owes to her also the definite and simple rule
and example that one lone, lorn woman can when necessary in
the United States have her debts collected for her by the Supreme
Court.

What more can any woman ask of her country?

2

If *you can meet with Triumph and Disaster and treat those two
impostors just the same—*

So said the estimable Rudyard Kipling—nevertheless I am
against shuffling the IF deck *if* it's possible to eliminate it. But in
the story of Margaret Sanger, whose service to womankind is
unequaled and unforgettable, it just *isn't* possible.

If Margaret Sanger hadn't been so beautiful that it moved all
hearts, even those covered by police badges or judicial robes, we
might be watching a fast-approaching end to our civilization by
famine and starvation. Mrs. Sanger invented the words *Birth
Control* and all they encompass. She fought the church, the medical profession, outraged public opinion and the more conservative
of her own sex banded together in Women's Clubs, so that Birth
Control could put a check upon a population explosion which
must in time have ended in the extinction of our race.

Dr. Gregory Pincus, principal developer and prime mover in
today's preventive use of the Pill, said publicly to Mrs. Sanger,
"The Pill is the product of your pioneering resoluteness."

Resoluteness.

What a word is that! The resoluteness of Margaret Sanger as she held to her purpose through arrest, attack, imprisonment, social ostracism and repeated failure still supports the bridge she built on which women walk across a chasm that once separated them from the liberty of Planned Parenthood, from selective choice in the size of a family they have decided they can educate and bring up in health and well-being. From world overpopulation with all its attendant ills, that might have eaten us out of house and home.

This tribute by Dr. Pincus giving Mrs. Sanger credit for her part in the Pill reached her not long before her death in 1966 at the age of eighty-two. She accepted Dr. Pincus' tribute as she was wont to do always, with calm and gracious conviction that she deserved it. She kept on being deliciously sure she deserved all the credit for Birth Control long after the Movement had passed from her leadership. Indeed, into a time when her name and all its association with the long, violent years of opposition from Church and State was a handicap.

All her resoluteness, her pioneer publicity, much of which was unpleasant and included headlines such as MARGARET SANGER JAILED ONCE MORE, her founding of a magazine of her own called appropriately *Woman Rebel*, might have been useless but for the fact that she looked like a combination of Helen of Troy and the Angel of Mercy, and not at all like an Anarchist, once dedicated to pulling down the Republic in favor of what we today would call Communism.

Of Margaret Sanger the famous, best-selling English novelist H. G. Wells, whose *Outline of History* remains one of the most successful books of all time, said, "She was so very beautiful, with wide-apart grey eyes and a crown of auburn hair, combining a radiant feminist appeal with an impression of serenity, calm and graciousness." This charm, what today we would inevitably call Charisma, he adds, went with a romantic, rebellious and assertive personality which she used shrewdly and with a sort of impersonal genius to get her own way in all things, to open all doors, and almost singlehanded to build one of the most important bridges of all for her sisters. It kept her out of jail often so that she could conduct a dirty, no-holds-barred, knock-down contest unrivaled in woman's long struggle for freedom and equality. *If* she hadn't walked in beauty like the night of cloudless climes and starry skies, the Pill as it is known and used today wouldn't exist, for that beauty allowed her to do the pioneer works which no battle-ax—as Mr. Hearst called some of the pioneer women leaders—could have accomplished.

No man ever closed a door or locked one on Margaret Sanger for long. And she used this weapon, which so many modern feminists scorn, frequently and dramatically. I remember seeing her being carted off to jail in the Black Maria looking like Marie Antoinette on her way to the Guillotine. The judge took one look at her and released her at once. The offense, by the way, with which she had been charged was the distribution of "obscene literature"—the obscene meant birth control and advice on prevention of conception.

Here we have a born revolutionary, strong, clever, and experienced as a trained nurse whose life met the death of another woman in full force with an explosion that was heard around the world and whose vibrations have never ceased. All things conspired to dramatize the death of Sadie Sachs in a slum tenement on the Lower East Side of New York. And they brought Margaret Sanger face to face with a Cause which she was to recall vividly when her teacher, adviser and friend Havelock Ellis told her she must find a Cause, One Cause, and not scatter her fire on every revolutionary battle going on anywhere in America.

She was dying when I got there, Margaret Sanger told me many years later, dying in pain and terror and remorse and despair. And she told me the story in words that were themselves heavy with that remembered agony.

As she spoke I saw the one tenement room, squalid and stinking, the six small ill-clad unwashed children, huddled together in a corner, and on the disheveled bed a woman with the gray shadow of death already on her thin worn face. Her hands were clenched into absurd little bony fists and every time the cries of the children broke forth, they opened wildly and then shut again even more tightly.

Mama, I'm hungry. Mama, I'm hungry—hungry—hungry—

At that moment, Margaret Sanger told me, she knew that all over the country there were children crying—Mama, I'm *hungry*— There must be a way not to bring children into the world to cry for food through their dirty tears. There must be a way.

The woman writhing on the bed in spasms of pain had tried *a* way. She had attempted an abortion, performed it by herself on herself—and a hideous death was the result, a death leaving even more lonely and hungry and desperate the plight of the unwanted children she had already brought into the overcrowded city. Her only, desperate way, and though she had done this to herself, there were many who went to the greedy, unprincipled abortionists with unwashed hands and money-hungry unconcern, who died likewise.

From that day forth Margaret Sanger was always and at all times and under any circumstances whatsoever opposed to abortion. *Prevention,* this was the word on the banner she was to carry into half a century of fight for it.

She ought not to have had any more babies, Margaret Sanger told me. *You can see that.* She was quite desperate—despairing and desperate.

The doctor came, Margaret Sanger said.

Always, I think, Margaret Sanger, though she served them well in her capacity as nurse, felt an envious resentment where doctors were concerned. She felt for sure that she could have done better, that she would in fact have been a much better doctor than any of those she met in her rounds either as a private nurse or when she worked as a visiting nurse in the poorest sections of the great roaring city.

She always remembered—she remembered when she was quite an old lady because she repeated it to me—what the doctor said when he came to give a death certificate for Sadie Sachs.

"She shouldn't have had any more children," said Margaret Sanger, tired and a little rumpled after a long day in uniform. "She couldn't take care of those she had. She didn't know what to *do.*"

"What she should have done," the hard-worked doctor said, "was make Mr. Sachs sleep on the roof."

"As though he would!" said Margaret Sanger. "Mr. Sachs or any other man."

Her feeling about doctors, of course, went back to the time when she had found there was no money, would never be enough money, in the Higgins family to send its daughter Margaret to medical school. She had wanted to go from the day she first knew the word. Little Margaret Higgins began early to tell her father and mother that she was going to be a *doctor*. Of course she was. Sometimes the other children in the little town of Corning on the banks of the Hudson River where she had been born and brought up in the large family of Michael Hennessey Higgins, teased her about this. They didn't believe she could ever become a *doctor*. It took time and money and position and power to get to and through medical school and the Higginses didn't have any of them. They were right, of course. There were too many children in the family—eleven in fact, of whom Margaret was the sixth—to find spare money to send any of them through medical school.

There is no doubt that young Margaret Higgins blamed this as well as the early death of her mother on the fact that Michael Hennessey Higgins had never slept on the roof at any time.

One way and another her father, a stonecutter by trade, an iconoclast by profession, had a most definite influence on his daughter's life. She referred to him as "a philosopher, a rebel, and an artist," revered his humanitarianism, his free spirit, absorbed his ideas, radical at the time, on feminism, socialism, the single tax, but refused absolutely the easy Irish love-of-life which kept him from being a militant combatant. She did accept his teaching, "Leave the world better because you, my child, have dwelt in it." It stirred in her a "world-hunger" which only a great cause would satisfy.

On the other hand she learned from him early that the free thinking she so much admired had a price. When her father invited the well-known agnostic, Robert G. Ingersoll, to speak at a meeting in Corning, they found the hall locked against them; Higgins, Ingersoll, and Margaret were pelted with vegetables. Subsequently the Higgins young were ostracized by respectable church families and called "children of the devil." The episode had financial repercussions as well. The Higgins family had lived about midway between the financial extremes of Corning, the poor of the flat-lands where Margaret's compassion was aroused by the dirt, hunger, overcrowding, unemployment, and the wealthy on the hill where clean, neat houses, women in pretty dresses and smelling of per-fume stirred her envy. Following the Ingersoll fiasco there were fewer marble angels for her father to carve for headstones in the churchyard. His income decreased as his family increased.

Margaret felt all this keenly and from the moment of her mother's death, medically attributed to tuberculosis, there can be no question that, while she continued to reverence Michael Hennessey Higgins the philosopher, she felt a good deal of re-bellion against Michael Hennessey Higgins the man.

That frail adored mother bore too many children too close together and this left a wound on Margaret's heart. Her first encounter with sex was in what she felt was the helpless, frightened degradation of that mother. In tenements, even in the more genteel poverty in which Margaret grew up, all too often children were familiar with sex in ways that were frightening and disgusting to them. I remember in my teens being told the story of the little boy who, locked in the closet as punishment, happened to be wit-ness to the relations of his father and mother and who later complained, "And that's the guy who beat me for blowing my nose without using my handkerchief." A fairly vulgar remark but one that conveys a little of what Margaret Sanger often spoke of in later years.

She thought of sex as part of the enslavement and humiliation of Woman. And unwanted children as the fruits of this degrada-tion.

No wonder, Margaret said later, so many women died young in those times. She remembered with bitterness that her mother died at forty-eight, her father at eighty.

And while the great sociological problem of population control and decent upbringing was uppermost in her motivations, it had another side. At another interview I had with her when her Birth Control Clinic had come by stages to occupy large head-quarters on lower Fifth Avenue, she spoke very frankly of this. "No wonder women used to be victims of female trouble, of backache and debility, so that they drank quarts of *Peruna*, a patent medicine whose alcoholic content was higher than whiskey. This was to overcome the pain in their backs and the nervous spasms in their stomachs. The terror of getting *pregnant*, of adding to a family already too large, of not having sufficient food or warm clothing, all this kept the average American woman of the lower or middle class in a continual frenzy. Part of my early anarchy and socialism and rebellion was no doubt rooted in the differences I saw along the banks of the Hudson. The magnificent estates where it seemed to me there were never more than one or two children, each with a *pony*. While near my own home in Corning the poor always seemed to have enormous numbers of children. Later when I lived in New York City I began to listen to Eugene Debs, as he led the Socialist Party and was its candidate for the presidency, heard John Reed, the young reporter who is now buried near Lenin in the Kremlin, and followed Bill Haywood of the IWW—the Independent Workers of the World—I became more and more rebellious against class distinction. The *poor* should not have such enormous families. Something should be done to prevent this from the simply sociological and political viewpoint.

There was, Margaret Sanger felt then and shocked the reasonably conservative press by stating publicly and printing in her own little magazine *Woman Rebel*, another major point here.

I still remember the hot and emphatic words in which she gave this to me, with again that strange contrast between her soft and clinging beauty and the aggressive personality and the dynamic forceful words.

"Much is said in psychology," said Margaret Sanger to me in one of our interviews, "about the frigidity of the American woman, the unsatisfactory sex response of the American wife. I am sure this came and will come from the terror of getting pregnant. Of adding to a family already too large for decency or justice to the children. Already beyond the wife's strength as housekeeper and mother of many. Nothing produces coldness in the blood like fear. Passion does not come to flower in an icebox and fear puts ice into the blood of every woman. Therefore that is another good thing Birth Control has done. It has freed women from the frigidity of fear of pregnancy. It has allowed them, unburdened of this fear, to be natural and normal and happy and responsive in sex relations."

Margaret Sanger's spirit of rebellion was always *active*. The action she took after the death of her mother was direct and drastic. Driven emotionally by loneliness, the drudgery of managing the household, the restrictions her father now placed on his beauty-blossomed daughter, she found herself longing in her heart for "romance, dancing, wooing, experience," beyond the narrow confines of Corning. Yet the thought of marriage, the conventional way out, was to her "akin to suicide." Stronger still in her mind burned that world-hunger, the desire for service intensified by caring for her mother in her last illness. She resolutely pushed aside her romantic longings. If she couldn't be a doctor, she would be a nurse.

At fifteen Margaret Higgins enrolled in nurse's training at the White Plains Hospital in Westchester County, not far from the city of New York.

These next three years, she was to write, "tested character, integrity, nerve, patience, endurance," highly desirable qualities in the pursuit of her humanitarian career. But when she transferred to the Manhattan Eye and Ear Hospital for a final period of training she found herself swept up in "dancing and wooing." In the city of New York she had time and inclination in this more leisured world to enjoy the romance for which she had longed. If the thought of marriage was still the same as suicide, the center of her womanly existence was a dream and in it she saw visions. So that when a young man she'd met at a hospital dance began to wait for her daily on the steps, she drifted into the only romantic feeling she was ever to admit. More beautiful than ever at nineteen, her beauty carried her out of her controlled, rebellious-in-a-cause career woman pattern, for William Sanger, making a good living as an architect but burning with the desire to be a painter and to live in the utopian world of artistic creation as he imagined it, fell so utterly violently in love with her that he enveloped her in flames and fantasy. After appearing daily for several months, he carried her off to a minister and married her.

By the time she stood beside the death bed of Sadie Sachs, Nurse Sanger had fought several battles, including one for her own life. A tubercular weakness had been hers at birth. Before she married she spent some months in a sanitarium in the Adirondacks, and after the birth of her first son she had to go back with her baby for almost a year. For the first and, so far as I can tell, only time in her long life Margaret Sanger was tempted by despair. The long confinement, the boredom, the uselessness, the months and years stretching ahead. But her spirit of revolt was stronger—and as always *active*. She refused to submit. In a surprise move she suddenly packed up, left the sanitarium, and returned with her son to her husband.

Now indeed for a time, in these next years of their delightful attempt at marriage, they were young Mr. and Mrs. Sanger of Hastings and Dobbs Ferry. They had three children, and the freshness of their love and their first contact with normal ways of living in the beautiful suburb of the Hudson kept the romantic dream alive in the only prosperous, conventional success-story of Margaret Higgins Sanger's experience. She floated on top of it in softly draped gowns of rose and gray and with smiling gentleness. Their house, designed by William, was beautiful as well as neat and clean. We may be sure the housewife smelled of perfume. It is interesting and enlightening that those who knew her during this period use the adjective *pretty*. Such a *pretty* woman, say those with whom I spoke who had known her then and not after she returned as the flaming crusader of Birth Control. Evidently it was a proper word for that period of her life when she at least kept up the fantasy of the bride, the wife, the mother, so much written of in novels of that day.

This satisfied neither the husband nor the wife.

William found making his living as an architect a dull affair and Margaret, disenchanted with what had become to her "petty middle class comforts," rebelled against the stagnation of her suburban Eden as she had once done against the restrictions of Corning. She could not, she felt, feed her world-hunger on a diet of "tame domesticity." In 1912, after ten years of married life, the Sanger family left Hastings-on-Hudson and moved to New York.

The Woman and Her Moment.

In the preface to his excellent biography of Mrs. Sanger (rather more objective than her own well-known works, *My Fight for Birth Control* and *Margaret Sanger, An Autobiography*), David M. Kennedy says: "There are historical moments perfectly fitted to the temperaments and personalities of certain individuals. The time from 1912 to the Second World War was such a moment for Margaret Sanger."*

New York City. 1912. A milieu of political unrest. Greenwich Village, the Liberal Club in MacDougal Street, Mabel Dodge's elegant salon. Socialists, anarchists, avant-garde artists, radical intellectuals debating everything from the theories of Freud and Havelock Ellis, sexual freedom, radical feminism to reform, rebellion, revolt.

The Sangers plunged in. Margaret absorbed new ideas like a thirsty sponge. She listened, she learned, and, being Margaret, she acted. Following her husband into the Socialist Party, she became a women's organizer for New York City. Her oldest son was sent to the experimental Ferrer School which drew fire as a center of anarchist activities. Resuming her career as a visiting nurse specializing in obstetrical cases, she encountered the appalling ignorance of the poverty-ridden, prolific immigrant women on New York's Lower East Side, and wrote a series of articles for the daily Socialist paper dealing so openly with venereal diseases and feminine hygiene that the *Call* was banned by the Post Office, her first of many such encounters. Wherever the action was, there was the delicate Mrs. Sanger, now with energy to spare. When she found the Socialists too conventional in their political approach she unhesitantly espoused the anarchists' tactic of direct action. In this her friend and mentor was Emma Goldman, agitator, conspirator, feminist, long-time unsuccessful advocate of "Voluntary Motherhood" as part of a revolutionary plot to weaken America. Arm in arm with the notorious Emma, who had already served a year on Blackwell's Island, Margaret marched in protests and on strike lines. And then, in that bleak cold tenement, with Nurse Sanger at her side, Sadie Sachs died.

Two years later, in a flat in Brixton, England, Margaret Sanger met the man who was to establish the foundation for the rest

* *Birth Control in America, The Career of Margaret Sanger*, by David M. Kennedy, Yale University Press, New Haven, Conn., 1970.

of her life, though there was nothing either romantic, passionate
or sexy about it in spite of the fact that he was known chiefly
for his researches and writings *on* Sex, including Sex in Relation
to Society. Havelock Ellis was twenty-five years older than
Margaret when they met and already famous as a psychologist,
sociologist and writer. The afternoon Margaret Sanger was invited
to tea with him was undoubtedly the true turning point in Mrs.
Sanger's life and the beginning of her work in Birth Control.
John Dewey, the leading educator of the time, has said of Mrs.
Sanger, "The death of Sadie Sachs was her Gethsemane, her meeting with Havelock Ellis was the beginning of her real mission in
life." Up until that time, she had scattered her fire. Hot fire it
was, no question about that. Always and at all times, always her
emotions, her feelings drove her as fire drives an engine, always
her heart beats controlled her head beats, though she had plenty
of both. The fascinating thing is that, now we are able to see
her and her career as a whole, it is quite obvious she had no idea
of this. She was quite-quite sure that her head, her mind, her brain
power was always in command not only of *her* but of all those
who had anything at all to do with her life and career.

Already in the wake of Sadie Sachs's death the Sangers had been
to Paris where, while William studied painting, Margaret studied
French techniques for contraception, a science she considered woefully backward in America, and fraternized with French rev-
olutionaries. Chestnut blossoms came and went. She scarcely
noted them. Finally convinced there was more potential romance
and fulfillment in the coming revolution that in an uninspired
marriage Mrs. Sanger left her husband more or less permanently
and, with her children, returned to New York. Here she set about
to shock society awake to the facts of life as she saw them. Her
views at that time were sweeping and not very clear.

When *Woman Rebel*—editor, Margaret Sanger—appeared it
advocated prevention of conception and promised to give con-
traceptive information. To do so would have violated the so-called
Comstock law which generally prohibited mailing, transporting or
importing *any* "obscene, lewd or lascivious" articles and specifically
banned all devices and information pertaining to prevention of conception. The church and the medical profession supported the ban.
Violating it would, as she meant to do, challenge a formidable

establishment. But as issues rolled off the press Mrs. Sanger's shock tactics, swept along by her emotional resentments, scattered her incendiary volleys in all directions. Inflammatory, brash, *Woman Rebel* attacked capitalists, marriage and "the marriage bed," published an article "In Defense of Assassination." There were, indeed, excerpts from a speech by Emma Goldman on "Free Motherhood," advice on using prevention of conception as a weapon to frighten "capitalistic classes" by weakening the work force, and in one issue she coined the phrase Birth Control. But the promised specific information on the how-tos of birth control was not forthcoming. This, based on techniques she had learned in France, Margaret had set down in a secretly printed pamphlet, "Family Limitation." Before it could be distributed, six out of eight issues of *Woman Rebel* had been banned, and Margaret found herself indicted on nine counts of violating the general intent of the Comstock law. No four-letter words, no pornography, as these came to be known years later, yet the United States Attorney held that the article in defense of political assassination, which she had not even written, "would defile the records of this court."

Thus Nurse Sanger, who had hoped for martyrdom on the test case of "Family Limitation" found herself faced with going to jail for nine other reasons. Instead, having arranged for release and distribution of the controversial pamphlet, she fled to England —and her meeting with Havelock Ellis.

It was Havelock Ellis who loudly, directly and specifically told her that she must direct her appeal to one Cause alone and only. That she must select this Cause and to his way of thinking it should be Birth Control, her own phrase, her own banner, her own description used and invented to describe her battle to give women the right to have children only when and as often and how they pleased.

Havelock Ellis, an English psychologist when psychologists were not as numerous as they are today by seven million, was the first doctor-writer who drew attention to the sexual behavior of woman. In America this had been a subject seldom if ever discussed in public and practically never speculated upon in fairly uninhibited language. Around him controversy and publicity swirled and leaped and very soon Margaret Sanger was known as one of his leading disciples, heavily involved in all his doctrines and tutelage. She never did anything by halves or three-quarters, come to it.

Just the same, it was Havelock Ellis who, with dynamic command and careful explanation, was able to persuade her that she was scattering her fire in such a manner that she wasn't really accomplishing very much of anything.

Concentrate, he told her. Choose your Cause and put your full power into that and that only. He agreed that Prevention of Conception had as much to do with the possibility of a happy and adjusted sex life for American women as any other single thing. He advised her strongly and persistently to *concentrate* herself, her beauty, her brains, her by now well-known name upon this and this alone.

Birth Control.

A fabulous phrase, he told her, and *her own.*

Two other things Ellis did for her: he systematically guided her reading and study of birth control, first at the British Museum, then sent her to Holland to study advanced methods there. And his influence tempered her bitterness—which had fed on class hatred—with his own generous philosophy and dedication to what Margaret understood to be "life more abundant." It was, in its way, a conversion and, while it did not alter her methods, always uniquely her own, it did change her emotional basis. It prepared her for the transition from what had begun as a revolutionary movement to the charitable cause it was to become, a cause in which, she truly believed, Sadie Sachs—and her own mother—had already given their lives.

Perhaps this was the only time that a man of full manhood and great power ever *concentrated* upon controlling Margaret Higgins Sanger. Her father hadn't cared that much. William Sanger sort of drifted around in her life and disappeared from it with hardly a ripple. And actually, though she was a conscientiously good mother, the same is true of her children. When later she divorced William and married the much older, very rich oilman, J. Noah H. Slee, Margaret insisted that she would keep the name she had made famous, and her own separate abode, though she readily permitted Mr. Slee to use considerable of his fortune in support of her work. Margaret Sanger drove only one mule—her career, her Cause, what she saw as her duty to build a bridge for her sister-women and for the world itself.

Controversy, said William Randolph Hearst, is the life blood of circulation. By circulation, of course, he meant the number of Hearst newspapers in New York, San Francisco, Chicago, Detroit, Atlanta, Los Angeles and Seattle. By controversy he meant the hot differences of opinion that made people buy newspapers, the arguments pro and con that keep readers vitally interested in any cause, personality, scandal or story. Woman and her many activities and personalities in this century have produced a lot of controversy. No more controversial figure and cause appeared than that of the exquisite, delicate, feminine figure of Margaret Sanger and Birth Control.

On her return to the United States she announced her stated objective—Propaganda—"to dramatize the situation—to focus attention on obsolete laws." Such as the Comstock law. Such as laws prohibiting doctors from dispensing contraception except in the treatment or prevention of diagnosable diseases. And dramatize the situation she promptly did. By making speeches across the country, educating and enchanting audiences. By *not* making speeches. In some states she was hustled off the platform and onto the front pages for discussing a subject "decent, clean-minded people" wouldn't mention in public. She was carried from one hall looking like a fragile madonna while the entire audience sang, "My country, 'tis of thee . . ." For six years she courted controversy tirelessly. She opened an illegal birth control clinic in Brooklyn and went to jail, to be greeted on her release by worshipful women singing the "Marseillaise." She wrote books, pamphlets, articles, distributed "obscene literature," sold contraband contraceptives, and went to jail again. And again.

In the Twenties she organized the First American Birth Control Conference, the bare little clinic on Lower Fifth Avenue became the American Birth Control League, and Margaret Sanger was a world figure, traveling to Europe to organize an international conference on the population problem. Her cause at home was becoming fashionable, the women's clubs, the wealthy and middle-class housewives rising slowly to her banner behind the moral and financial support of such courageous pioneer women as Mrs.

Dwight Morrow, Mrs. George Rublee, Mrs. Gertrude Minturn Pinchot, Mrs. Franklin Delano Roosevelt. Fashionable, not respectable, for as late as 1929, with the unwitting cooperation of the police who raided her perfectly legal birth control clinic, Mrs. Sanger was back on the front pages again.

By the Thirties, however, she had so thoroughly aroused the public that she could concentrate all her fire on the obsolete laws and the medical profession. The law yielded first in the famous *One Package* decision. Resolutely Mrs. Sanger propagandized nearly every member of the American Medical Association House of Delegates, where she had more enemies than friends. Her blatant bid for publicity, so necessary to her early cause, had scandalized many in that conservative body. And elsewhere. But hers was a Cause whose time had come. In 1937 the AMA endorsed Birth Control.

It remained only to persuade government agencies to full acceptance and participation. This she had already attempted with Presidents Coolidge and Hoover, only to find her name anathema. But the president to follow Hoover into the White House was one whose wife had long upheld her, who personally admired Liberals, both male and female. In 1942, with the support of Franklin Roosevelt and his First Lady Eleanor, Mrs. Sanger saw Birth Control officially adopted into the federal government through public health agencies.

For Margaret Sanger, Her Moment was over.

In her own words she "left the front." The front no longer existed. She was a combatant, a fighter. The battle was won. She, who had been the movement's greatest stellar asset in its disreputable days, was a liability now that she'd made it respectable. Yet she could believe and cherish the telegram sent to her after the AMA victory by a leading gynecologist, Dr. Robert Latou Dickinson: "Among foremost health measures originating or developing outside medicine like ether under Morton, microbe hunting under Pasteur, nursing under Nightingale, Margaret Sanger's world-wide service holds high rank and is destined eventually to fullest medical recognition."

That women today have the Pill and the right to use it, that neither Church nor State now makes any loud noises in opposition thereto is owed almost one hundred percent to one woman.

A lot of people called her a sinner, as she attacked systematically, in campaign after campaign.

Later, women—benefiting as of course they did by her victories —called her a saint.

I don't want to mix similes or metaphors—my grammar is non-existent—but this butterfly carried a sting like a submachine gun.

What put that halo on her flaming auburn hair for me was the story of Sadie Sachs, which I was privileged to know at first hand. I *knew*—I had to know—that Margaret Sanger was right, and that Birth Control was something that would benefit women and make their lot easier, happier and more productive of good. I came to believe that and still do. As I watch the young women around me I feel that the Pill is a good thing and that this present generation is about to restore the Family, in a smaller but even more powerful unit.

There is no way not to give admiration and accept the greatness of Margaret Sanger. H. G. Wells, who had raved always about her beauty, said also that she was "the greatest biological revolutionary the world has ever known."

That great and saintly woman Helen Keller, who overcame the handicaps with which she had been born, once wrote to her, "You are among the women I most love because you so labor and suffer that the life of the human race may become safer, finer and more creative. You are a free, world-illuminating spirit."

A physician named Dr. John Favill is quoted by David M. Kennedy as telling her "your vision, courage and achievement make you the world's greatest woman."

When I knew Mrs. Sanger, when I wrote interviews with her as she became more and more newsworthy and of more and more interest to American women, I recognized her beauty. I have known most of the great Hollywood beauties, I once saw the Empress Eugénie driving in Hyde Park, and I lived in the same house during the war with Madeleine Carroll. I agree beyond question that Margaret Sanger was beautiful.

I salute her service to women—which may well be as great as that of any woman of whom I can write—and continues now that she has been dead for almost ten years, and will continue probably as long as we have this world and a human race.

I admired, respected and looked up to her and whenever I think of Sadie Sachs I love her. Sometimes it is easier to love than to like.

For years I have kept on wondering why I didn't like her. I wanted to! I wrote of her with admiration and appreciation. I treated her with respect and the same kind of courtesy I showed Eleanor Roosevelt.

When I wrote *Final Verdict*, the book about my father, Earl Rogers, in it I said I had tried by writing it all down to come upon the answer to the one great unanswered question of my life— whether I had done right about my father in the courtroom that day.

This of course is of trivial and impersonal unimportance compared to that.

Or is it?

What I—a woman—think of the great women I knew, how I feel about them is surely part of my life and character and relationship to God.

I know what I as a woman owe Margaret Sanger.

Allright. As in *Final Verdict*, writing this has brought me the answer. I tell it with that humility which comes to take the place of pride after it has had a fall.

It is highly possible that this next paragraph won't be in the book *at all*.

I didn't like her because she didn't have a sense of humor.

Not a scintilla.

Perhaps her Cause, her particular Accomplishment, was of a nature to shut out the smallest modicum of humor, the possibility of laughing at a joke.

On the other hand—Saint Cabrini—Jane Addams of Hull House is still remembered by newspapermen for her wit—I've always believed that it was just possible Amelia Earhart laughed at the Japs just before they shot her. What could have embarrassed them more? And *belittled* their victory?

Anyhow, right or wrong, in writing this I've discovered and must admit that is why I didn't *like* that great humanitarian Margaret Sanger. Maybe our Tavern can make Mrs. Sanger laugh once in a while. Then we can love her all the way.

3

This gentle lady.

So Senator Abraham Ribicoff described Rachel Carson in Washington's National Cathedral during the mid-Sixties after her explosive book *Silent Spring* had been published and caused more uproar, acclaim, accusation and applause than any book by a woman author since *Uncle Tom's Cabin* started a great war.

Silent Spring also started wars, civil, scientific, and political.

Enemies called it an overzealous and inaccurate myth. Its supporters in the millions called it one of those rare books that change the course of history.

This gentle lady, I saw her testifying before the Senate Committee which had been summoned to meet the challenge of her book. So complete was the impression of gentleness that I backed out, convinced I'd come to the wrong place. I was looking for that impassioned, embattled, pugnacious *biologist* who had halted a vast industry manufacturing DDT and other pesticides in its money-making tracks, who had pinched and prodded a reluctant, negligent and complacent governmental agency off its fat rear end to cope with this menace to public health. No question I had a *thing* about Rachel Carson. I still have. At this minute my typewriter begins to stutter for fear there is *no way* for me to do justice to this woman without whose unflappable courage and teaching a lot of us might not be alive today. I admire her as a woman of Science, as a Teacher of that Science, as a writer about it, and she exemplifies all that women can and do accomplish, even if she *was* a lady. That never stopped her anywhere, any time.

A woman of the species smart enough to take all the advantages a lady gets from men! Who accomplishes more than other women because she has the full help and active support instead of the opposition and antagonism of the men she encounters in her professional life. Who can enter into a creative partnership with men she finds cooperative and willing to back her visions and desires. This gentle lady has to be a joy and blessing to all and so Rachel

Carson was. Could we spell it gentlelady—in one word? Jack Dempsey, who seems to remain the Champ for all time no matter who holds the title at the moment, once explained to me that he had been called a gentleman in spite of being a prizefighter because he had learned to be *gentle* for fear he might hurt somebody. I don't think Rachel Carson had to learn to be gentle. She was born that way, and long, close, deep companionship with her gentle mother, as they walked the woods together in her youth, extended and reinforced this. But she had to learn—when the time came, the time of attack and vituperation—to be the counterpuncher, a woman who refused to stay down, a crusader who could never be turned back, a fighter against such potent forces as enormous industrial corporations, governmental agencies and scientists fighting for their lives against their own mistaken shortsightedness.

This, her being a gentle lady, is my first big joy in the American woman named Rachel Carson whom I discovered in *The New Yorker*, a "popular" magazine, along with Dorothy Parker and Robert Benchley and Alexander Woollcott. Totally characteristic of her that she didn't want to write only for the Fish and Wildlife Service publications or the scientific journals and pamphlets. So often those with special knowledge communicate it only to other specialists and we are the poorer for it. But Rachel Carson? A natural-born teacher, she was eager and fervent and predisposed to reach those who didn't know, to awaken interest in the world so they would *listen* to what she had to teach them about the *wonder* of the universe.

Once when, long after his presidency, I was talking with Herbert Hoover, he spoke of Teaching, Teachers and the Teaching profession in words I've never forgotten. He was, perhaps, not everybody's ideal as President of the United States, but as an engineer he had no equal here. Graduated from Stanford, he had practiced his profession as a mining engineer in Australia and China as well as the United States, and finally in England he became the chief consulting engineer of his time. The efficiency of his work as Food Administrator in the trying times of war and famine made him more popular than his term as president and when I knew him he lived at the Waldorf in New York and was the center, actually, of the engineering world. Nobody seemed to build a dam or a bridge or enter into any engineering development anywhere in the world without first coming to consult the former president.

"Speaking," he said to me, "not as a religious man, not even as a Christian—which I hope I am—the greatest Teacher who ever lived was Jesus. His teaching is beautiful, brilliant, persuasive— and above all, he taught anyone anywhere, by the roadside, on the Mount, on the sands of the Sea of Galilee. They didn't have to have credentials or grades, they just had to have interest enough to stand still and *listen*. And his Teaching has come down to us over centuries as no other teaching has. Not too long ago the New York *Times* listed his Teaching from the Mount as the most important event in all history. He had something wonderful to say and he said it wonderfully and it still means more to us than anything else that ever happened."

A *Teaching*.

Rachel Carson was actually first and always a teacher and I think her favorite teaching was Wonder. I know it was her favorite word and many of her early articles had it in the title, in *The Ladies' Home Journal*, the *Atlantic*, as well as *The New Yorker*.

I wonder about the trees, Robert Frost once wrote.

Perhaps that was why two of her favorite books, two she quoted frequently, were *Alice in* Wonder*land* and *Through the Looking-Glass*. Once in an interview at a time when she and *Silent Spring* and her ecology theories as a whole were under fire she brought up a dialogue between Alice and the Red Queen:

> "One *can't* believe impossible things," said Alice. "I daresay you haven't had much practice," said the Queen. "When I was your age, I always did it for half-an-hour a day. Why, sometimes I've believed as many as six impossible things before breakfast."

"And that," said Miss Rachel Carson, "is a very necessary thing to know and to do. You start believing in them in spite of their being impossible, and the first thing you know they aren't impossible any more."

I'm sure that is what she would have said about flights to the moon. Quite impossible, our ancestors said. And here we are, looking at a moon we know men have walked on.

"Help Your Child to Wonder" was one of the first of her magazine articles—in *Good Housekeeping*, I think—and I remember very well that I cut it out and tried to use it with my own children.

A great deal of this she learned from the child she adopted when he was only four, her grandnephew Roger Christie. As far as any of us knew, there was never any question of marriage for the author of the classic *The Sea Around Us*. I can't recall any rumors of engagement and love affairs or attachments surrounding the name of Rachel Carson. Asked by a rash reporter why she had not married she replied kindly, "I didn't have time." Nor, indeed, would it seem she had.

Her early life was spent in her native Western Pennsylvania, her nearest friend the mother who passed on to young Rachel her own deep regard for and love of wild things. As a student at Pennsylvania State College for Women, at Johns Hopkins, later at the Marine Biological Laboratories at Woods Hole, Massachusetts, her life was crowded with studies. She got her degree, passed the civil service examination, and accepted a position with the United States Bureau of Fisheries, where she remained for fifteen years. But always, even when she became editor of the Fish and Wildlife Service publications, she managed to do her own writing at night, to pursue her studies in marine biology, to wonder at the almost impossible beauty she saw in nature. In Washington she joined the Audubon Society, an ardent "birder" sometimes scouring the countryside, sometimes rising early after a late night of writing to watch migrating flocks in their dawn colors. When, in 1951, *The Sea Around Us* became an immediate and immense success, she left her government job to devote full time to her studies and her writing, but her new-found fame brought with it such demands that somehow for a while Rachel Carson seemed to have less time than ever. Because she couldn't find the home she wanted, she finally built it for herself, a big early-American red brick house on a wooded acreage about twenty miles out of Washington, in Silver Spring, Maryland, and at about the same time she added a wing to the family cottage overlooking Sheepscot Bay at Southport, Maine, and for the rest of her life went there as often as it was possible to fit it in.

It was after she had completed and moved into the house in Silver Spring that her four-year-old grandnephew and his mother came often to visit with her—and when his mother died Rachel Carson adopted the small boy, and her first teachings of the wonder of the woods, and its birds and small wild life and the fish in its little stream were given with joyous comradeship and love of teaching so nobody noticed it *was* teaching.

In those days there was a phrase—it even became title of a smash Broadway play—*The Old Maid*. Although Rachel Carson never married it would be absolutely impossible to call her an old maid. She not only expressed femininity, she dressed it. She did her brown hair in soft curls, she wore delicate bits of jewelry at her wrists, in her ears, pinned in the laces at her throat. A single lady. *Not* an Old Maid. And her devotion to her adopted child and his friends, her habit of taking them on strolls through the woods and telling them tales of those woods around a campfire or as they sat down to eat the lunch she'd brought in a big wicker basket, showed a gentle motherliness.

Yet it was this gentle lady who got such blasts of ridicule, such insults and barbs of wrath as few figures in our history have known. At no time, when hundreds of other scientists and alleged experts pooh-poohed her theories and findings, when governmental authorities insisted that Miss Carson was a dangerous alarmist, and a false alarmist at that, a person who didn't know what she was talking about in her wild and inaccurate book *Silent Spring*, that her facts far from being facts were ridiculous fantasies, guesses about the future which it would take hundreds of years to prove or disprove, not even when she was openly called an Impostor—at no time did Miss Carson cease to be a gentlelady. Perhaps sometimes this was a performance, as beautiful and gifted as Judy Garland in *The Wizard of Oz*. Perhaps it was the role she thought most effective in her beleaguered position. Every great teacher finds and portrays the warm, burning yet somehow *calm* infallibility no matter if the personal life behind it is disturbed or anguished. Rachel Carson went through the Gethsemane of doubt, of the unfounded charges against her, of the scorn and bluster bombardment which met her on every hand.

"I hope to complete my work on the chemical poisoning of the environment by insecticides during the summer," Rachel Carson wrote early in 1958, and nothing stopped her, and at all times and against every effort she maintained her poise as a perfect lady.

My second delight about Rachel Carson is that she brought together that sensational, unequivocal combination—a true talent for teaching, perhaps even genius, *and* something *wonderful* to teach. She didn't always sit behind a desk in school or university, or simply give lectures at the many colleges around the country where she was bidden.

Her deep desire was to teach *people*, all people, all kinds of people, young and old, rich and poor, big and little, black and white to know the full *Wonder* of their environment and to allow nothing to deface or destroy it. To allow nothing to poison its purity.

Ecology was the other word she brought into our active minds, souls and vocabularies. Most of us had never heard it before when Rachel Carson began to use it along about 1955.

> *Biology*   the science that deals with the origin, history
> and physical characteristics, life processes, habits, etc. of
> plants and animals; it includes botany and zoology.

> *Ecology*   the branch of biology that deals with the
> relationship between living organisms and their
> environment.

The science of—

Rachel Carson as a biologist turned this science into poetry, drama and philosophy. She taught it as all three. As she first attended college she wanted to be, she thought, a writer. She majored in that subject. In Biology, a required course which she entered without much interest, unexpectedly, to her total surprise, she found her focus. In time, Miss Carson was to say, "Eventually, it dawned on me that by becoming a biologist I had given myself something to write about"—which would in her case necessarily mean something to teach about, and so enchanting was her work that William Shawn, editor of *The New Yorker*, welcomed all she could write about the birds and trees and stars and their relationship to their environment and to us and the *wonder* of it all.

This of course because, along with being a biologist and a teacher, she was a *poet*. So said even the critics. Rachel Carson herself, when accepting the National Book Award for Non-Fiction after publication of *The Sea Around Us*, explained this very simply. "If there is poetry in my book about the sea," she said, "it is not because I deliberately put it there, but because no one could write truthfully about the sea and leave the poetry out."

Somewhere, I think it's in *The Light That Failed*, the finest prose writer in the English language, Rudyard Kipling, says that no amount of fancy color and decorative design will cover up bad drawing. I am sure that no eloquence will hide inaccuracy, fatuity, unsubstantiality or absurdity. No amount of saying nothing poetically or brilliantly or significantly can make up for having nothing to say.

The letter killeth, but the Spirit giveth life, said the greatest of all Teachers.

Doubtless there have been as great teachers as Socrates, but apparently he had some burning inner fire as he taught. No one ever forgot a word he said. In my short senior year at Hollywood High School I had an English teacher named Elizabeth Wood. I remember every word she said to me and she had more influence on my becoming a writer by profession than anyone else in my life.

Two outstanding teachers and scientists of our time have written and taught with the power and poetry and tremendous command of their subject that gave them power to teach. It's a circle. At Princeton, Einstein proved a most moving and inspiring teacher and not just because he was *Einstein*. The two times I talked with this *great man* I found in him this gentleness of so many of the *truly* great, but I also found that he could and did explain to me the theory of relativity so that I could understand it, and it changed my entire perspective of the world. And I found, too, in him a deep and scientific and unquestioning belief in that other young Jew who taught the Science of Christianity, Jesus of Nazareth.

Rachel Carson taught officially at Johns Hopkins, where she had once been a student, and at the University of Maryland. She taught—she told me this once—because she thoroughly enjoyed it and because she felt, as she put it, a need to tithe her knowledge, her wisdom and her experience. Unofficially she taught wherever she went. Her lectures to groups all over the United States to bring them up to date on ecology, on the dangers of pesticides and pollution were actually the work of a fine teacher who could talk to and explain and instruct any class-group-club-fraternity-league or combination. In her appearances before the Senate, in her work with William Shawn of *The New Yorker*, in her assault on the Department of Agriculture, she was teaching everybody ecology and when she was through the word and the fact of ecology were part of the life of the United States of America.

All this, the final course and subject of her teachings, had been determined for her the day she received a letter from her dear friend, Olga Owens of the Boston *Post*, telling of the increasing number of poison sprays being used. This and a warning published under the name of Roy Barker of the Illinois Natural History Survey at Urbana, Illinois, which said that robins were dying because they had eaten earthworms sprayed with DDT as it dropped from the trees where it had been used to halt Dutch elm disease. As Margaret Sanger's revolutionary activities were focused down to Birth Control by the death of Sadie Sachs, so Rachel Carson's teachings about nature, about the sea and the sea winds and the woods and trees, were centered upon the fight against pollution by pesticides when she found robin redbreasts, her beloved playfellows as a child, dead at the foot of the trees because of the poisoned ground and worms.

Convinced now that she must put aside other projects to concentrate on this one, encouraged by her publisher, by William Shawn, by other farsighted research scientists, she began work on what she hoped would be "a synthesis of widely scattered facts that have heretofore not been considered in relationship to each other. It is now possible," she wrote her editor, "to build up, step by step, a really damning case against the use of these chemicals as they are now inflicted on us."

Writing did not come easily to Rachel Carson. She once told me that she wrote slowly, she wanted to discuss *writing* with me because my newspaper training had made it possible and imperative to write quickly. "I always wanted to write," she said. "I felt this was the best means of teaching. With it, one could reach more and more people. But it was always *drudgery*, it was always slow."

"That," I said, "is partly because you are a perfectionist, and partly because you are working with facts that haven't quite come into existence yet, so you are always fighting to be accurate and also to persuade others to see your point of view. I must say I admire your fortitude and determination. If it had been that tough for me I would have quit cold in the second year."

Writing on pesticides, she was also forced to work as quietly as possible. No one knew better than Rachel Carson the massive and powerful nature of the opposition. "As you know, the whole thing is so explosive, and the pressures on the other side so powerful and enormous that I feel it far wiser to keep my own counsel insofar as I can until I am ready to launch my attack as a whole." This to her friend and confidant Clarence Cottam, Director of the Welder Wildlife Foundation in Texas.

The summer of 1958 came and went, and another summer, and another, and Rachel Carson did not quit. She wrote a friend: "I am pressing ahead just as fast as I can, driven by the knowledge that the book is definitely needed."

It took Rachel Carson four years to complete her work on the chemical poisoning of the environment by insecticides. The book: *Silent Spring*.

> It is Miss Carson's particular gift to be able to blend scientific knowledge with the spirit of poetic awareness, thus restoring to us a true sense of the world.

So said Henry Beston, author of Rachel's beloved *The Outermost House*, who should certainly know whereof he speaks.

There is another imprisoned splendor about Rachel Carson.

By the time she came to sit before a Committee of the United States Senate as the leading authority on Ecology, by the time her testimony sounded an alarm in that august chamber for that powerful body, which said alarm would force awake the sluggish government agencies in the Department of Agriculture who were responsible for the environmental welfare of the country and its millions of people, by the time *Silent Spring* had become not only a beloved bestseller but a momentous historical document impossible to ignore, Rachel Carson knew that she was dying.

For some time she had been walking hand in hand with death. As she and young Roger wandered in the woods together she knew her teaching career, her adoptive motherhood, above all her fight to keep the birds singing in the spring—all these, the doctors had told her, were now *terminal*. Inoperable cancer was the diagnosis and this cut her off from at least ten, perhaps twenty, years upon which she had counted to be sure her guiding conception, what some said was her imaginary divination, became *fact*.

Oh yes, she knew. This gentle lady with the innocent and candid eyes, the low sweet voice such as becometh a woman, she knew well the army that would march against her and her attempt to save us all. But save us all she did! Never allow yourself to hear the name Rachel Carson, to read it, without acknowledging that it is highly possible she did more to save us and our children from contamination and corruption than anyone else who lived in our time. Or any other?

What a falling-off was there! Shakespeare once remarked, though about what I have forgotten.

But as the birds grew silent in the spring a falling-off there must have been—in time, one of fatality and famine.

Her health, in spite of the initial fragility and slender delicate body, had been excellent most of her life. Often without sleep, she had worked day and night, twenty-four, sometimes forty-eight hours at a stretch, overcome by a driving conviction of the enormous need for all she had to say in *Silent Spring*. It may seem now that she could have spoken forth in articles, on TV, in *The New Yorker*, on the front pages of newspapers and all would *listen*. This is not usually possible for pioneers. I believe it is more possible all the time, because all too often those "kooky" pioneers have turned out to be right. I am always reminded at this point of the sister of the Wright Brothers, who invented airplanes. She told me once, when we were thinking of making a movie around their work, that for years they were treated with opprobrium. They had things thrown at them on the streets, they were threatened with incarceration in a mad house, "and then," said Miss Wright, "one day, it *flew*." Nothing so instant and spectacular could happen to Miss Carson's attempts to save human society from itself. Roland C. Clement, of the National Audubon Society, has somewhere compared the attacks upon Miss Carson and her demand for action to the Overkill policies manifested in stockpiling nuclear weapons. With her own small hands, Miss Carson had to break down the locked doors of the USDA Plant Pest Control Division. She had to cut through all the Red Tape always existing in Regular Channels.

There she met with ridicule and obstruction that it is now difficult to credit. I myself can testify to one member of this official body in whose hands our lives and breathing and that of all the birds in the world rested—a long-faced somber gentleman who looked down a lengthy nose to tell me not to waste my time on that "troublemaker" Miss Rachel Carson. "Her ideas are certainly disturbing," he said. "They become less so when you realize that they are totally without basis in fact. *In fact*, we may call most of them feminine fancies." Her refusal to accept DDT as a savior of mankind without a fault at a time when the Department of Agriculture was willing it should be used as an overall panacea without any concern as to its outside effects or after menaces made Rachel Carson, so the Department said publicly and privately, an enemy, not a help, in preventing and halting pollution.

At this point, I stopped to reread *Silent Spring*.

Once or twice in a generation does the world get a physical scientist with literary genius. Thus the New York *Times* after *The Sea Around Us* was published.

Once or twice in a generation? I hope so! I should say Rachel Carson may well be once in the century of which we are wobbling to an end.

Three American women have written books that changed the world and blessed all humanity.

In the nineteenth century—

Harriet Beecher Stowe, who wrote *Uncle Tom's Cabin*, which started a war that saved the Union and kept us one nation under God (we hope).

Mary Baker Eddy, who wrote *Science and Health*, which not only started a new religion but has now infiltrated many churches with her demand for a return to apostolic divine healing as commanded by the Master and Founder of Christianity.

In the twentieth century—

Rachel Carson, who wrote *Silent Spring*, which changed the course of history and, as Frank Graham, Jr., predicts in his magnificent follow-up, *Since Silent Spring*,* compels us to recognize that the time has come to make crimes against the environment on a par with crimes against humanity.

No book by any other woman at any time has ever caused such furor, uproar, brought forth such attacks upon the author on one hand, and the applause and cheers on the other. For me there is one word that sums up Rachel Carson, whose purpose in life was to see that as little damage as possible was inflicted on our environment by a careless, vicious and indifferent application of chemical pesticides. For this purpose she was one hundred percent *unflappable*.

I would like to go back to the day in the Senate when, to support her theories and her accusations against our Agricultural policies and leaders, to vindicate her demand for more *action* in the Agricultural Department, Rachel Carson appeared before the Senate Committee called to investigate this vital matter.

Here too she was absolutely Unflappable.

In his truly and absolutely essential book, if you are interested in Rachel Carson—and more and more each year you should be —Frank Graham, Jr., has this quote from someone who worked with and for her when she edited the Fish and Wildlife publications: "She was a stickler for both accuracy and readable prose and she was furious at some of the stuff the lesser writers turned in to her. But she never lost her outer calm—she was absolutely unflappable."

Unflappable. To meet with triumph and disaster just the same.

* *Since Silent Spring*, by Frank Graham, Jr., Houghton Mifflin Company, Boston, 1970.

To hold firm in giving the best to God and man, to develop a habitual spiritual consciousness that makes prayer a listening ear *immediately*. True, she had intended *Silent Spring* to shock the inert government agencies, *and* the apathetic public into some active awareness of the dangers inherent in the ecological abuses going on with almost imbecilic negligence. But the storm that broke, the abuse hurled at her, the fury of ignorant and unfounded accusations had taken her by surprise.

Nevertheless, as a counterpuncher she remained Unflappable.

So she was absolutely Unflappable in the face of the diagnosis of inoperable and terminal cancer.

Rachel Carson knew. Sitting that day before the Senate Committee, the folds of her black gown falling about her so gracefully, the lace at her throat held back by a pearl pin, her hands so still in her lap, she knew that her time was short and her urgency was not to waste a moment of time in her Crusade. Dearly as she loved her small son, her big house, her friends—her teacher's soul raced only to give her message as much as she could.

She was only in her fifties, and as things are nowadays when the old Biblical three-score years and ten is referred to as "an early passing," that was young to know for sure the date of one's own death.

I didn't ask Rachel Carson for her views, her reactions, her feelings about this. I wouldn't—I somehow wouldn't have felt that I had the right. This was always a lady who suggested to you in this very, very *public* age that she had her own privacy, not to be invaded.

But in a Senate waiting room, it came up quite naturally. We were talking one day. She mentioned it, so I asked her what her reaction to a death sentence was.

Curiosity.

That was the first.

Second was to use every moment she had left to *teach* everyone what Ecology meant.

Let me say here as my last words those that were spoken by Senator Ribicoff in Washington's National Cathedral on April 14, 1964, when scientists and all those who knew of her work and many who knew her gathered to pay her final loving reverent tribute:

". . . this gentle lady who aroused people everywhere to be concerned with the most significant problem of mid-twentieth-century life—man's contamination of his environment."

After she wrote *Silent Spring*, the debate would never be the same—because Rachel Carson had the evidence.

So this gentle lady was a *great* lady in every way a woman can be!

Let us send her a prayer of thanks wherever she is helping to beautify and purify the landscape now.

4

More than any other woman, Dr. Miriam Van Waters—of whom you may never have heard but are about to in tragedy, comedy, melodrama and even farce—had a lasting impact on my life. And yours, as you'll find out. If you got into Dr. Van Waters' orbit, you had a tiger by the tail. From there on, no matter how you were separated from her by time and space, you were driven, coerced, seduced, stapled and garroted by what she, the world's leading authority on juvenile delinquency and prison reform for girls and women, thought of you, said to you or about you. Miriam did not mince words. She'd heard them all and they crackled out in her crisp, cultivated voice with Old Testament ferocity and dignity.

"I am an *ass*," I once heard her say when she had attempted conciliation instead of counterattack with certain Boston politicians, who accused her of misconduct in office. "I am Balaam's own ass!" (If you do not know Balaam and his ass, you will find them in the Bible in the Book of Numbers.)

From the moment I met her, when I was working on the Los Angeles *Herald* and she was head of the Juvenile Hall of Los Angeles County and Referee in one of the first Juvenile Courts in the United States, she was hypnotic and pervasive upon all who came within her sphere of influence. Without raising hand or voice, Dr. Van Waters could and did quell three hundred rioting girls armed with pitchforks and barbed wire. I saw her do it.

Saw her? I can still see her!

"That little woman?" everyone said at first sight of her.

I suppose she was little. It would have taken three of Miriam Van Waters to make one of Babe Didrikson Zaharias, but Miriam at five feet two and scarcely more than a hundred pounds had the same belligerent, dedicated determination to get from here to there that made Babe the greatest woman athlete of the twentieth century. And heaven help you if you got in the way.

Physically small as she was, she suggested to anyone who was with her the disciplined strength and control of a dancer. That quality made it possible for Miriam to stand on her feet in a witness box under fierce attack for nine hours, and *still* have the air of cool, vehement distinction at the end as at the beginning. "I am somebody," she seemed to say. "The place whereon I stand is holy ground because I know what I am talking about, and don't you forget it." This daughter of a minister was a *practicing* Christian from the day of her birth. She was able to cope with squalor, degradation, vice and lawlessness as Christ had taught his disciples to deal with sinners, and she was ready to walk on the water if it proved to be necessary. Dark-eyed, with straight *black* Egyptian eyebrows, dark hair early streaked with silver, which somehow danced out of the smooth straight coiffure she tried to impose on it, coming up in an explosion of curls. She kept flattening those explosions *down* with one commanding hand, but without success. Her eyes danced, too, with war-like rage, threats, power, hot challenge against and to what she recognized as evil. As well as delight in the drama of life and all the humor she felt in it.

Many people can easily be identified with some kind of animal. Rat, coyote, wolf, lion, friendly bear, tiger-tiger burning bright, peacock, Pekingese, maybe even Jonathan Livingston Seagull. I skip over that game and am inclined to place people in some sport. Naturally, I saw Dick Nixon as a quarterback having a bad season, Kissinger as a basketball forward, infinitely forward, running up and down with the ball like Bill Russell or Jerry West. Burt Reynolds isn't up to Mark Spitz but he might be if he wore a pair of trunks; he looks sort of self-consciously *silly* with no clothes on at all! I always saw Doctor Miriam Van Waters—A.B. from the University of Oregon, Ph.D. from Clark University in

Worcester, Massachusetts, Honorary Degree from Bates and others, world famous as a penologist by the time she was thirty—as a shortstop. She had the lean dark face of Phil Rizzuto, the best who ever played it, always wildly alert both of them for fear a grounder would take a bad hop and get by them.

We wore hats in those days. Miriam's was always worn at a kind of rakish angle, like a baseball cap.

Stylish but stupid.

It seems incredible but those were the words under her picture in the Annual of St. Helen's Hall, the exclusive school she attended.

Style she always had. On a thousand platforms, in tailored gray satin, in her office as superintendent of a vast women's prison, wearing heather tweed in winter and tailored Chinese silk in summer, or in the candlelit court and orange-scented gardens at the Riverside Inn, most romantic setting in California, where young Hans Weiss of Switzerland or young Stanley Arnold, of the Attorney General's office in Washington courted her, she wore gay combinations of colors in cottons or organdy with lace collars and embroidered berthas. Always tailored on her job, she never even in prisons and reform schools lost an almost excessive femininity.

At the time she knew she would be a candidate for the presidency of the National Federation of Social Workers in San Francisco she went shopping and wrote to her mother:

> I have a new black lace evening gown to go with my exquisite shawl. I have an ensemble suit in black, a black coat, an orange jumper with a figured green skirt. It sounds gayer than it is. I would wear it in New York and not be too conspicuous. A black hat goes with it; then I bought a silk dress, gray, tan and blue for court (note: Juvenile not Buckingham Palace) or morning wear. It will do well for the Conference, also a tan polo coat and a dull sage-green sports hat. The two pairs of French slippers, and some underwear and sand-colored stockings, complete the outfit. I hate to spend so much money on myself but I am *not* going to look like a social worker.

It was actually at this very conference that she first introduced Social Service as a new profession for women, in days when professions for women were few. As an early example of her impressiveness as a public figure and a vote getter she won the election by a majority of the four thousand delegates in spite of or perhaps because of making sharply critical speeches concerning conditions in many of the juvenile courts and institutions which those very voters represented.

There (and everywhere thereafter)—as she had at Juvenile Hall when I first knew her—Miriam kept running into what she called her three P's.

Prejudice. Politics. Public Opinion.

"Ladies," I heard her say once in a speech to the ultra-conservative Friday Morning Club in Los Angeles, "you will always encounter these three P's. To go forward is to stick your chin out for assault, it always has been. Nevertheless, let us refuse ever to take a backward step for fear of them. Let us meet them with the three P's of *Prayer, Poise* and *Prevention*."

They gave her the first standing ovation I ever witnessed.

Women, I have been told in academic circles, have been left out of the history books. Well, I am about to propose Miriam Van Waters, Doctor of Anthropology (the science that treats of the origin and development of man) and Philosophy (the story of the Truth), world authority on prisons and prison reform for women and in our century still of *Youth in Conflict*, author of a book by that title, even today the best book available on the problems of juvenile work of all kinds. Under a grant raised by women headed by a multimillionairess philanthropist in Chicago, Miriam soon became the leading investigator of the orphanages, reform schools, prisons, juvenile courts, probation offices in twenty-six of the forty-eight states and made a report on these to officials and federal powers.

In the history books, Thomas Mott Osborne, once warden of Sing Sing, is listed as the great Prison Reformer.

But

"You drove Osborne to suicide," Dr. Van Waters once shouted at some of the New York political bosses. "Do not think I will so accommodate you! I am not the suicide type."

Does it seem to you that the *woman* who went through hellfire and brimstone, survived all attacks of the three P's, including the last one in Boston, and came out on top should be in history rather than, or at least as well as, the man who tried but was in the end defeated?

The story I must tell you breaks down as do most stories into three acts. But before I start them, there is one historical fact, one penological reality, which must be understood and accepted as the climate and surrounding in which Miriam Van Waters did her work. Else her fight may assume a quality of Don Quixote tilting at windmills. For the truth of that time is difficult to accept.

In spite of the fact that in our day sometimes it might seem that the pendulum has perhaps swung *too* far in prison reform, softened into laxity and encouraging riots, at the time Dr. Van Waters entered the field of prison conditions for women and children those conditions were foul, fetid and medieval. On my own first story at San Quentin, I remember the shock of finding all the men branded in striped convict suits, heads shaved to the bone, women sitting around idle, many of them wearing handcuffs, with five minutes for talk and fifteen for exercise out of the twenty-four hours. No way they could in any wise use all this time they were serving to improve their minds, repair their educations, learn a craft or trade, so that they might re-enter society as decent citizens and not return to prison within the shortest possible time.

Dorothea Dix, noted social reformer and journalist, had after a careful investigation exposed some of the horrors existing in women's prisons. No American writer had done the fabulous job Dickens did with *Oliver Twist*, *Great Expectations* and *Little Dorrit* in England, but Dorothea Dix had accuracy and appeal and for the first time this country had its attention called to and fixed upon conditions that it is difficult to realize existed within the memory of many still alive. She found, Dorothea Dix told the country, drunkards, raving lunatics of every species, drug addicts, diseased prostitutes in the same cells and beds with twelve-year-old girls held as material witnesses, pickpockets and shoplifters handcuffed and chained, in fact she found naked women chained in icy cellars, subject to every kind of attack, beatings and rape. Sometimes she found the corpses of babies at the feet of their helpless mothers, often there were small children kept in prisons, reformatories and almshouses with their mothers but without care, clothes or food.

In these United States of America? I'm afraid so. To this minute, it takes constant vigilance. As late as 1970, the infallible *Christian Science Monitor* published a series of carefully researched articles on conditions in reform schools that showed how swiftly con- ditions reverted to horrors.

My chronicle of Dr. Miriam Van Waters breaks into three acts, as I said in the beginning. Let's look at the program:

I. Scene: The Pig n' Whistle, a candy shop–restaurant
    where one day at lunch Dr. Van Waters
    discovered I was Earl Rogers' Daughter.
II. Several years later.
    Scene: El Retiro, a new type of reform school for
    girls, in the San Fernando Valley, where Dr.
    Van Waters as its Superintendent insisted Girls
    who'd gone wrong could be taught to go
    right, while the three P's of Prejudice, Politics
    and Public Opinion shrieked from platforms and
    papers that Dr. Van Waters was *pampering*
    these little monsters instead of punishing them.
    Maybe that makes two more P's that were to
    pursue Dr. Van Waters—the difference between
    Pampering and Punishment, as her enemies
    called it. Miriam called it the difference between
    Prevention and Punishment.
III. *Many* years later.
    Scene: A courtroom in Boston, Massachusetts, where
    Dr. Van Waters as superintendent of Fra-
    mingham Prison for Women was on trial for
    her very life, where my own papers were all
    part of the three P's against her and where I,
    for the first and only time in my life, had to
    defy the great Walter Howey, our top editor.

To go back to the beginning.

It was because of my father that I knew Dr. Van Waters early in my work and hers. She was at first violently opposed to all publicity in juvenile cases, feeling that it increased the problems of each girl or boy by magnification and dramatization. It wasn't until much later when on tour of the country and she needed to call attention to some of the things she found that she began to be on the front pages.

"A national figure at thirty-four," her favorite Uncle Charlie commented.

But when she was the first referee of one of the first Juvenile Courts in the country, she didn't want to put herself *or* the children with whom she dealt into the limelight in any way.

The Pig n' Whistle was near the offices of my paper, the Los Angeles *Evening Herald,* where I had worked earlier and was still going back for special stories or for some months of regular work. My husband, Ike St. Johns, was secretary to the Mayor about then, and since the City Hall was only a block away we could go back and forth together and he didn't mind my going back to work so much. While the ladies' table at the Pig n' Whistle never became as famous as the Algonquin Round Table, as I look back on it from here I find it impressive, even a bit melodramatic from time to time. Gathered about it for the midday meal were the women who carried more power than any others in that growing politically powerful part of the State of California, the part south of the Tehachapi Mountains, not to mention Hollywood looming on the western front where D. W. Griffith was making something called a Movie and entitled *The Birth of a Nation.* At that time I do not think any of us gathered at that table noticed what we represented. If we were leaders in our field, we had accepted the new responsiblity with good will and some prayer. This all belongs right here because it is an illustration of what women had begun to accomplish by a method of doing the job as well as—even better than—anybody else.

There was, for instance, Estelle Lawton Lindsey, the first woman to run for elective office in Los Angeles. She ran for and was elected to the City Council. Thin, gray, dynamic, a woman of middle age, elected for her courage and competence by an all-male vote, the women as yet not having any. Her aim was to improve conditions for women and children. All men trusted her and worked with and for her projects. There was Nora Sterry, principal of a school in the slum area down by the always-dry river bed of what was called the Los Angeles River. Nora was big, heavy-set and belonged to a famed California family. According to the testimony of doctors, police, sheriffs, priests and press Nora had prevented the spread of the Bubonic Plague in Los Angeles, the worst scare we ever had in the city. When a case was discovered, the district was quarantined, Nora's grammar school in the center of it was closed, they were not going to allow her to pass the lines. Real danger threatened, the city shook in panic, the health and medical authorities and even their religious advisors couldn't control the population of the plague area. Most of the population was Mexican, spoke no English, was deaf, dumb and blind with panic and refused to obey orders, to burn old clothes or to take drugs or baths or to use disinfectants. They wouldn't stay where they were told, but sneaked out and away to other parts of the town as fast as they could. The possibility of someone carrying the plague and spreading it as a holocaust became great.

Miss Nora Sterry walked through the quarantine lines, defying any doctor, cop or sheriff to put a finger on her, and within two hours the whole situation was under control. In their own language of Spanish, she spoke to the fathers and mothers, called all the kids by their first names, and they accepted her commands and directions, she stayed there until all signs of epidemic and panic had vanished. For which, of course, she was much heralded and decorated. That school was just across the First Street bridge and so she was able to come to the Pig n' Whistle to lunch from time to time.

Also we had Mabel Walker Willebrandt, one of the first women lawyers to practice in California. Mabel became *the* first woman to be an Assistant Attorney General of the United States and she was in charge of cases that came from the Bureau of Federal Prisons. I am sure that her knowledge of this, which brought about that appointment, started at the lunch table where she and Miriam Van Waters often sat next to each other discussing women's prisons and what was to be done at Juvenile Hall, itself a prison for the young. Grace Stormer was in charge, as a vice-president, of what we would today call Public Relations for a big bank. Ida Koverman, who became the greatest political power in the State of California and selected Earl Warren to run for Governor, was then with the Mayer studios out at the Selig Zoo, and we also had Mrs. Randolph Huntington Minor, society leader de luxe, and one of our top philanthropists, Dr. Hammond, who headed a big hospital, Orfa Jean Shontz, the first woman elected to the Superior Court bench in California and Miriam Van Waters who acted as referee in that court. The referee in that early work with juveniles being the one who went and found out all about the case—the family, the surroundings, the school conditions—and then made the recommendation for what the judge ought to do about it.

I bring this up in detail for much of it was before Women's Suffrage, and was our method of working up to being able to take part in the things that affected women and children.

Conversation echoes back to me as Miriam says across the table to Nora Sterry, "Nora, what used to be the first principle of living for the Family? Even down in your part of the city where they have so little money to work with?"

"A house where there is room for the children to have a play-room, where there is a dining room big enough for the Family to sit around it, above all a Yard, back and front if possible, so the children don't have to play in the streets," Nora said.

"Within a few generations," Miriam said thoughtfully, "we have begun to change the emphasis and it will radically change conditions for the worse. From vigorous rearing of healthy children just *naturally*, not with substitutes in every field such as I begin to see the Boy Scouts trying valiantly to do, substituting Scouting and Scout masters for their fathers, in a few generations American life is changing and will be changed beyond belief. I have seen worse things than an outdoor privy myself. Modern conveniences, however, will take first place. They will all want to be near shopping markets. Room won't be the first thought—that will be places to spend money and where to find entertainment."

"Well," Mabel said, "so far the contribution of America isn't art, or education, it's plumbing."

I remember clearly that Miriam seemed to be concentrated on this talk. She seemed not only to see those hundreds of youngsters who still passed under her supervision at Juvenile Hall, who paraded before her in juvenile court, she was peering into the future. She said, "Listen, listen, please listen. The need of the child spirit is for faith. The need of the child mind is for its own adventures. Above all, the need of the child heart is for true love, at least one person who truly loves him. I hope we shall not forget these things as we grow into a richer and more powerful country, and population flows from the country into the cities. When the State has to take over more and more and function in more ways, we sometimes do not have the time or the vision to remember the mind and spirit." She turned directly to Mabel and said, "The law about children is your business. Unless the law is based on true principles it is no good."

"Hear ye, hear ye," said Judge Shontz with a twinkle.

When Judge Shontz and Dr. Van Waters got up to go back to court, I asked if I might go with them. For some time I had been trying to get a series of stories about their work and always I had been refused. This time my luck was in, for at that very moment, Orfa Jean asked about my father and something she said conveyed to Miriam Van Waters who my father was. Obviously she had not associated young Mrs. St. Johns of the *Herald*, to whom she was definitely hostile, with her idol, Earl Rogers. Earl Rogers, that champion of the underdog, the one man she felt understood and shared her views and convictions—she remembered well the things he had said about the very problems that absorbed her burning interest. That was when Mr. Rogers was trying to clean up what was then known as the Tenderloin, including the red-light district, the saloon belt and the adjacent slums. Here, Mr. Rogers had said, hunger, ugliness, poverty and ignorance are the grounds in which to breed crime, where it can come to full harvest for young and old. "I am against grafters and crooked politicians taking a bite out of every tax dollar that ought to be spent on clean government, better schools, more parks and playgrounds, adequate fire and police protection, city and county hospitals, reformatories run by trained personnel, charity for the old and sick when needed and help for any criminal young or old who could possibly be saved and restored to our society as a worthwhile citizen." Rogers had said that on front pages during a recent political upheaval, and, to be sure, he himself had started, stirred and sometimes finished quite a few of these upheavals.

No wonder Miriam Van Waters idolized him. This put forth
what she was always talking about—*prevention*. A second chance.
A restoration of health with a new outlook. How many of the
great American women have dedicated their hearts and lives to
prevention in one form or another!

So it was as Earl Rogers' daughter that I got invited back that
day after lunch to see Miriam Van Waters' juvenile courtroom
and her handling of some of the young people who came into it.

I am going to try to see it as I did then. Dr. Van Waters became
referee, I think, along about 1920—very early in this work—and
I was already staying home part time with a baby or two trying
to write fiction. But in those days it was not only possible but
happy for everyone to have a Mammy and/or a Nanny to make
up a household, where it was all one family, and so I was able to
go back to the City Room part time or on those special assignments,
so I am going to try to see it as I did then, a young woman reporter
with a deadline beginning as usual to throb on the presses only a
couple of blocks down the street and also from where I sit now
in my place above Time and the River, as I've explained I'm
trying to do all the while.

Remember, I have spent a lot of my life in courtrooms, from
the Boyd case when my feet didn't touch the floor, to the famed
San Francisco Graft trials, into that chamber of the Immigration
Authorities where we fought to save the Queen of Chinatown
from deportation, to the Riverside chambers where the smell of
orange blossoms filled the air as Judge Wellborn thundered
against my father that threat of disbarment that was to haunt me
all through the years. All this I told in full in *Final Verdict*.

The courtroom I entered with Miriam Van Waters was as
different from any I'd seen as she was from any judge-on-the-
bench in my experience, and, as I look down upon the whole
sequence of them, still is.

Dim light. Plain walls. No Bench, no jury box, no court stenog-
rapher taking down every word to be on record forever. No
witness box, that seat which can be one of terror and inquisition
as it had been for me when I waited for my father to cross-
examine me. Austerity was the word for Miriam's set, and if
many people are given to dramatizing themselves and their activities, Dr. Van Waters was tops at *un* dramatizing anything she

had to do with. Orfa Jean Shontz, a small, plump woman with soft graying hair was in one kitchen chair, and Miriam slipped into the other, adding to the gray austerity. She belongs right there.

Within, I should say, about thirty seconds everything in that room had faded except Miriam Van Waters and the youthful defendant. I wouldn't say that Orfa Jean was an easy fader, nor I think am I, but of course in my case I was more than willing to disappear because I was one hundred percent sure that if I moved an eyebrow, if this boy with the jutting chin and the thin shoulders glanced in my direction, I would be evicted, Earl Rogers or no Earl Rogers. As for the *Evening Herald!* Miriam's only loyalty then was to Our Children.

This boy, according to Miriam, needs a dentist. A *dentist?* Miriam concludes judicially that his teeth not only pain him almost constantly but that they interfere with proper breathing, and make him defiantly self-conscious. The verdict is that we should get something done about these rotting, protruding teeth—and then see what can be done about his failure in schools. So he is removed; I presume, to go to the dentist.

The skinny girl is under sixteen, yet it is necessary to describe her as a *fading* blonde. More pitiful, since the charge against her is soliciting gentlemen. It had been disappointing soliciting—she was skinny because for at least two years she hadn't had enough to eat. Years later I was to find that half the young runaways from home, who ended up with guns, hypodermic needles and four-letter-word vocabularies were *hungry.* No one had bothered about their diets, their needs as they *grew.* They were often jittery from lack of any decent sleep in any place where it was possible to get decent sleep. All this Miriam van Waters saw *then,* and she rattled through her notes and found a farm to which she could send this girl to do what work she could and, as Referee Van Waters pointed out, to get fed for a while. The brain, she commented, has to be fed—young people who are not properly nourished often have half-nourished thought processes.

A family I was to know later on in an elegant suburb of San Francisco had a son whose conduct was unsatisfactory and seemingly inexplicable. I began begging for an overall physical examination, when I found this hadn't been done, and when I

remembered how this had been an absolute must in the Van Waters'
method of coping with these problems. *Mens sana in corpore
sano*, as Juvenal said. Sure enough, there was an obscure eye
difficulty which made his school work nearly impossible and when
that was cared for his whole life changed.

The second girl was a different story. Prettily plump, as was
allowed in those days, brassily blond, ten cents a dance, fifteen
cents for additional time and attention, she was up for shoplifting
and assault with an attempt to steal an old lady's purse. In those
days conspicuous lipstick was synonymous with the scarlet letter
A for adultery, and it was plain to all of us that this girl enjoyed
being bawdy, that she welcomed prostitution as not only the oldest
but the easiest and most profitable profession.

It was years before that in Clark University that young, shining
Miriam Van Waters from Oregon had startled a famous in-
structor in psychology by stating, "But a prostitute is not a *type*.
A prostitute is a human being and each one is different."

The girl in the Van Waters' courtroom, as I saw her, would
plainly grow more defiant, more dangerous, as she spread disease
and degradation without even knowing she was doing it. No one
had ever taught her anything about the warm satisfaction of self-
respect, or the joys of the mind and vision, or the possession of a
soul as spirit above both mind and body, or the possibilities of love
that was not a physical act.

What's to be done with her?

I cannot tell you how young Miriam Van Waters achieved
that combination of authority and friendliness and interest which
is *concern. Somebody who cares.* Nor how she managed to awaken
an *ambition*, somehow conveyed *You can do better than this.* Let's
enjoy a gamble—let's try improving you so your horizon widens.
Let's sell you some of the truth about life as it can be lived walking the Way Jesus taught. She never used the "religious" words
but the Teaching, the faith, hope and charity, love, were in everything she said.

Now there is a boy not more than twelve surely. He has run
scissors into another boy, deep, almost fatal. He snickers constantly.
The scissors had operated exactly as a switchblade knife would do
today, but between snickers he keeps shouting that he never did
nothing, the other boy ran into him, the other boy was trying

to get at him, he just held the scissors and the other boy ran himself into them, the old plea of self-defense.

What he needs, it appears to Referee Van Waters, is *discipline* and lots of it. Careful discipline and regularity upon which he can depend. Where he can lose his fears of all those around him, growing from the careless, cheapening abuse he has received from his parents. He needs someone at a school who is steadfast and where there is a work and play schedule. So he is sent to a Reform School, which is not of course ideal but seems the best available solution. Here Dr. Van Waters can keep an eye on him and it seemed to me as I knew her work that she would need as many as the hundred eyes of Argus to keep them on those she desired to help and oversee.

The next boy is obviously of foreign origin, strangely pale eyes, large head, accent that obscures what he thinks he is saying. Part of the melting pot that lands in San Francisco and San Pedro. He and four or five other boys have broken into a warehouse and stolen marketable goods. These boys, Dr. Van Waters says, need work, hard work, as hard as their growing minds and bodies can endure and perform. She pauses to think, she says, "We must invent some kind of reward for their work. Something to show them, to convince them, that *if* and *when* they work they will get as much of whatever it is as they would if they were stealing. We must become better salesmen for honesty. There must be time off for good behavior and they must understand this as a reward. They must know they will have recommendations for jobs, or that we will try to find good homes for them to live in. Good conduct must give them better lives than bad conduct."

The drama here is real. Real real real. As I sat in my corner silent and as near motionless as possible, I was growing more and more aware that this drama was real. These, I said to myself, are real children. Real, American children, their dialogue as they speak it is real, their heartaches are real, this slim woman with the black hair in a sort of bang, dressed so becomingly and properly in gray, is as real as a flame. This is what Victor Fleming, the greatest of all motion picture directors, meant when he kept hollering at me when I worked with him at MGM after he had directed *Gone With the Wind* and *The Wizard of Oz*, the two greatest pictures ever made. We were trying to find stories for Clark Gable, just back from the war. Real life, Victor used to say, real life is what I want to get on the screen; I want what actually happens in real life, not tragicodramatic or comicfarcical, or ham-hammy. The difficulty is to make the story work, to confine it within lengths, to use the technique of the movie screen to produce a slice of life. Once he and I did try to make a picture that way, just letting it happen, begin and end, as though it was real life. That did not work. Perhaps it was because I had seen so much of real life, real people, that I was never able to respond to any of the kind offers I had to become a screen actress. For quite a while Mr. DeMille kept at me about a part he insisted I must play, he couldn't understand that it seemed to me the most deadly *bore*, now that I was grownup, to go around pretending to be some-body else who wasn't real and who did things that weren't real. That was, I am sure, why Clark Gable found it so difficult to be an *actor*, which he had become because of looks and personality. It wasn't until in *Gone With the Wind* Vic Fleming made him feel that Rhett Butler was *real*, he was *really* Rhett Butler, that Clark Gable gave us reality in his acting.

Again now, even now, I can feel the real emotion that almost overcame me as I watched Referee Van Waters in court that day now long ago. The certainty that these children had lives to live, these children were, as Kipling said, the Men and Women of To-morrow, this aroused me to want to know What tomorrow, Where, how, why. If she has to send them all to the only kind of Reform Schools we have, I thought, won't they be hardened into crime without hope?

Now we have picked up the key, then and always, to Miriam Van Waters.

Hope.

Hope is one of the three greatest things in the world as Jesus offered them to us. In the greatest sermon since Jesus preached on the Mount, Dr. Henry Drummond holds *hope* as part of Love, which is what he calls *The Greatest Thing in the World*. God's darling daughter hope, as the poet says, is an essential part of Love. This is the light that so often guides our way. The inspiration that gives us the strength to work, keeps us able to go on.

A girl who years later testified for Dr. Van Waters in the

famous trial when Dr. Van Waters had been accused of misconduct in running the big women's prison of Framingham kept
saying from the stand, "She gave us hope. She let me hope it
wasn't too late for me to try to live a good life. I'd never had any
hope before about anything until she gave it to me."

Yes, yes. Alone and singlehanded on that referee's bench, after
all the damage the juvenile system as it was then had done to these
children who stood before her, the slimy little prostitute, the boy
committed to stabbing, smashing, violent robbery, the others who
came often so riddled with disease that it made them moral
idiots—somehow this young woman-Daniel-come-to-judgment gave
them *hope*. They did not sink down and down into worse crimes
and hells. The quality of mercy in her was distilled into practical
hope.

Progress is the law of life.

I am sure this was a Miriam Van Waters motto, for it is a line
from Robert Browning and Miriam Van Waters lived at a time
when Robert Browning was the most read and most popular of
all poets and she did at one time belong to a Browning Society,
as so many of us did.

Her progress—

Juvenile Hall, where she was Superintendent.

El Retiro an experiment in Juvenile work which Miriam Van
Waters called a necessary progression and the three P's insisted
was a useless waste of money and dangerous pampering of young
criminals, in a world that was becoming conscious for the first time
of Juvenile Crime.

Juvenile Court and Juvenile Hall, of which Referee Van Waters
was head, worked in close coordination. They were pretty much
one operation.

El Retiro comes next and was to Referee Van Waters the most
important step taken up to then in the world of Juvenile Crime,
what we would today call Juvenile Delinquency, and actually in
the life and progress of Miriam Van Waters herself.

Obviously, the words translate into a place, time, and condition
of retirement. A place into which to retire at the proper time and
under helpful conditions.

El Retiro as such had had a most difficult time in coordinating these into a progressive whole.

It had been built originally by a group of doctors as a sanatorium for patients with tuberculosis. Apparently, it wasn't ideal for this, and of course at that time the San Fernando Valley, north of Los Angeles, was by no means the exclusive suburb and real estate development it later became. Far otherwise. It was a heterogeneous collection of truck gardens, hen coops, manure piles and turkey hatcheries, and had no more social standing than a briar patch. After its failure as a sanatorium there seems to be an interval described as "a center of Moral Hygiene," which again can be translated as an institution for milder forms of derangement such as eccen- and idiocen-tricity, kleptomania, delirium tremens and hypochondria, where those who came to Southern California purely for relaxation in the climate could hit bottom. Thus arrived a time when a lot of social workers suggested to Los Angeles County that here were buildings, acres, and a usable setup for sale at a bargain price. Somehow the package was presented to Superintendent Van Waters of Juvenile Hall. "What had we better do with this?" "What we'd better do with this," said Dr. Van Waters, "is to make it into a school for girls, from fourteen to nineteen, who are wards of my Juvenile Court. I can run it from Juvenile Hall with the same staff. Thus there will be no additional cost." For a long time, Dr. Van Waters had been talking of, hoping for a place where she could try her methods of reclamation, rehabilitation, restoration and recovery.

Often she quoted Tolstoy, who had said, "You may think you can do this work without love, but you cannot."

El Retiro would become such a school. "Where Girls Go Right," so Dr. Van Waters wrote of it in a magazine article. Girls who had gone wrong would not be *com*mitted, they would be *per*mitted to enter there. They must stay for a year. A girl who felt the need could remain until she was twenty-one. The court order read:

Jane Doe is permitted to go to El Retiro until further order.

Five entrance requirements were written out by Dr. Van Waters:

1. An earnest desire to make good, proved by an
   unbroken good-conduct record at the detention home

and an expressed willingness to undergo a period of
training.

2. Freedom from infectious disease.
3. Candidate must be of normal or borderline mentality
   —no diagnosed cases of feeble-mindedness can be
   accepted.
4. Girl's home situation must be one that prevents her
   successful re-education there. Such a home as one unfit,
   weak or broken.
5. Evidence that the candidate cannot earn her living
   outside without harm.

When questioned by practically everybody, including the
California State Board of Health, Miriam offered a pamphlet in
which she explained that she wanted El Retiro to build sufficient
moral muscle so the girls could protect themselves in the world
outside. Severe requirements, once in, for exercise, hygiene and
diet were to promote health and Miriam enforced them with a
firm hand. When they entered, the girls took vows never to bring
dishonor to El Retiro and there, under the olive trees, within sight
of the purple foothills, Miriam Van Waters began a concentrated
experiment in trying to restore *bad girls,* girls who had committed
crimes, to a faith in the integrity of human life.

There, in that work, as always throughout her life, Miriam Van
Waters believed in, lived by, and offered as the inspiration, daily
help, and expected miracles a simple real and shining faith in God.
God as Our Father. God who loved them and would welcome
them home as prodigal daughters. In fact, one of Miriam's talks,
throughout her life at El Retiro and ultimately at Framingham in
Massachusetts, was that God welcomed home the Prodigal
Daughter as well as the Prodigal Son.

The three P's of Politics, Prejudice and Public Opinion still
haunted her. At first, some churches wouldn't allow the girls from
El Retiro—a Reformatory, they called it—to come to Sunday
Services to hear the words of the Man from Galilee. Also it took
an appeal to the Board of Education to get them their right to
attend high school. Politicians would frequently grab a front-page
headline by insisting that the regime at El Retiro was too loose,
by demanding a prison strictness be enforced there.

I was sent once to cover what we had been informed was a

A steady diet of good reading

Mail this card today to receive the next 11 issues of Moody Monthly for only $10.95 . . . $1 savings off the regular $11.95 price!

☐ One Year @ $10.95

☐ Two Years @ $19.95

☐ Bill me later ___Please initial___

☐ New

☐ Renewal *(attach mailing label)*

Add $3 a year if outside U.S.

Mr.
Mrs.
Miss _____

Address _____

City _____ State/Province _____ Zip/Postal Code _____

A36

serious "riot" by the girls of El Retiro. It turned out that the girls had marched nineteen miles under a hot California sun to beg Dr. Van Waters at Juvenile Hall to deny that she was "forsaking El Retiro." That she wasn't coming back there any more. When —with tears—Miriam Van Waters assured them that El Retiro was her child, that she could no more abandon it than she could her own child, they went peacefully back to the school.

And by this time Dr. Van Waters had taken into her life a "child of her own," a small waif named Sarah who came before her in the Juvenile Court. Sarah turned out to be as mischievous as the proverbial cage full of monkeys, but she became the recipient of a rare maternal love which reflected in health and wholeness for the child and great joy and fulfillment for her foster mother.

Trying to make the small budget stretch over the two institutions of Juvenile Hall and El Retiro, studying to pass both her Bar and Civil Service exams, having to engage in a prolonged legal battle with a woman doctor whom she had to fire and who thereupon sued her for thirty thousand dollars, Miriam wrote to her father, the Reverend George Van Waters: "The whole thing is politics and I am so sick of it I can hardly stand it." And to her mother: "Dear sweet darling beloved little mother; How blessed we are in our health and strength and happy family love. All I do, all I am, is the result of the love and faith and stimulus I received in my home through my parents. No matter how much study people get nowadays, they cannot surpass what you and Father did for me in my childhood. I am no Christian Scientist but I do believe if we are happy, busy and courageous we don't get sick." Which, indeed, was what Mary Baker Eddy believed. And Mrs. Eddy thought, as I'm sure did Miriam Van Waters, that it was the Father Himself who made it possible for His children to be happy, busy and courageous.

I have thought often that the two women I have known who gave all credit for their strength, their success, and their courageous lives in very public places to their parents and to their upbringing and what they were taught in their homes were Miriam Van Waters and Katharine Hepburn. Certainly no two women showed higher standards and finer principles and more love for their fellow man. And fellow woman.

It was while she was still in Los Angeles and acting as Referee in the Superior Court of Judge Orfa Jean Shontz that there entered into the life of young Miriam Van Waters the *angel*— Miriam's name for her—the angel who seemed to her to have been sent by and from God to help her in her work and to make it possible for her to do the many things, to try the experiments, to save the girls, to spread new truth and reformation across our country.

Progress is the law of life, Miriam said it again and again.

El Retiro's chief aim is to establish by modern intensive methods, self-respect, self-government and sturdiness of purpose in its young students.

To do this, beset as she was by Politics, Prejudice and Public Opinion, she had true need of help.

One day a Presence arrived in Miriam's courtroom, when Miriam as usual was dealing, quietly, firmly and lovingly, with an unusually heavy load of juvenile cases. Cases, Miriam told me once, that all seemed terribly difficult of solution because the *homes* were contributing factors to the evil.

Strange how quite unpoetic newspapermen and hardboiled cops and even other women referred to Ethel Dummer as a Presence.

We felt a Presence— Suddenly there was a Presence— A Presence seemed to welcome me—

Entirely without any advance notice Mrs. Dummer drifted quietly and inconspicuously into the Juvenile Court where Miriam Van Waters was sitting and Miriam told me later that something happened, a light—the proportions—the whole scene changed and became a background through which she moved.

I felt it myself the first time I met her.

Actually, Ethel Sturges Dummer, in the Social Register as Mrs. William F. Dummer of Chicago, was and had been for years a well-known and highly respected humanitarian and philanthropist.

But it was more than that. This Presence had power, it brought light. Above all, I should say, looking back upon it, this was as though an angel came into your everyday life and experience. Not a guardian angel on your shoulder, not an angel to fight your battle, like Michael, or comfort you like Gabriel—this angel was a messenger to prepare the way. *I will send my messenger before my face.* Here is a messenger of mine. And neither snow nor rain nor heat nor gloom of night ever stayed Mrs. Dummer on what she considered to be her appointed rounds.

From the first moment in the Juvenile Court of Los Angeles there can be no doubt that Mrs. Dummer considered irrevocably and consummately that Miriam Van Waters, who knew and understood more about Juveniles than anyone she'd ever seen, was part of her appointed rounds. This dark flame of a young woman, blazing away there behind that ordinary kitchen table that was called the Bench, must at once and as soon as possible have a wider field for her work, more opportunity to exercise her wisdom, a greater sphere of activity so that the Nation and not just one small western County could benefit.

One thing about Mrs. Dummer. As a most elegant and truly spiritual Presence, she was also willing to pick up the check.

Once years ago at a table in the Twentieth Century-Fox Commissary where at lunch Harry Brand, super-genius of Publicity for Zanuck, Gene Fowler, Doc Martin, husband of the unequaled Louella Parsons, Mark Kelly, Damon Runyon and others of us used to gather, we were discussing the great *lines* and quotations from poets and dramatists, as to the greatest, most beautiful, most memorable. Kelly was all for the one from Keats: "The same that oft-times hath charm'd magic casements, opening on the foam of perilous seas, in faery lands forlorn." And Fowler had a description of the statue of Josephine in the square in Martinique, and suddenly Harry said, "Come, come. The most beautiful words in the language are when somebody else says, '*Bring me the check.*'"

Those were Mrs. Dummer's favorite words.

As soon as she could she persuaded Miriam Van Waters to ask for a leave of absence, and then she paid for a trip through twenty-six states on which Dr. Van Waters could study and coordinate the work being done, the most pressing need of juvenile work and

schools and prisons, the plans or parts of plans being put forth
by other workers and experts in this field. There is no question
that this not only gave Miriam vast and useful information but it
made her well known throughout the country—she knew how
to take advantage of the publicity opportunities to awaken the
women of the nation to the situation.

All women's clubs and organizations responded to Miriam Van
Waters. More than to any other crusader among all the great
women of America. On the platform, she was irresistible. A fiery
and at the same time amusing and entertaining orator. I think I
heard them all and I would pick Miriam as the best woman speaker
I ever heard. So that the vast power of the women's clubs—which
were then indeed a power—was opened to her. The Friday Morning Club, the Council of Jewish Women, the Business and Professional Women's Club, Catholic and Negro groups, the Junior
League, the PTA—wherever she spoke she not only wowed 'em,
she made them part of her fight for better conditions for young
people, she brought them into active work to reform schools and
prisons before they were supposed to reform their inmates.

"My dear, my dear, you gave me freedom to write my book!"

This was what Miriam herself saw as the great earth-changing
thing which came to her as the result of Mrs. Dummer's help.

Youth in Conflict the book was called, and both the reviews
and the results were magnificent. A critique in the influential *Survey* spoke in superlative terms: "Every two or three hundred years
we get a total eclipse of the sun. Just about as often we get a
thoroughly satisfactory book—one that you can recommend to
your friends without reservation. Dr. Miriam Van Waters' *Youth
in Conflict* is such a book."

It still is. Still is the best book on the subject *right now*.

At the time, its reverberations brought about startling changes
for its author. Representatives of the Laura Spelman Rockefeller
Fund arrived in Los Angeles to ask her to undertake a major
research project on American adolescents, and offering her all the
help she needed. The findings of this would then be sent to all
workers in this field in every state in the Union.

As soon as the book was published, she was overwhelmed with
pleas that she would come here, there and everywhere to speak.
I was touched to find that one of the first places she went was

to Stockton to the College of the Pacific, and of it she wrote that she was amazed to find a Methodist college so truly liberal. I wish she could have met my grandfather, the Reverend Lowell Rogers, a minister of that church and at one time president of the College of the Pacific when it was still called Napa University. I am sure she would have realized that great Christians, who follow in the footsteps of the Master, as my grandfather did, are aways liberal with love.

As Miriam's speaking tours, in answer to invitation, increased day by day it became impossible for her to continue them as impromptu and spontaneous speeches, which was the way she liked to do all things. To her it seemed that the gusto and gumption of things that gushed up from the heart, filled with desire, could not be duplicated by any that had been prepared, no matter how carefully, ahead of time.

But as her position as the leading spokesman for the cause of how to cope with juvenile problems became more and more recognized, as with Mrs. Dummer's financial backing she was able to travel extensively wherever she felt she could do the most good, she saw that she could not do justice to so new and complex a cause at the impromptu level. People wanted exact information, they wanted the truths it had taken her so long to discover. So her one-shot talks as well as those which she now gave as a series of eight were arranged and the titles are now specifically illuminating:

One Shots
1. The Juvenile Court and the Community
2. The Mental Hygiene Movement
3. The Child Guidance Clinic of Los Angeles
4. Youth in Conflict
5. Child Versus Parent
6. Certain Problems of Adolescence
7. The Major Problems of Social Diagnosis

Series
1. Modern Goals of Child Welfare
2. The Emotionally Unstable Child
3. The Unadjusted Child and the Community
4. The Movement Toward Mental Health
5. The Normal Mind in Action
6. The Disordered Personality

7. Personality and Social Relationships
8. The Modern Teacher of Social Psychology

At that time there can be no question that Dr. Van Waters was the leading authority on all these things of which she spoke, many of which were new to our thinking about children, good or bad, in families. And she was in the fortunate position of being able to continue the work in her laboratory, which was composed of the Juvenile Court, Juvenile Hall, El Retiro and the investigations Mrs. Dummer's backing made it possible for her to pursue.

Soon she was to be asked to work on a proposed Harvard Law School Crime Survey. After a little opposition, she was given a leave of absence to do this, and for the next few years commuted between her "eastern" office in Cambridge and Los Angeles where she continued to supervise her courts and her institutions.

There are many pictures, many estimations, many appraisals and computations of Dr. Miriam Van Waters during this time.

She was by now front-page headline copy, a fact she had come to accept, and one of the most famous women in the country.

She made the front pages when she rescued three of her own Juvenile Court girls who were on probation from the White Slave traffic which then operated in California. Miriam herself went down to Chinatown and remained hidden with a friend of hers, a Chinese lady of high degree. There were no Chinese juvenile delinquents in San Francisco, Los Angeles or Watsonville because the old people ran the Families, but this Chinese lady admired what Dr. Van Waters was doing for the poor uncontrolled American young people. When the girls were located Dr. Van Waters waited until the moment they came out of the house where they'd been hidden. She simply went over, grabbed them, and put them in her car and sped away. Re-kidnapping them seemed the simplest way.

The Encyclopaedia Britannica asked her to write the article on Children's Courts and this delighted Miriam because it so pleased her father.

A manuscript of a second book to be called *Parents on Probation* was destroyed in a fire that consumed the little hillside house where she lived with Judge Shontz and her own small foster daughter, Sarah Van Waters. Somehow she never got it rewritten, and I can understand why. If you'd *finished* it, and known that moment of supreme joy and relief, it would be impossible to start all over! That is why I keep a set of carbons in a steel dispatch box and *never* allow anyone to burn up any of the pages I throw away.

At UCLA Dr. Van Waters taught some classes in the work of Children's Courts and they were so popular that there was talk of founding a department, but somehow no budget was ever available.

In these years, we always kept an eye on Dr. Van Waters, who was NEWS. We knew when she had romantic escorts at that most romantic spot, the Mission Inn at Riverside, with its beautiful Wedding Chapel. Though several romances crossed her path, I do not think myself that Miriam Van Waters ever in her life thought seriously of marriage. In spite of the fact that she had grown up in the home of a happy marriage, the rewarding marriage of her adored father and mother, I still don't believe she thought of it for herself.

This was one hundred percent a Career Woman before the term was coined.

From her first moment in Juvenile Hall, her Career had absorbed, satisfied and glorified her, it took all her energy, all her knowledge, all her imagination and all, all, all her love.

Which is perhaps why she felt so keenly the heartbreak of El Retiro. She had not forsaken this "child of my own flesh and blood." When she left for Harvard Law School and her work there with Felix Frankfurter on the survey of law as it applied to juveniles, she left her "students" in the charge of a handpicked superintendent. On her first return to Los Angeles she found her superintendent ousted. El Retiro had reverted to a regular Reform School, with guards and guns, and as this was in the midst of those recurring waves of public sentiment against "coddling" juvenile lawbreakers there wasn't anything she could do about it. The three P's had taken over. She managed to save her Juvenile Court but it was too late for El Retiro. She was to wait five years before she found another opportunity to put these ideals into practice.

The first step came with an invitation from Washington, D.C., to be a member of the Wickersham Committee. This was a group and a crusade formed by President Herbert Hoover for Law Enforcement. Since she was notified of the possibility of this by a telegram from Felix Frankfurter, it is probable that he recommended her. And that same year she was elected president of the National Conference of Social Workers.

The Women's Reformatory for Girls and Women at Framingham.

This rates a line, an act, a climax treatment, for as Dr. Van Waters said it was the place where she could put all to the test. This was to be both Gethsemane and Calvary to this Christian on the pathway of Penology.

Miriam's progress had been steady, endlessly busy, challenging. Juvenile Hall, Juvenile Court, El Retiro, Harvard Law School, the Wickersham Committee where under the President's orders she worked for the Government on juveniles in federal prisons. Finally, accepting the appointment as Head of the Massachusetts Reformatory for Girls and Women at Framingham, just out of Boston, she was truly uplifted by a sense that here she could follow through her program of salvation. At a time when she was offered the State Commissionership of Wisconsin she stated positively, "I shall never leave Framingham, because I want to demonstrate here in this one place that Christian penology can bring fruits. *By their fruits we shall know them.* Here I can plant, I can water and cultivate, I can sew and reap as it were. One can never escape politics and other obstacles but when you have time to *prove* your Christian methods, then you can offer the results."

Certainly she never meant to leave Framingham of her own free will. I interviewed her there shortly after she took office. I was working then on syndicated articles for International News Service and she was, of course, by this time one of the most famous and interesting women in America. I think it was at the first interview that she said, "I would rather be head of a great prison for women than be President of a college. Here I can fulfill my life's work in the reclamation of women and girls who have strayed into the world of crime. Our aim, surely, is to return them as worthwhile citizens of the United States of America and that is what I intend to do with Christ's help. Surely, surely this is better than having a prison that through nothing but punishment sinks them into a deeper place in the world of crime."

When in March 1932, the leading woman penologist of her country, she came to take charge of the Women's Prison at Framingham, all that she knew, felt or dreamed was wrapped up in that one package.

She took with her all that she had learned in her years of service, the thousands of cases that had passed through her firm, loving hands. Above all things, she took with her her father's spirit.

> His is more and more a part of my everyday life. Not in any vague, remote fashion, for he was so practical, so human in his *service*,—but as a realistic inspiration and guide. Never miss an opportunity to be with your loved ones: he says that to me. Be moderate; be tolerant; be merry; make people *enjoy* life; enjoy it yourself; *never* say a harsh word; never criticize; never get discouraged; be *good* but don't talk about it. All this flooded through me this morning.

Framingham Prison for Women—the Women's Prison at Framingham—where for the next fifteen years Superintendent Miriam Van Waters was to establish the finest record for running a big prison ever conceived.

I remember my beloved friend Warden Halloran of San Quentin once telling me that they had all learned much of what could and could not be done from the work of Dr. Van Waters at Framingham.

Oh God!
I knew the format so well. I knew exactly how it was done. I had done it myself so often.

The Exposé, we called it.

Great for circulation. Rated tops, however, only if your Exposé was so interesting, important and extensive in appeal or actual *news* that all the other papers had to pick it up and begin to cover it.

In my time, I had exposed the County Hospital. That was a laudatory and praiseworthy one. It sure needed exposing when we found corpses in the corridors because they'd been given the wrong 606 (for syphilis) medicine and died of it. I had exposed the alleged Charity organizations during the Depression in a spectacularly successful series on Unemployed Women. I posed as one, and made the sacrosanct Community Chest get into line where they had a little *charity* and less sanctimoniousness. I had exposed a man in charge of the County Jail who'd allowed a woman prisoner he fancied to skip across the Mexican border in spite of the murder rap against her. A crooked Mayor and his believe-it-or-not love letters, a corrupt Police Chief and even a Hollywood star or two. And a phony Talent Agency that promised jobs to kids who might soon follow in the footsteps of Jackie Coogan or Shirley Temple. Here again I ran into Dr. Miriam Van Waters, for one of her chief concerns was the teenage girls who came to Hollywood with the ambition to become Movie Stars and very little else. Their money ran out, there were no jobs, and Miriam tried to keep a fund so that when they were broke and discouraged she could send them home. She helped me once with a series of short stories I did for a magazine and called *The Port of Missing Girls*.

Sometime in 1949 I was in a hotel in New York, I was working for INS, and into our office came our Boston paper, the Boston *American*. One look at its headline shook me as though I'd been hit by a tornado. We had an Exposé going, and as a result, a couple of Irish politicians had fired Dr. Miriam Van Waters as head of the Framingham Prison for Women—which our Exposé had insisted was corrupt, slack, a mess of homosexuality among the women prisoners—

We—my own Hearst Press in the person of our Boston paper—were exposing Dr. Miriam Van Waters. And it was a lulu.

Frantically, I reached for a telephone. My training had always been to reach for a telephone, *do something*, about whatever it is do *some*thing, get hold of whoever it is that can do something about whatever it is, call Mr. Hearst at San Simeon, call the City Desk of the nearest paper, call Joe Connelly, head of INS, or Barry Farris, head of Universal Service, call the White House,

the Supreme Court, the FBI—you are the Press, you can always
get through to them. This time I felt the call was a matter of
life or death. I was talking aloud to myself while I waited to
get *Howey* in Boston. Walter Howey, our greatest editor, who
had become advisor to Mr. Hearst on his various properties, was
doing a stretch on the Boston papers.

I kept on *talking*—into space—to myself—

Of all the ridiculous, unfounded, vile and stupid bobbles, blun-
ders, bungles, buttons and bows this gets the Brown Derby—
oh sure, sure, Dwyer and McDowell or O'Donnell or whatever
or whoever a couple of those wormy Boston politicians with
softening of the brain and collapsed arteries (this was pre-Ken-
nedy)—Dwyer and McDowell to the front—okay, Howey, put
on circulation, never mind who you run over in the process—go
ahead EXPOSE somebody, anybody—

My call went through and there was Howey at the other end
yelling blasphemously—I went right on talking, I was too mad
to be able to stop—

                      —expose 'em never mind
whether you know what the hell you're doing or not, trying to
expose Miriam Van Waters you must be out of your goddam pig-
headed—you gotta be dead from the neck up, you silly bastard,
you've got yourself flummoxed by some of those ambitious Irish
political pumpkins, you're not getting senile are you, Howey?—I
mean, babies like Dwyer and McDowell or O'Donnell or whatever
—I've known Dr. Van Waters for years, she's the greatest authority
in the world on women's prisons and correctional work among
girls and detention homes—and she's absolutely incorruptible,
don't you realize she was on the President's Committee—

About here, Howey's roar was loud enough to shut me off.
Besides, I was beginning to sob with rage and frustration.

"A girl hanged herself!" Howey roared. "At the goddam Reformatory. She hanged herself in the barn because she was disappointed in love with another girl inmate. Get that? There's
plenty of that doll razzamatazz going on in there they tell me—"

"WHO tells you?" I shouted back.

"Dwyer tells me," Howey continued at top pitch, "and he's
head of Corrections for the State of Massachusetts and he's been

your pal Miriam's boss for quite a while and he says she's too goddam *slack* and *soft* and she plays favorites so maybe—"

"Howey!" I said and he backed off and began again "—okay, Dwyer says she lets 'em walk in and out like it was a resort hotel and not a prison. Dwyer says she got some bug about *reforming* them and saving these little bums—"

"Look up reform in your dictionary if you've got one," I said, "and I'll be up on the next train."

"Nobody asked you to come up here," Howey said. "When I want you on a story of ours I'll send for you—"

"If I wait for you to send for me on this one," I said, "you will have made a mistake that'll blight your reputation the rest of your life like burning Joan of Arc at the stake—" I can almost feel again the pain of the breath I drew about then. "Listen— please, Walter, listen? I am a great exponent of the Exposé myself. I've done 'em for years. You don't think I'm altogether a fool about *news*, do you? I tell you this is ALL WRONG. You are exposing the wrong story and you NEED me whether you know it or not—"

"Did you ever know the time when I didn't know what I needed?" Howey said icily.

"No," I said, "but as Queen Isabella said to Columbus, I'm going to bet a lot on your finding the first time. Keep Mr. Dwyer on ice for me, please. In the morgue or out."

The answer was, after all, pretty simple.

Dwyer and McDowell, politicians of high position and some power, did not approve of Dr. Van Waters, nor her principles on penology. There may be something stubborner, more hard-mouthed balky and impervious to reason than a small-time political boss who dare not change his mind because he doesn't know why he made it up in the first place, but I've never encountered it.

"Howey," I said, "it is only an error in judgment to make a mistake, but it argues an infirmity of character to stick to it."

"You never thought that up," Howey said.

"No," I said, "but I know all about Dwyer and McDowell. I've watched Miriam Van Waters battle prejudice and public

opinion and above all politics and politicians ever since I first
went to work for you right after the Civil War when you were
trying to find out what kind of whiskey General Grant drank.
Remember?"

I did know all about Dwyer and McDowell, though they
were new to me under those particular names. They were against
all this modern *reform* crap, all this Prevention not Punishment
flapdoodle. Get *tough* with these half-grown streetwalkers and
pickpockets and shoplifters, hell, half of the ones in Van Waters'
jail got took up for sticking a knife in some guy's back. Some
day they were bound to catch her slipping up, and Dwyer and
McDowell kept active—and hostile—watch on the Reformatory
and it's famous head at all times. It was their privilege to give
jobs and they hadn't given this big one to this *dame* in the first
place.

When Toni Di Marco, one of the six students—as Dr. Van
Waters insisted on calling them—who were in what was called
the Barn Group, was found dead hanging by a sheet-rope, the
verdict was suicide—with a nasty, sinister whisper about *murder*
and an even nastier one about the cause, whichever it might be.

Toni was a big girl, it was probably suicide, but immediately
one of the Hearst papers in Boston began a series of stories which
featured the sinister, the salacious, and the scandalous. Our
American put a crime reporter named Jim Delaney on it, and
before long Jim with the best intentions circulation-wise had
stirred up McDowell and Dwyer and shortly thereafter with
their help they'd poked and prodded State Senator LoPresti of
Boston's North End, reawakened his suspicions of Framingham,
which had been the means of sending him to "investigate" the
Reformatory several times before.

So—there was the array against Dr. Van Waters. Dwyer,
McDowell, Senator LoPresti, and the Boston *American*.

It began to look as though when Toni Di Marco put a rope
around her own neck she might have put one around Miriam
Van Waters' as well.

In the minds of hundreds of girls and women whose lives they
insisted—and testified—she had changed over the years, she was
a saint, an angel of mercy, Joan of Arc protecting them. The
love that had nourished Miriam in her own childhood, the love

of her father and mother that had been with her in her teens and on into her adult life and benevolent professional achievement, had proved impervious to the corroding influence of human misery and depravity she had dealt with. In all her dedicated career, she never shirked her full responsibility to find out if there was anything to hope for or about, any way to bring hope forward, any way that hope could lead to healing. In a fine biography, which I recommend to you with all my heart, called *The Lady at Box 99*, written by Burton J. Rowles and published by the Seabury Press, New York, the steps are taken and prove her incredible healing and saving work with delinquent girls and youthful criminals, and her platforms and blueprints for better parents, schools and corrective institutions.

But when I arrived in Boston, by the next and fastest train, neither Dwyer nor McDowell nor the *American* and its editor Howey saw it that way.

REFORMATORY HEAD CHARGED WITH CONTRIBUTING QUIZ DR. VAN WATERS ON INMATE ESCAPEES STATE HUNTS MISSING VAN WATERS WITNESS DR. VAN WATERS DENIES FATAL BEATING

By Tim Riley and James J. Delaney

Dr. Mirian Van Waters, superintendent of the Women's Reformatory at Framingham, today emphatically denied charges of State Senator M. LoPresti that she operates the Institution behind an Iron Curtain. However, the renowned penologist refused to discuss the reopened probe into the death of Toni DuBenedetio, 21, whose family charge she was fatally beaten by another inmate last November. "There were frequent fights among the girls," Dr. Van Waters said. "Some girls called other girls names. That usually starts it. With so many girls who have records of lawlessness thrown together in such numbers as these are, there are bound to be some instances of hostility."

"You drove Thomas Mott Osborne to suicide. Do not think I will so accommodate you! I am not the suicide type."

So said Dr. Miriam Van Waters. But the politicians, the under-
world and, as so often happens when politics makes strange bed-
fellows, some of the churches—all for different reasons—were
making an effort in that direction.

The day I got up there the morning story by Riley and Delaney said that Dr. Van Waters was on the stand and remained
serene and unruffled. The way they wrote it suggested a hardened criminal, but knowing her I was sure that she would remain serene and unruffled until she fell over dead because of her
full consciousness of innocence. Which would be as good as driving her to suicide, as far as the end results of getting rid of her
and her *reforms* was concerned.

I talked to and yelled at Howey, but found him too committed
to his Exposé *and* the powerful news-controlling politicians behind it to be swayable—though I had a suspicion that he was
beginning to wonder if Dr. Van Waters' side might not have
been a bigger circulation-getter.

Persecuted Female—and her pictures were not cheesecake, to
be sure, but they were sort of—decorative—at that.

So—I called Mr. Hearst.

By then he was living in Marion Davies' house in Beverly Hills,
San Simeon being too remote for doctors and hospitals. This
house was where I was to see so much of him as we put together
my memories of the Movies in a series for our *American Weekly*,
which by then had the biggest circulation in the world.

I poured it out the way I always had to him. I explained that
probably Howey might be reluctant to move against so much
concentrated political power—the Boston Irish have the longest
memories of anybody. They lay in wait, they do. I reminded
him, however, of Dr. Van Waters' work at Juvenile Hall when
I was a young reporter, and the series I had done about her sensational headline work at El Retiro, where she had handled and
reformed hundreds of wayward girls. I said, "Oh, Mr. Hearst—
she couldn't do the things they say she does and has done. You
always taught me that there are some things certain people can
do—but others they simply could not. Certain murders they
might commit, others they simply couldn't. You know Boston
Politicians. Miriam has always told me that Politics, Public Opin-

ion and Prejudice worked against her and here they are altogether in high. Dwyer and McDowell are the Politicians, but we've got Riley and Delaney in there on the story and Jim Noonan on the City Desk at the *American* and—Howey—I mean, he doesn't know Boston as well as he did Chicago and New York—and he won't listen to me about Miriam Van Waters. He says all reformers are hypocrites. You want to know what they claim is one instance of how *soft* she is with these girls? She took some of them to an AA Meeting! You know, Mr. Hearst, you had me look into AA for you not too long ago and you decided Alcoholics Anonymous was great. Remember?"

Remember! I should tell that original elephant memory to remember!

"Perhaps," he said, "we have chosen the wrong side of this particular Exposé. Perhaps I can suggest to Mr. Howey that you can be of some help to us in this matter."

Suggest he apparently did, for while Walter didn't turn out any brass bands over my arrival, and his one good eye was almost as expressionless as the glass one, he did arrange for me to go up to the courthouse.

"You understand this case is as upside down as *Alice Through the Looking-Glass*, don't you?" he said.

"No," I said. "What's upside down about it?"

"They are not suing her," Howey said with an evil chortle. "She is suing them."

"I do not know what you mean by that," I said.

"They fired her," Howey said. "They fired her as superintendent after fifteen years for misconduct in office and failure to function properly as head of the Reformatory. In fact, they allege that she has been performing improperly as Superintendent of Framingham, allowing the inmates to do as they pleased. But the almighty Dr. Van Waters—I tell you there's a woman thinks she can get away with *anything*—she refused to be fired. More nerve than anybody I ever heard of—*she* brought the thing into court to make *them* prove she'd failed in her duties!"

"Could that be because she's innocent?" I said. "That sounds like my Miriam all right. I should think you'd be on her side. It's not like you to uphold some wormy politicians trying to do a girl out of her job. What do the inmates on the whole say about it?"

"On the whole"—Howey was intent on the copy before him—"they're on her side. But they'd be that if she was soft with them, wouldn't they?"

"Your reporters ought to—" I began.

"Oh shut up!" Howey said, loudly enough for the whole city room to hear. "Are you supposed to write me a piece?"

"Not you," I said. "INS."

"Allright allright," Howey said. "Go on up and take a look. You always know so much more than anybody else."

"All I know is Miriam Van Waters," I said. "She's about a hundred years ahead of our time. I don't suppose Boston can bear that. They prefer to put anybody that can see beyond their nose in the pillory or hang 'em in the public square with a scarlet letter on."

"I suppose you'll want me to erect a statue to your Dr. Van Waters," Howey said.

"Somebody should," I said. "And when somebody takes time to look back on how we treated any juvenile who did wrong before Miriam Van Waters came along, we probably will."

I still say it.

Somebody should.

If possible, it should be exactly as I saw her when I arrived at the State House where this upside-down torture chamber was located. My reporter's luck was in (as it so often was!), for Dr. Van Waters was standing in the witness box and had been for four hours already. She was to stay there, small, vivid, on the alert, wearing the same—or it looked like the same—elegantly cut gray suit, the same bright scarf, the same gray hat that looked like a baseball cap. Probably she had been yanking it over her right eye from time to time, for it was at a more rakish angle than usual and I could see very soon that she was allowing herself more emotional outgo than I had ever seen in her before. Naturally, I had to go back to that first austere little courtroom, with its kitchen table and two kitchen chairs, where she and Orfa Jean Shontz had dealt with "wayward children" in this new pattern designed to preserve and protect rather than punish and penalize. Over a quarter of a century had gone by and Dr. Van Waters was less changed than anybody I had ever seen. Still cast in steel, I guess. She had to be.

It didn't take long to size up the situation.

I saw a bishop in Dr. Van Waters' support. Two outstanding club women whose names I recognized. These women really worked for reform in many areas and were highly respected by one and all, including the newspapers and Walter Howey! There were present also several civic and state leaders who were not part of the Establishment, as we would call it now.

I called Mr. Hearst again.

Many years later I was in Boston, trying as I have for so many years to get the Christian Science Church to let me write a real true life story of Mrs. Eddy, getting nowhere as usual against their determination not to show her as she really was, the greatest fighter for Christ and the return of apostolic divine healing we've had since Saint Paul, but as they wanted to keep her, a saccharine little figure like the bride on a wedding cake. This time when I hit Boston the Teddy Kennedy story at Chappaquiddick had just broken and I was sitting in to offer my small word and vote about what could be done without violating the integrity of Freedom of the Press to save Rose Kennedy, whom we all loved. I was there by accident and sat next to a Hearst editor and publisher whom I'd known and admired for years. I brought up the name Van Waters and he said she had retired but was still living in Framingham. Then, after a moment's thought, he said with puzzlement, "I never understood why we got called off on that Exposé of her right in the middle of the trial. How could Mr. Hearst have suddenly switched like that—what did he find out?"

"I can't imagine," I said.

A fine newspaperman named Sam Mornstein, who is now head of the combined newspapers in Boston, was kind enough to send me the file clips from those old days. These were of the news that made history, since it preserved and protected Dr. Van Waters so that she could continue her amazing work. I have tried to spot exactly how and when the Exposé changed into sound, unprejudiced reporting. I can't. It was done cleverly and quietly, as became good, sometimes brilliant, newspapermen of vast experience. It was done soon, for there is now a headline which says

DR. VAN WATERS SUPPORTED BY CLERGY

Over the exaggerated charges of suicide among the girls, of open homosexual practices permitted by the superintendent, of accusations regarding her too lenient policies in running this Reformatory—little by little emerged her own clean-cut practice of Christianity. *He came to save sinners, not the righteous.* In fact, Dr. Van Waters used those words as she stood there, used them to explain her policies and management, and I had to think of her father, the Episcopal minister, in whose Christian doctrine Miriam had been brought up and which doctrine she had lived by ever since.

A *practicing* Christian. Indeed.

While I was writing the novel *Tell No Man*, in which a young minister set forth to follow Our Lord, day by day, I truly often thought of Miriam Van Waters. I have not known many who made this attempt.

When Dr. Van Waters said on the witness stand, This is an experimental reformatory, she meant experimental in trying to follow in the Way.

Yes, said Dr. Van Waters, here girls are taught trades. Each goes out into the world once more with a means of supporting herself instead of becoming a burden to the state or returning to crime or prostitution to make a living. No girl is under graver temptation than when she hasn't anything to eat or any place to sleep. (I remember how well I came to see this when I myself had posed as an Unemployed Woman.) Yes, said Dr. Van Waters, they are allowed to keep their babies in my Reformatory. We try to teach them how to care for babies, how to bring them up, above all to love them. This often proves an incentive for real reform. They want to make a home for them. Most girls love their babies and if you give them half a chance will try to keep them. Yes, I have taken them to AA meetings, where there is an alcohol problem. A goodly percentage of my girl and women inmates were drunk when arrested. Many of the crimes were committed when they were intoxicated. Naturally, I felt that the work of Alcoholics Anonymous would be of great benefit to them. It had the best record of bringing alcoholics to a happy sobriety with the help of a Higher Power. Fear only makes a "dry" drunk, and that's no good to anybody. Yes, we have music in an attempt to soothe their troubled and savage breasts, to smooth out their jittery nerves, above all to give them hope.

"I wanted them to know," Dr. Van Waters said in a clear voice that pealed through the crowded courtroom, which seemed frozen silent and motionless, "that there was one person who loved them, who wanted to trust them. I wanted to give them hope, for I do not believe anyone can reform unless they have hope."

Over and over the witnesses from the Framingham Reformatory said, "She had confidence in me, so at last I got up the nerve to have confidence in myself."

What can you give a pitcher besides confidence? I go on and on quoting Red Schoendienst, who offered that explanation of his ability to get more out of his pitchers than any other manager in the Big Leagues.

In forgiveness lay healing, seventy times seven.

"I try," said Dr. Van Waters with one of her brilliant twinkles, "to teach them *how* to go and sin no more. It's not easy, you know. They have to make a living, they have to eat."

And of course in those days there were not as many jobs open to women as there are today.

Eleanor Roosevelt came once into the courtroom to support her friend Dr. Van Waters and showed plainly that she not only believed in her complete innocence but admired her greatly. Francis and Jessie Wilson Sayre (daughter of President Woodrow Wilson) were also at her side and, as the headline said, many of the Boston clergy.

Taking the witness stand, Austin MacCormick, one of the highest ranking prison authorities in the world, said, "She is not just the leading penologist of our world as far as women and children are concerned, she is a true life-saver who brought a spirit of rebirth to the inmates of Framingham and to many, many others throughout the world. If I were asked to name the American citizen who has saved more souls than any other, I should have to consider Miriam Van Waters."

And so should I! So do I!

Of course she was returned to Framingham "without a stain on her work ability or character" and I admit I like to think that the change-of-face of our papers contributed a bit to that sane and sound decision in favor of one of the greatest of all American women.

Chapter Nine

Harry Hopkins, staring at the newly sworn-in President of the United States, Harry S. Truman, *and* his wife Bess, standing as usual at his shoulder, said simply, "This is going to be a team effort."

A *team* effort?

The Presidency of the United States?

Yet who should know more of such things or be better able to predict their future than Harry Hopkins, right hand of that magnificent, controversial figure, Franklin Delano Roosevelt, whose death at the beginning of his unprecedented *fourth* term had put Harry Truman and his wife Bess into the White House. Because Harry Hopkins was right, I have selected Bess Truman as the First Lady belonging as though by divine right among the women of irrepressible spirit to whom this country owes no less than everything. For as half of that team Harry Hopkins foresaw, Bess Wallace Truman came closer to *being* President than any woman ever has or ever will be again, since women today are rapidly attempting to abrogate the rewarding partnerships of an inspired marriage.

"I never make decisions unless Bess is in on them," said the President.

Never, he said.

Decisions   decisions   decisions

To fire General MacArthur, the world's hero.

To use presidential power to end the midwar steel strike, in

spite of United States Steel's double-truck attacks in all newspapers. "You are not," said the President, "going to tie up this
country in wartime. If this is the way you want it, I'll stop you."
And did.

To attend the Potsdam Conference with Churchill and Stalin,
then representing England and Soviet Russia, and make the *decision* concerning the disposition of the conquered German Reich.

To found the United Nations in San Francisco.

To allow and oversee the conception and manufacture of the
Atom Bomb.

To drop it on Hiroshima.

"The final *decision* of where and when to use the atomic bomb
was up to me," President Truman says in his Memoirs. "Let there
be no mistake about it. I regarded the bomb as a military weapon
and never had any doubt that it should be used."

I never made a decision unless Bess was in on it.

So a woman was in on that most difficult of all decisions to use
the bomb and save thousands—maybe hundreds of thousands—of
American soldiers.

Then we come to speeches.

"I *never* make a speech without going over it with her," said
Harry S. Truman when he was President.

Speeches   speeches   speeches

Campaign, congressional, inaugural, state-of-the-nation, to a pol-
itician, senator, president, speeches are the voice of his spirit, his
policies, his exchange with the people to whom he is or will be
responsible.

"Unfortunately, and I say that advisedly, unfortunately a dark
fog of mistrust has risen between the Soviet Union and the West,
distorting and confusing our relations. It is clear that little progress
is likely to be made in settling disputes between the western
powers and Soviet Russia as long as there is so much mistrust. In
recently considering sending a special emissary to Moscow, my
purpose was to ask Premier Stalin's cooperation in dispelling this
poisonous atmosphere of distrust which now surrounds the nego-
tiations between the western powers and the Soviet Union."

That was to the American Legion in 1946.

OR

"In performing the duties of my office I need the help and prayers of every one of you. I ask your encouragement and your support. The tasks we face are difficult and we can accomplish them only if we work together. Today marks the beginning not only of a new Administration but of a period that will be eventful, perhaps decisive, for us and for the world."

So, indeed, they were, those years of making peace, of returning to peacetime living and economics, absorbing back into civilian living a vast army of young men, supervising the new powers of Labor.

That speech above was the second Inaugural Address, before a hundred thousand people in the great open space between the Capitol, the Supreme Court, and the Congressional Library. *Now* he was not Roosevelt's Vice-President come to the White House when that elected president died in office. Now Harry and Bess, after a team campaign in which Bess participated as no wife had ever done before, and with sensational success, now they were the overwhelming choice of the people. Out in Missouri, Truman's mother—to whom he wrote or telephoned every day—could congratulate him. This she had refused to do when, as she put it, he was merely backed into it. In effect, she followed the line Congressman Vandiver had made the slogan of their state, "I'm from Missouri, you have got to show me." Now that native son Harry Truman had showed 'em, and any of the population who couldn't believe that the farm boy from Missouri could lick the Governor of New York, Thomas E. Dewey. I remember this one real well because I won enough money from my Republican friends in Chicago to build a new guest cottage on the Hill.

When Senator Truman became head of the Committee to investigate the Defense Industry, which committee came eventually to bear his name as the Truman Committee, Bess was his official assistant. The press who covered it could see her influence on Headstrong Harry, as we had come to call him. Always sitting there at his elbow, she had laid a restraining hand on his arm from time to time *or* put a paper in front of him and shoved him into stronger action.

At his elbow Bess had certainly been when he wrote the campaign speeches that got him elected County Judge in their home town of Independence. (Miss Independent from Independence we came to call Bess when she was First Lady.) In fact, there is a legend around there that she wrote 'em before he had decided to run, and that it was her idea, after his failure in business, that he should go into politics. In that, his first race, and all those that followed and brought him to Washington as a Senator, then as President, and for many years afterwards when as Ex-President he was the best-loved and most influential Elder Statesman this country has ever known, Bess was never absent. When he was working on a speech—and he was a man who worked meticulously over each one himself—the picture was always the same. Sometimes framed in a window of the old Wallace house on Delaware Avenue, sometimes in the President's office, sometimes in their private car as they toured from state to state. There he was, paper before him, pencil in hand, head bowed as he wrote. And just outside the circle of light, with *her* paper and pencil, making suggestions, putting in a phrase, strengthening an opinion, reaffirming a position or policy or principle, was his wife.

His everloving wife—as Damon Runyon's characters said.

I never write a speech—

This isn't just a phrase, it is a simple statement of fact.

He never did.

While she seldom held a press conference of her own, we were just as apt to rush to her for information about what the Senator —or the President—was going to say. We knew she'd know, because we knew he *never*, etc., etc., etc.—

Who was she exactly?

Sometimes we know a great deal about the women who are elected to the White House along with their husbands. To the country at large, Bess Wallace Truman had been called the Woman Nobody Knows.

To begin with, I'd like to say that of all the women I ever met or worked with—or on—as a reporter, the one to whom photographers did the most injustice was Bess Truman, and it wasn't their fault.

"I do take lousy pictures, don't I?" she said to me once with that truly *amiable* smile. One that seemed to include you in her love-of-life, her faith in God, her sense of well-being.

She did indeed. Possibly today the cameras could do her more justice, more kindness, for her beauty—and she had some—was entirely a matter of color. There never were bluer eyes, never a fresher rose-and-cream complexion, never hair more golden. Your first impression, the one you carried around, was of that radiant color.

Even before his accession to the presidency in 1945, Harry Truman was well known as the Senator from Missouri, a popular Democratic spokesman, a leader in the party. But as long as she could Mrs. Truman clung to her right to be a Private Citizen. Long after it had ceased to be true. As a Senate wife, she was utterly happy in Washington and did, on the whole, live a private life. Played bridge very well, a strong and aggressive player she was. I once heard her deliver a classic lecture on the fact that you could lose as many points by *under*bidding as by *over*bidding— and she toted it up on a score pad where not bidding the rubber, then having the next hand won by the opponents, actually was more than an average big *set* of a hand. She went to the ball game and that was an experience you'd never forget—going to a ball game with Bess Truman. She stopped worrying about being a Private Citizen and became a *fan*, a real fan, who rooted, yelled, suggested killing the umpire or at least seeing that he went to an oculist, and spotted nineteen-year-old Willie Mays as a coming *great*—maybe *greatest*.

But her insistence on as much anonymity as possible was, I suppose, particularly notable following Eleanor Roosevelt, who had never been—or wanted to be—a Private Person even in her cradle.

"I," Bess Truman kept saying, "am a Private Person."

The truth is, she was first, foremost and always a *wife*.

But it has to turn out that the wife of the President is not even legally a Private Person, for private persons are not followed and cared for at all times by members of the Secret Service and, though this was one of the things she most disliked, Mrs. Truman was. No one, no one, who lives at 1600 Pennsylvania Avenue, in the most public house in all the world, is a private person.

Perhaps this is a delicate balance of semantics but to me it seems vitally important: Bess Truman was *the President's wife* before she was—if she ever was in her own estimation—*the First Lady*.

You can see why this made her the all-time All-American favorite with the Washington press. At the time, I was the only woman covering the White House for news. Every newspaperman had his own ideas and ideals about a wife—come to it, for that matter, so did I.

On the whole, my own experience of wives had been, has been, to say the best, negative.

To say the worst, in what I like to think of as a forthright manner, I have seen a lot of good men ruined by wives who could have been disposed of with a Flit gun and nobody in the world would have been a Tasmanian tulip the worse for it. I have seen what might have amounted to genius in a couple of writers turned into soap opera rejects by women no other man would have given house room to in an Eskimo hut in January. I do not understand how they do this. There is a certain kind of wife who enters your consciousness at the Scott Fitzgerald hour of 3 A.M., who *somehow* has a whammy on a fine, upstanding, interesting man with enough talent and character to contribute light, joy and hope to the Universe. And I have seen this gentleman as determined to escape as a prisoner just transferred to the neuropsychopathic ward at Dannemora, yet, after one wistful glance at the free horizon, return to duress vile because they couldn't do that to *her*, which is equivalent to saying you couldn't bear to pull up a hunk of devil grass that is ruining your lawn. Anybody, as Thurber once said, can survive editors and publishers because look how many of us have. It takes a superman not to show the whites of his eyes when a wife begins that *after-eighteen-years* routine. I suppose a good psychiatrist would identify this with my own sense of guilt as a wife failure, which I was, but then I've rarely met a good psychiatrist. The last one I had to do with believed in Confrontation as the solution for those who hated each other. This resulted in two murders and in the third case, where it didn't, left hundreds of innocent bystanders wishing that it had.

Often had I recognized the forlorn and nostalgic longing for the right wife in my newspaper confreres and I was always glad that *that* at least was one problem I didn't have to solve. I felt honestly sorry for my husbands and let it go at that. I am ashamed of this now and recognize my own selfish limitations, for a *wife* I was not. We once had a song written in the upstairs room of the Stork Club, sacred to newspapermen, and George Gershwin called it *The Life of the Wife of a Newspaperman*. It was certainly not an occupation to lure anybody with good sense, attractive as Bill Corum and Damon Runyon were, but I never knew happier wives than some of them—they were never bored.

Every masculine member of the Press in Washington envied Harry Truman. Not as President, not even as Senator, a job which most of them would rather have had of course. But they openly envied him his wife. In their cups and out, they all wished for one just like her.

For a long, long time Bess Truman struggled against a personal entry in *Who's Who in America*, that listing of celebrities, insisting that she should appear there only as part of her husband's. After m.

m. Bess Wallace, June 28, 1919.

Finally she had to give in, and wrote one of my favorite pieces of *literature*. The art of writing *short*, as all writers know, is given to few and achieved only after years of struggle. When I got down to Santa Ana on a big murder case one time and was told I'd only have to do six hundred words a day, I suppose the inexperienced would have considered that easier. It took twice as long as the twelve hundred I'd been used to. I got fired from the Journalism Department at UCLA, where I was giving lectures on feature writing, because, when the head of that department asked our students to write a report of facts and color it had taken them six months to collect in seven hundred and fifty words, I said if they could do it they were ready for a job on *Time* and shouldn't bother to go to school any more.

I give you Bess Truman's masterpiece:

> Truman, Bess Wallace (Mrs. Harry S. Truman); born Independence, Mo.; graduate Independence High School; student The Barstow School for Girls, Kansas City, Mo.; married Harry S. Truman, June 28, 1919; one daughter, Mary Margaret. Democrat. Episcopalian. Charter member the Missouri Chapter, P.E.O. Sisterhood in Washington.

Home: Independence, Mo. Address: The White House, Washington, D.C.

Note for a moment how much this tells you about the President's wife.

Home was still Independence, Mo.

The White House, Washington, D.C., was an address.

The Barstow School for Girls is an illustrious and exclusive seminary for young ladies and many women would have forgotten about Independence High School, for, as far as Kansas City can, the Barstow School ranks with Miss Spence's in New York, Miss Hamlin's in San Francisco, Immaculate Heart out of Philadelphia, and Foxcroft of Washington. And she seems to consider that stating the White House as her residence is all that need be said about the fact that the young haberdasher she married finally was given the biggest job in the world.

Her pride in Harry's success was enormous, she believed he could and would, with his liberal policies and his understanding of the cause of labor, do much for the People. But she wished to conceal as much as possible her own part in these accomplishments, she refused from the beginning to take any position or personality for herself in them.

True, we often got a picture of her sitting beside him as his first Assistant on the Truman Committee. She managed to make herself as impersonal as the chair she sat in. This was when most of us first knew her, at the time the Truman Committee began to be news. Up to then she'd just been another Senator's wife and there were a hundred or so—sometimes it seemed more—of them around the Capitol. Some you knew, some you didn't, a few were photogenic even before Jackie Kennedy came along. We first registered Mrs. Truman because she was the only senatorial wife who was always there.

A *team* effort.

Mrs. Truman was with me—*Mrs. Truman* and I—*Mrs. Truman* arrived—

In public he always called her Mrs. Truman. As far as I know, no one ever heard him say Bess and in the Memoirs, which are extraordinarily good and informative reading, except on rare occasions, he still speaks of her as *Mrs. Truman*. F.D.R. often spoke of his First Lady as Eleanor—to me and many others. As all who recall that last day in Dallas will remember, when President Kennedy explained that it took his wife longer to get ready than it did him, he said "—but *Jackie* is prettier when she finishes."

To H.S.T. his *wife* was Mrs. Truman.

No man who occupied the position had a higher regard for or more reverent understanding of the power and responsibility of the Presidency than Harry S. Truman. He made all of us feel it and respond to it.

> *There is no office quite like the Presidency anywhere else in the world. It has great powers.*
> *Within the first few months. I discovered that being President is like riding a tiger. A man has to keep on riding or be swallowed.*
> *I now had a responsibility without precedent in history. The decisions I had to make could well influence the future course of all civilization.*
> AND
> *I never made a decision without Bess—*

There you are. No other President as far as I can find out or as far as I saw them from Woodrow Wilson to Richard Nixon ever said or even indicated that. F.D.R. used to keep me after press conferences to tell me, with applause and laughter, something *Eleanor* had done. But I never had the feeling that they were *one*, as I did with Harry and Bess.

And it was Bess who often kept Headstrong Harry of the violent temper, of the sometimes unrestrained vocabulary, of an occasional one drink over the limit, out of serious trouble.

The boys in the Washington Press Club still love to recount the day when President Truman went up to the Press Club Bar and ordered what was obviously not his first bourbon and water. As he picked up the glass, the phone rang, the bartender turned from it to say, "Your wife's on the phone, Mr. President," and Mr. President put down the glass, turned and walked out without tasting what was in it.

"She can look after them," we always said, "she can look after both of them—she can handle 'em."

By this we meant the President and their beautiful daughter,

Margaret, who was, as he often said, the apple of his eye. And who aspired to a career as a singer, concert and even operatic.

> The Washington Post . . . By Paul Hume . . .
> She is flat a good deal of the time . . . She cannot sing with anything approaching professional finish . . . She communicates almost nothing of the music she presents . . .

Reading this in the afternoon paper, the President didn't wait to return to his office desk. In long hand, on a memo pad headed *The White House* . . .

> I have just read your lousy review buried in the back pages. You sound like a frustrated man that never made a success, an eight ulcer man on a four ulcer job. And all four ulcers working. I never met you but if I do you'll need a new nose and plenty of beefsteak and perhaps a supporter below. Westbrook Pegler, a guttersnipe, is a gentleman compared to you. You can take that as more of an insult than a reflection on your ancestry.

This he took out at once and with his own hand put in the mailbox outside the door to Blair House, the temporary White House where the Trumans then lived. Few White House letters have ever received wider circulation, more front pages and headlines, more editorial comment, most of it adverse. The editorial writers, a breed unto themselves anyhow, we reporters always thought, not really to be included among newspapermen, descended upon Harry for what they referred to as lack of dignity and decorum—but the country as a whole was *delighted*.

They had always liked Harry and cheered for him—now they loved him. He was a father after their own hearts, just because he was *President* he hadn't become someone above the ordinary human feelings, he was the Man from Missouri—and bigod and bijeminy he'd show 'em if they tried monkeying around with saying mean things about his daughter.

Not long after this, Headstrong Harry blistered Representative Edward Hébert of Louisiana and his proposal that the churches set aside a day of prayer in which to appeal to God for guidance and wisdom and Harry said, "I am extremely sorry that the sentiments expressed in your letter were not thought of before the

November 7th election when the campaign in your State of
Louisiana and in Utah, North Carolina, Illinois and Indiana was
carried on in a manner that was as low as I've ever seen and I've
been in this game since 1906."

These he mailed and on the whole with the general public they
increased his popularity.

But Bess decided they must not take any more chances. So far,
he'd gotten by with these epistles written late at night and now
and then with a couple of late night snorts. The next one—who
knew?

It was then rumored around the Press Club Bar that Bess Truman had a false bottom put in that particular mailbox—and after
Harry had gone to bed she, as the more careful head of the team,
went out and collected whatever envelopes had been mailed, read
them carefully and made the decision as to whether to put them
in a *real* mailbox or not.

I never made a decision without Bess—but now and then perhaps Bess made a decision without Harry.

Stories about Bess soon began to come our way.

From the diplomats and their Embassies, from V.I.P.s who
attended dinners and luncheons, from the Congressional members
and their wives who attended official meals and receptions, came
the astonished statements that it was now possible to *eat* the food
in the White House. Eleanor had been a grand First Lady in
China, Africa, London and Paris, all the states of the Union,
traveling many miles for her husband who for many reasons left
Washington as seldom as possible. But the meals at the White
House during her time there were awful. The Roosevelt sons,
young men with normally healthy appetites, complained bitterly
and in public and still do. Now, competently and quietly, Mrs.
Truman, the President's wife, was doing for him what any man
has a right to expect from his wife, she was serving him, his family,
his friends, his guests, his tremendously important political as-
sociates, and even his enemies, meals they never forgot.

How she did it on the White House budget for food, which
had continually bugged Mrs. Roosevelt and which the Kennedys
augmented with their own additions, nobody quite knew. The
Trumans had no private fortune to draw upon for anything.

"I have a good many Missouri recipes," Mrs. Truman explained, with that amiable smile. "We like to eat hearty in my part of the country, you won't find any better food anywhere, but we're not extravagant. We most of us know the value of a dollar—or a dime for that matter."

"You know," Clark Gable said to me after he had been a guest of the President and Mrs. Truman, "she's a very, very attractive woman."

Harry Truman thought that from the time he was eight until he was past eighty.

When he was taken to Sunday School at the age of eight and met the other members of his class ". . . there was one," he said one day at a Press Conference. "I became interested in one in particular. She had golden curls and the most beautiful blue eyes. We went to Sunday School, to public school, through high school, graduated in the same class and marched down life's road together. For me, she still has the most beautiful blue eyes in the world."

Sentimental.

Yes, and how wonderful, for the rather stern face of the President warmed into a smile as he spoke. I felt that as long as he knew Bess was at his side this man would have faith in the ultimate power of Good. She was, indeed, his better half.

A great many of us have confused change with progress. We have in some measure subscribed to a doctrine called permissiveness. This somehow always appears to be permitting ourselves to do what we know to be wrong. Many of us have wished that this Truman kind of lifelong love, devotion and *trust* had come to us.

No, Mrs. Truman did not hold regular press conferences, but she would usually grant you an interview if you had something specific in mind. On a magazine article I was to do about her, I said I thought she had been blessed to find the other half of her team in Sunday School, to have him grow into the right man, to marry him for all time, and to have ended in the White House as a team effort.

Her quick look was direct, honest and a little amused.

She said, "You may find this right man in Sunday School, or high school, or college. Staying married to him is another matter and the important thing. No man stays the same. You must see that the young man who went away to war, who later failed in business for lack of capital, the Senator who fought to keep the Defense Industry and its huge spending appropriations honest in a later war, the President who had the guts and heart to allow General MacArthur to come home and address Congress and the nation after, as Commander-in-Chief, he'd been obliged to fire him for insubordination—all these can be men of different growth and thinking. A wife must adjust to all of them daily."

I spoke then of the terrific responsibility of the President, who was without question the most powerful man in the world, the man upon whom more of humanity's safety and future depended than any other.

"Yes," Mrs. Truman said, "but in answer to that I once heard President Roosevelt say that the man in that office should feel that the country and the world were lucky to have him there!"

The Buck Stops Here.

That sign stood on President Truman's desk. It embodied what Mrs. Truman had said to me.

And I came to know for sure that it was Mrs. Truman who placed it there. It has, of course, become a legend.

No truer word has ever been said of the Presidency of the United States.

Once upon a time when that greatest of all pitchers, Grover Cleveland Alexander, had been called out of the bull pen to pitch the final innings in the seventh game of a World Series in which he had already won two games—one the day before—he was asked if he hadn't felt that final demand was almost too much. To which Alexander replied, "No—I just thought how lucky they were to have me."

Bess Truman felt this same steady, blessed confidence in her husband. At the end of the greatest war in history, faced with all the problems of ending it in a manner that would make it possible to prevent another one, in a time of one crisis after another in domestic affairs, Bess Truman felt how lucky the United States was to have Mr. Truman there in the White House where the buck of world affairs stopped. You couldn't pass it any further.

And how lucky Harry S. Truman was to have a *wife* who shared with him every moment of that responsibility and whose one object in life was to help, to preserve and protect her husband.

Once many years ago I was standing on a balcony of the Ambassador Hotel in Los Angeles with that noted wit and playwright, Wilson Mizner. As we watched the steady stream of traffic go out Wilshire Boulevard, Mizner said, "I wonder how many of those men are going home to somebody who believes in them and cheers for them. That's what man needs most."

That was what Harry S. Truman had most of.

And that is why I choose her for this company—an irrepressible woman and the best wife I ever saw! It seems to me that these are the requisites of a great First Lady.

Chapter Ten

In the beginning I said, *Today's Woman ought to know a good deal more than she does about the irrepressible spirit and the gallant character and the never-say-die methods of her predecessors*. There are many such. I had said to my friend Colleen Moore Hargrave, who has that genius for inviting the right people at the right time, Remember, if we ask them to the Tavern at the End of the Road, we shall be stuck with them for all Eternity. We must have some criterion.

Even their enemies must love them.

Colleen said this quietly, these words Father Passy had spoken to Alyosha in *The Brothers Karamazov*. In other words, they couldn't be wishy-washy, or goody-goody, or milksop or peace-at-any-price. Strong enough, valiant enough in a Cause, audacious and undismayed enough to make enemies. *No coward soul is mine*, said Emily Brontë. Yet of such heart and soul-fire that none can feel enmity.

At that moment, I felt deeply moved. For looking back over my whole life I know it was at that moment that I knew my enemies can love me only if I am trying to love them. Women of irrepressible spirit love their enemies even when they battle them to the death for worthy ends.

"What a collection!" I said.

A saint, a sinner, crusaders meek and crusaders with an axe in hand, a spy, a genius, a writer, a Follies Girl rubbing elbows with a Ph.D. and a chambermaid with a First Lady. Now I could read too that Colleen's hostess mind was busily pairing them off with the men in the Tavern, I could tell by that Pixie look which once made her the greatest Movie Star of that time that she was ready for mischief. The pairs would most certainly be unorthodox. As she scrawled and murmured to herself, I caught lines—

Clark Gable was to offer his arm to that *attractive* (his word) lady from Missouri, Bess Truman. Same expression Clark wore when he bowed to that other great lady Melanie Wilkes in a time now Gone with the Wind. Of course it had to be Mark Kelly, sportswriter with whom I'd been sent to South Bend to keep him sober while he negotiated the first Notre Dame-USC football game, who would escort Carry Nation, carrying in one hand an axe and in the other a Bible as she tried to warn us and head off the Alcohol menace which she foresaw would destroy us if we didn't watch out. And the fascinating Paul Gallico, having written *Mrs. 'Arris Goes to Paris* as well as *The Snow Goose,* must hand in Elsie Parrish, a sort of Mrs. 'Arris herself. Mr. Hearst, I noticed at once, wasn't available. He'd brought along Marion Davies as naturally as he'd brought his right arm. And I know Damon Runyon, All-Time All-Star reporter, was handcuffing Amelia Earhart—there'd always be a *story* where she was.

A Mixed Bag indeed. A Motley Crew I had come by. All had spirit, all had got up off the floor one time or another. I might well call them a Gallant Band.

At this exact second Colleen came up with a valid demand. "You'll have to explain the people you don't ask," she said. "It's as much the people you don't ask to a party as the ones you do. You won't go to cocktail parties because you say you get stuck with people you're not interested in. The truth is, those people shouldn't have been invited in the first place. They belonged at some other party. But you're leaving out a lot of people who will surprise *everybody*."

"Such as who?" I said.

"To begin with," Colleen said, "the two women alive today you admire most."

"Anne Morrow Lindbergh."

"Rose Kennedy."

To me, the greatest living American woman is Anne Morrow Lindbergh—the lady who can and does drive three mules with sparkle in her eyes and strength and gentleness in her hands. The best woman writer in the United States today—mother, wife, citizen interested in many things—and if you have had a glimpse of her soul as she offers it in *Bring Me a Unicorn* you know with what a pure flame it shines.

But—I cannot ask her to my table at the Tavern because of course she would have to bring her husband, Charles Augustus Lindbergh, the first man to fly the Atlantic, and not only would the Colonel not wish to come but—to be frank—we wouldn't want him. The Press, I mean. There was—there always has been —let us call it a misunderstanding between Lindbergh and what is today known as the Media, I believe. Looking at it now, squarely, across the years, it is easier to comprehend than it was then. I think it became clear to me when I saw a picture of tall young Colonel Lindbergh together with the Prince of Wales— receiving the cries and plaudits of multitudes in London. The Prince of Wales was a beloved idol and a member of the Royal Family. He had been brought up to know this and to accept his duties, to handle crowds and adulation, to smile the royal smile and wave the royal hand. Young Charles Augustus Lindbergh had been born in the United States of America, an ordinary boy in the vast Northwest of our continent. He had been an airmail pilot, he had saved and worked and finally a small group of men banded together to buy him an airplane called *The Spirit of St. Louis*—and in this, with incredible bravery and cold nerve and the ability to be *alone* in the very Universe, he had flown where only eagles had been before. Landing in Paris—we could no longer call him the Lone Eagle—he was catapulted into fame and such hero-worship as no man had known in our country before, or since. Writing to a friend some time later, young Anne Morrow said, "Apparently, I am going to marry Charles Lindbergh. Don't wish me happiness—wish me courage and strength and a sense of humor. I will need them all." And she did—and, I rather imagine, does.

She wrote *Gift from the Sea*, and I would frankly rather have her at my table than any other woman in the world. But—she wouldn't come without her husband, I'm sure of that, and it wouldn't be proper or useful to ask Colonel Lindbergh to a Press Table—

So—I will have to settle for Anne Morrow Lindbergh as my first living candidate for the Women's Hall of Fame.

Is it all wrong of me not to invite the almost divine Rose Kennedy? I think so myself because we will miss her so much. I know no woman who is better company than Mrs. Kennedy. Of course she belongs immediately and without any ado in the Women's Hall of Fame which I hope any women who are reading along with me will wish to start. But you must see why I can't invite her to the Tavern at the End of the Road.

She has a table of her own. And around it sit several generations of people, all of whom I'd love to have in my Tavern, but her table will be, as it always has been, as I know she will wish it to be, a *family* affair.

There is another magnificent woman I've left out who will certainly surprise *everybody*. Helen Keller.

That great soul over so many years rose above every physical handicap a woman can have. I can still shut my eyes and see her plainly as she came floating across the lobby of the Institute for the Blind in downtown New York with the grace and joy that made it impossible to believe that she was deaf, dumb and blind.

The other night at the San Marino home of Robert and Carole Finch—Bob was secretary of HEW in the Nixon Administration, and was for many years the guiding light of Nixon's relations with the Press (things haven't gone so well in that department since Bob came back to California where the majority of people of whatever party hope he'll soon run for *something*, governor or senator probably)—one of the guests was Theodore White, who writes classic books about Presidents. And as my host and hostess were kind enough to inquire about my book telling the stories of great American women, all the guests spoke up to ask what women I had chosen and which woman they would select first. Besides Teddy White there were also present Jess Marlow, one of the news commentators who has a full grasp of the news he broadcasts, Harry Collins, publisher of the Pasadena *Star News*, a leading executive of MCA, and several powerful club-ladies.

The first name that came out from everybody was:

Helen Keller.

They put her forth as THE great American woman and when I said I hadn't included her in my book at all they stared at me with incredulity and censure. But why? they said in unison.

"She will of course be in the Hall of Fame," I said. "The Women's Hall of Fame. On a high pedestal surrounded by blue-birds and angels with her Seeing Eye dog at her feet. But it seems to me she is a case so exceptional, her gallant spirit is one so different from that of any average normal woman that she must have a place all her own."

Let us look together into this Women's Hall of Fame which some day we must achieve. When we have it, there will be en-shrined there forever the great women of our land whom we all know, have known and will know into eternity, as we do Nef-ertiti and Queen Elizabeth and Betsy Ross. Modern Woman has been swept up in Flumdoodle and Falderal about being *lib-erated*—they never say from what—so that they've had no time to show forth and immortalize the American Woman over the centuries from 1600 to this present day. Here in the Hall will stand the American women already known to every American:

Mary Baker Eddy
Helen Keller
Anne Morrow Lindbergh
Rose Kennedy
Eleanor Roosevelt
Babe Didrickson
Jane Addams
Emily Dickinson
Louisa May Alcott
Dr. Margaret Mead
Aimee Semple McPherson

There are also a few who are famous indeed, who accom-plished many things, but they didn't pass the tests. Without those tests, this would all be meaningless.

Begin with Isadora Duncan.
In the native land of De Tocqueville, who claimed superiority

for American women, the only one of them who is distinguished. Or ever was. Again and again, I saw the people of Paris fill the streets to watch her pass, stand from early dawn in lines for a chance to see her dance to the Paris Symphony, led by the top conductors of all Europe.

Dance?

Like no other dance that ever has been. Rather it was as though some glorious statue came to life while you watched. As though one of Rodin's masterpieces of Isadora herself yielded to the magic of Pygmalion and moved to rejoice. *Dancing,* in terms we had known, it was not, and hard as she tried Isadora was never able to teach it to a student or imitator. Her efforts to open and conduct schools in several countries failed—first, perhaps through lack of organization, and second, I think myself, because Isadora's dancing was unteachable. You had to *be* Isadora. In Moscow she did have some classes and she marched her pupils down the streets in red tunics with the permission of Lenin himself, but after she left Russia the school soon ceased to be.

Paris always cheered her to the echo—and never ceased to weep with her for her children, the two beautiful, shining little ones who were drowned in the Seine because of some freakish accident when the car in which they were riding leaped over the chauffeur as he cranked it. Many who knew her declare she was never alive after she went that night to the morgue in Paris and saw the still bodies of Patrick and Deirdre, that actually she joined them in death there.

But—

No no, that *but* comes later.

We must see first that millions had sat entranced as the Paris— or London or Berlin—Symphony orchestra played and the curtains parted to show a Grecian stage with simple pillars and in a tunic of soft veils or a cloud of silver gauze out came one woman alone. Sometimes she didn't move six inches in six minutes and yet it seemed the movement of the cherubim to the music of the spheres, or the dance of Salome in her indecent triumph or some strange illustration of the tales of Scheherazade that stirred the imagination. She was cast in drama, or melodrama, in tragedy and sex masque, and the Muses were her patronesses. And she was—she *was*—in many ways the first Modern Woman.

I'm sure she would have accepted things addressed to

Ms. Isadora Duncan

because

she was never sure whether she was Miss or Mrs. nor cared.

Her claims to be the first Modern Woman totally LIBerated are many.

She regarded marriage as a degradation and—until circumstances forced her to enter into it with a mad Russian poet so she could take him out of Russia with her, and thus increase all the desperate financial difficulties under which she so often suffered—she would have nothing to do with this remnant of an outmoded society. Her freedom and her career were paramount. She made much of them, to an extent that sometimes makes the reader of her life story find his reason tottering. For of course she wrote her life story and of course she called it just that. *My Life.* Dorothy Parker, as a book critic, wrote, "Out of this mess of prose come her hope, her passion, her suffering; above all, comes the glamour that was Isadora Duncan's. And the glamour of Isadora Duncan came from her great, torn, bewildered, foolhardy soul." And later in reviewing an opus by a then actor—matinee idol named Lou Tellegen called, believe it or not, *Women Have Been Kind,* she says that in only a few pages does Mr. Kiss-and-Tellegen give out glamour: "That is when he writes of Isadora Duncan. It seems impossible for any writer to speak of that woman without conveying something of greatness."

True true, and I am putting all this in out of fairness and to convey *something* of greatness.

Something but not all.

By no means all.

For—a champion has to get up off the floor. No? Yes! Yes yes yes.

Ray Barbuti won the 440 at the Olympic Games and when I interviewed him in Amsterdam afterwards I said, "The 440 is known as the toughest of all races—*a long sprint.* You win it. How do you do this?" Ray gave me a friendly grin and said,

"Oh, it's not all that tough! I run the first 400 yards as fast as I can—and then I sprint." A champion.

Isadora ran the first 400 yards as fast as she could and doubtless broke all records for the distance. Then she quit cold.

Yes she did. She *quit*.

So—is she a champion? Of irrepressible spirit? A get-up-off-the-floor gal?

I know. It's tough. Lots of people quit. Some very fine and important people didn't get up at the count of nine. I *know* this ('deed I do). And I love Isadora. I loved her when I knew her as a comet of amazing brilliance in our sky. She was another of those whose enemies had to love her and even though her own country, the United States of America, rejected her for "indecent exposure," the very same city once rejected Miriam Van Waters, and Dr. Van Waters, after refusing to be rejected, kept right on counterpunching for almost a decade. Isadora fascinated even her enemies—such as hotelkeepers on whom she managed to drape unpaid bills all over Europe. These things—the unpaid bills, the broken furniture, the mad marriage, the wild carryings-on—these are all part, as it were, of the Artistic Temperament, which is part of Isadora's glamour.

She was *Isadora* and even the people to whom she owed money loved her.

But—

Now I go back. I am on the Riviera. I have been told—in unencouraging tones—that Isadora has a Villa nearby. Not one of those magnificent villas of the type Paris Singer always gave her as evidence of his lifelong adoration. Nor the one given her by the actor-son of England's great actress-star Ellen Terry, where her babies were born. When I finally found it my heart began to beat even harder—oh yes, it was beating hard, no one nowhere no time ever approached Isadora without an increase in circulation. And to this I now added the lifeblood curiosity of the reporter. She hasn't danced for her public in a long time. No concerts where thousands in North and South America and Europe waited from dawn to dark to see her. So great and so popular an artist! Is she too *old?* No, no, in her early forties—in shape she would look far less of course. And who cared anyway? *Age cannot wither her, nor custom stale* . . . Those dances were more than Greek statues coming to life, they were the motion of winds and waves, the flight of birds, they could go on forever. I had interviewed her after the tragic incident in Boston, when they closed her theater and branded her Art as "indecent," and later once in London, when I realized that she was the only American woman artist famous—*known* at all—in Europe. A San Francisco girl who had made good—and bad? We were fellow countrywomen and came from the same forever beloved city by the Golden Gate. Surely she would allow me to call upon her, these some years later, in her semiretirement or whatever it was.

The villa was small and—rather dilapidated? As I approached, it seemed unusually quiet, poised in stillness and silence. I—didn't at all like the feel of it. Peeking through a window when there was no response to my knock, I was reassured by the famous blue velvet curtains, hanging around all the walls of the big room. They—surely they weren't as faded, as—blurred as they looked at first glance? The shiny spots—the limpness—and then I saw against them on a small, priceless antique table a bottle, half-empty, and some glasses, and behind them a Rodin statue of Isadora dancing—

Isadora didn't get up off the floor.

When you've seen one drunken woman you've seen 'em all and by any name it smells of the end of the world. It was when the *women* began lying around the swimming pools that Rome fell. Remember?

Oh, this is absurd.

I am *crying*.

I had been warned. Newspapermen in Paris had said with shrugs, She drinks. So? I had known too many who sought something they never found in alcohol to be shocked. I had compassion plus for this tragedy. I had seen it destroy my father. When I saw her there she had been drinking, too deeply. God help all women adrift on *that* sea. I know—her children, who had died so *idiotically* by a senseless accident. Yes, coming age was slowing down her body, which was the temple of her genius. Poverty—extreme poverty, obviously. (But—she could *earn* any amount of money if she—) And I supposed the desertion of her husband and lovers—Isadora had cared more for having lovers, many of them, than for the lovers themselves. I don't find that she ever actually loved a Man. They were all complements of Isadora Duncan and her Art—she always spelled that word with a capital.

Only in her forties. When she stepped into that fast racing car in front of her Riviera villa and, crying aloud, "*Je vais à gloire*," flung her scarf around her shoulder so that it caught in the wheel as it moved and strangled her instantly—she was still at seedtime of life, *the teeming autumn, big with rich increase.*

I hope she went to glory. She loved it so.

Dorothy Parker, to whom she remained the epitome of glamour, says Isadora ran ahead where there were no paths—I grant this—but so did Mother Cabrini. Great women do not come to bad ends! Tragic ones, to be sure, getting burned at the stake like Joan of Arc and tried as by fire like Miriam Van Waters or being shot like Amelia Earhart or finding fame and fortune almost too difficult to bear like Margaret Mitchell. Or little Judy Garland. Judy got up before you could count to ten so many times, and in the end death won the final bout. But Isadora had given up before she died—quite a while before she died. The incredible courage of a Lil Tashman was beyond her!

"And what," said Colleen coldly, "about Clare Boothe Luce?"
Oh dear!

This was, of course, bound to happen. If Colleen had to do with the Guest List of women to be asked to the Tavern at the End of the Road, we were sure to have to deal with Mrs. Luce. Her favorite!

"You," I said, "are the only *friend* Clare Luce has—"

"No," Colleen said, "I am not. But if I was, it would only be because she was—always has been—too busy serving her country and being a good wife and full partner to a man like Harry Luce to have time for friendships."

It may be, I see this for the first time, possible that I am just plain jealous. I do not have a jealous nature—it just doesn't hap-

pen to be one of my faults—but I have cherished being Colleen's
best friend over many years and nevertheless I have been fond
of her many other friends—Mrs. Loyal Davis (Edie to us) and
Hope McCormick with whom she takes trips around the world
and beautiful Mary Hansen who lives near her now in Paso
Robles and is a joy and delight to all. She took Mary around the
world with her but then she often invited me on this tour and
I have refused. First, I don't ever have time and, second, I don't
like *travel*. But there was something in her excessive admiration
for Mrs. Luce—or *I* called it excessive—and Mrs. Luce's for
her that I found upsetting.

The truth is, I resented the fact that when Colleen said Clare
Boothe Luce was the most remarkable woman in the United
States and that no *man*—or hardly any man—had ever accomplished anywhere near as much as she had she was speaking the
whole and *nothing but*—

"Clare Boothe Luce is just the biggest Success Story of all
time," I said.

"What more do you want?" said Colleen. "She was a brilliant
young editor on *Vanity Fair*. She married the richest and most
eligible man in New York when she was *nobody* and every unmarried woman in the highest circles was trying to catch him.
She wrote a smash play—a really fine top American play that
stands out in our Theater Art. Then she married the most powerful publisher in America and was his partner and helpmate for
many years. She was elected to Congress and served well and
she was appointed Ambassador to Italy by Eisenhower and did
a magnificent job in that trouble at Trieste—or over Trieste—
or whatever it was. I've heard men in Rome say it was a diplomatic feat of first magnitude. She was the opening speaker at a
Presidential Convention—no other woman ever has been."

"She's so successful it's positively repulsive." I had said it once
and I said it again. "If you tried to write it as fiction nobody
would believe you."

"Then why don't you try to write it as truth?" Colleen said.

I felt that I was perfectly willing that Clare Boothe Luce
should be in the Hall of Fame. Has to be! A beeg niche. I'd even

burn a dash of incense to Success. In its way it was a Rags to
Riches tale such as all American readers love—for little Clare had
been born on Riverside Drive after that lovely boulevard along
the Hudson had become a sort of high-class slum. Her family
was poor and unknown and except for the fact that she won her
first recognition at eight years old by enchanting Mrs. August
Belmont, who forthwith sent her to a fine and fashionable school,
she might have been lost among the many girls who were grateful
to have a chance to earn a living as secretaries or nurses. Opportunity would not have knocked.

Her accomplishments are beyond possible question.

Success without failure—success without really having to try
—success at everything—I am not her enemy, heaven forbid, so
I do not have to love her and I think that is my reason for excluding
her with all her endorsements, records, archives, memorabilia and
adversaria from my Tavern. I mean, she does not seem to me
in any way to be *lovable*. Is it possible that there must be some
weakness, some human failings, some failure for a woman to be
lovable? As there must be tears for a comedian to make you
laugh?

And that brings me rejoicing and shouting Hallelujah to the One
and Only.

I understand it is a plebeian trait to love the dawn, to wish
to be awake and able to see sunrise. In order to get some sunrises
into my life style, today I am perfectly willing to be plebeian.
And thus a couple of mornings ago I woke as a rosy-fingered,
dewy, incense-breathing Dawn came up sweetly out of the East.
I sat on the edge of the palisade that comes up out of the Pacific
Ocean below my house and it was so clear that I could plainly
see Catalina Island twenty-six miles across the sea.

Early morning thoughts more than any others, it seems to me,
take off on their own. I began a simple meditation of gratitude
and hope—something I once made my own out of Joel Goldsmith
—Father, this is Your day, You made the sun to rise . . . as the
heavens declare the glory of God so must I show forth the
Glory of God—this day use me and let me glorify God—and let
me see how beautiful that Island is—I love *islands*—Who said

There are no islands any more?—I know—Millay—(Edna St. Vincent)

> This little life, from here to there—
> Who lives it safely anywhere?
> (The tidal wave devours the shore:
> There are no islands any more.)

There are islands any more because there *is* one right in front of me. It's not a desert island, of course. When I was little my father and I used to go to the Metropole Hotel on vacations and there is a picture of me trying to pretend I just caught three enormous barracuda. I haven't been there in years. I wish it was —no, no, I wish I knew of a nice desert island where you could go and *think*. The only island like that I know is a drawing room on the *Super Chief* from Los Angeles to Chicago.

Suppose I was actually cast away on a desert island. Would I be able to endure the loneliness I think I want so much?

Or would it be better and happier if I had someone—some *one* —just a companion who'd sort of mind her or his business most of the time but surface by the campfire for brilliant and witty dialogue of tales of whatever they have tales to tell of—*Leather-stocking*—or Natty Bumppo—told them of his life among the Indians, *Tales of a Wayside Inn*, Kipling's *Plain Tales from the Hills*, which filled my youth with joy—maybe I'd like someone on my desert island with me and I think I want Tales of *Life*.

Of how to live it, how to make it glorious, how to know the people one meets and do a job of work whatever the work may be.

At first it didn't come to me that it could be a woman and then—little by little—I brought my thoughts to women with wings, women of irrepressible spirit, women of *tenderness*—the way Marie Dressler was with the man she loved who was in a wheelchair so long—or as she was with Jean Harlow when Jean had to come back to work at MGM after she'd seen her husband Paul Bern kill himself, or with Frances Marion when Frances' sister was killed—and with me.

There used to be a game when we all selected what ten books we'd take with us *if* we were going to be cast ashore on a desert island—I can still remember mine—

The Bible (has the best stories, as Harry
            Truman said in *Plain Speaking*.)
The Jungle Book
The Complete Shakespeare
Pride and Prejudice
David Copperfield
Untermeyer's Treasury of Poetry
Alice in Wonderland
Agatha Christie Omnibus
Oxford Dictionary
Macaulay's History of England
Plutarch's Lives

So much for books. I can revise it ten times a day.

Suppose I had the chance to select one woman—not in my family, because frankly I would prefer my daughter Elaine to any-body I know or have known and after her my granddaughter Kristen and *her* daughter Jessica and likewise my granddaughters Kathy and Tracey and Sunny and her daughters and great-grand-daughters Liz and Bernadette and Julie.

Outside of these ridiculous proofs that blood is thicker than anything, I read *Robinson Crusoe* with enjoyment—it being among the all-time superlative adventure stories—and faced some of the things that would come upon us if by any off chance we found ourselves resident in what is intended to be the loneliest of all places—a desert island. For in this overcrowded age on earth we have come to understand what loneliness can be. On a desert island I might have blessed solitude but I would also cope with boredom, fear and many kinds of hunger.

One woman.

Not one second of hesitation. Not one flutter of indecision. Which has to prove that I, anyhow, had One Woman, a One and Only. True, true, and I am flooded with gratitude that I knew her. That she was my friend. I can still hear her laughter and the roar with which the world responded.

For this is the woman from whom again and again the world borrowed its mirth, having none of its own.

During a great war, during the Depression which historians now say was the worst thing that ever happened to our country, worse even than the Civil War. During so many of our everyday lifetimes, when pain and sorrow and betrayal, when fear and despair and disillusion and failure hit us, as they do everyone sometimes. There she was! Offering us irresistible laughter.

So often I saw the world borrow its mirth from Marie Dressler.

So now we wind up not with Cinderella or the Sleeping Beauty or even with Dorothy of Oz—we wind up with the Ugly Duckling.

The Ugly Duckling which turned into a Star.

Several stars, several times.

She kept coming back to Hollywood, for instance. Having failed signally three times. Another name for Marie Dressler would be the Comeback Kid. Once she left to go back to New York because the picture she'd done was a miserable failure, through no fault of hers. Once her friend Frances Marion wrote a super-part only Dressler could play—we'd have to have Marie Dressler for that, Irving Thalberg said, and those big stage stars won't come to Hollywood. But Frances knew Marie was not only "through" in that particular moment of the Theater, she was broke, and so she increased the part and sent for Marie, to play Mrs. Callahan in *The Callahans and the Murphys*. But the Irish decided to have one of their less endearing moments and boycotted the picture, saying that in it they had been insulted and belittled and so made it a miserable affair that never got off the ground.

And down Marie Dressler tumbled once again.

Her whole career, Marie sometimes said, was founded on *falls* of every kind.

At the age of five little Leila Koerber, her real name, was placed on a pedestal with nothing on but a bow and arrow. This was in a Church Social, for her mother had a theatrical gift and only this means of expressing it. And in this tableau—tableaux were very much *done* in those days, in costume and with living statues—in this particular one the one-day-to-be Marie Dressler took a leading part as Cupid. And very effective she looked when her mother placed her up there on the tall pillar. The trouble was she couldn't stay there and came tumbling down in a superb fall that sent the audience into hysterics.

And so you see, said the by-that-time-most-popular Movie Star in the world, my first impact on my audiences was a pratfall. (A pratfall being one that lands the faller on her rear end, her *der-*

rière. Marie once, when trying to raise money for some big cause, used what she thought was the word delicate and proper for one's posterior, namely *derrière*, and thereby shocked the older generation of Rockefellers, who, like their founder, were easily shocked.)

Anyhow, at five, Marie fell off the pedestal and landed on her, she says, already fairly large behind—surely one can say *behind* of a five-year-old—or maybe it should be tail—I am being all this meticulous and almost prissy because of Marie—she so detested any kind of dirty words, or obscene humor, *not* she said on moral grounds but because they and it are an admission of failure.

"Great Comics do not need to resort to the vulgar to get laughs, she said, "and the only ones who laugh at themselves are those who can't get anybody else to laugh at them."

I am having some trouble trying to follow any chronological order in bringing Marie Dressler into my Tavern at the End of the Road. Scenes—lines—expression—bits and pieces of things she did and said keep coming through and I am sad and uplifted at the same time. For what Marie said and did stayed with us always. It changed our lives, it influenced our actions.

For instance.

When I was covering Washington and the White House during the Roosevelt Administration, when things were simpler than they are now and F.D.R. used the Press both for Ideas about our country and for how to carry them out, I was working for that great lady of the Press, Cissy Patterson, on her Washington *Times-Herald*. Often I went out to spend the night at her country estate, called the Dower House, which it had been to Lord Baltimore, and on this particular occasion I'd had a blazing row with the man I was going to marry, Ray Helgesen. He had driven us out into Maryland at his usual insane speed, and here is what years later in *The Honeycomb* I said of this:

> In the dark room at the Dower House, smelling faintly of potpourri, with my too tired too busy brain chasing its tail in my aching skull I had an impulse to get off the bed and go on my knees—Marie Dressler used to say Life knocks you to your knees because that is the position that leads you to pray.

I remember when Carole Lombard was killed in a tragic plane accident during the War, Ralph Wheelwright of the publicity department took her husband Clark Gable up to the Nevada town nearest the wreck. And Clark wanted to climb up to it, before the airlines had had time to clear the spot and remove the bodies.

"I didn't let him," Ralph said. "I had to hold onto him for a couple of minutes. But he was too shocked to have his real strength and I managed to keep him down there. I kept recalling what Marie Dressler said to me once, 'Never let human beings torture themselves if you can help it. They all have a tendency in that direction but it never does them any good.'"

I remember what Marie Dressler said or did—

How many of us say and do that even now.

The why is perhaps in some of Dressler's own words again.

Philanthropic women of high social standing and financial power in the early days of the War asked Marie Dressler to find the right woman to represent the Stage in some big war work they were planning. Said Marie Dressler, "It should be a woman who has lived, loved, suffered, sacrificed, fallen, fought and won."

You know who they selected?

Marie Dressler, to be sure. And the war-shocked and sorrowing world borrowed some of her mirth as she went around the country selling more Liberty Bonds than anyone else in the world.

No other actress, no other Movie Star, not even Mary Pickford ever was the close and beloved friend of the great and powerful as was Marie Dressler. Her real buddy after Frances Marion was Anne Morgan, sister of the money colossus J. P. Morgan. She rode down Fifth Avenue with Mrs. Stuyvesant Fish, the greatest Society Leader we've ever had in this country, she toured Europe with Hallie Phillips, Mrs. Robert Morris Phillips of the Social Register and Park Avenue, she led the Equity march, as we know.

> Marie Dressler used to go out on the stage and sweep away the troubles of an audience, heal them with laughter, comfort them with fun, clothe stern reality with a glorious respite in the gay garments of comedy, while in her dressing room in a wheelchair beneath the very shadow of death sat the man she loved, the man who was kept alive only by the vitality of her presence and the flood of her love.

That appeared in an article called "The Private Life of Marie Dressler" in *Liberty* Magazine, then a circulation in the millions weekly, sometime in the early Thirties.

And the article began with a description of the royal triumphal ride of a Movie Star down Park Avenue, while crowds swept off the sidewalks and tried to touch her and cried in chorus, "We love you, Marie," and Marie made them laugh by crying—and then making hideous faces at them. "I love you too," she cried to them. And she did—that is the real answer to Dressler. She *loved* People.

Once she said to us when we were sitting around her dressing room, "You know Jesus never asked anybody anything before he healed them! He knew if he healed them they would know the Presence of Christ and that would change the lives of many of them—even if only one in ten like the lepers."

She had—I beg you to believe this—she had a true, faithful everyday *love* for Jesus Christ. She used this when she comforted the Baby, little Jean Harlow, the first day Jean came back to work on the day after she'd seen her husband Paul Bern commit suicide, leaving a note which named her as the cause though he pretended it didn't, the louse. He was, you know, covered with Intelligentsia and Art and whatnot—but a louse just the same.

So many of the remarkable women through the years were *little*. In fact, my blessed typist, Nancy, who works stride by stride with me, said the other day that as she typed the women with wings in this book she was inclined to get an inferiority complex, since she is five feet eight. Marie will comfort her—Marie was *big*. Really BIG. She gave you always an immediate awareness of how big she was. She weighed anywhere between one hundred and sixty-five and one hundred and ninety-five pounds, depending on what she was doing at the time. When she was young and exciting, because of her Canadian coloring and glowing vitality, she was already over five feet eight inches. In all the old pictures of Weber and Fields, the leading comedy team of the American musical stage for many, many years, she is always taller than any other member of the cast. She towers over both Weber and Fields and even over Lillian Russell, the Beauty, after whom theaters were named and multimillionaires gathered in pursuit, and the Beauty was a fair height herself. Incidentally, Miss Russell was one of Marie's earliest fans, and Marie told me once that it was

Lillian herself who persuaded Weber *and* Fields to let them do a skit together.

Her Hollywood career, when it came, was another of the Ups and Downs, now you see it and now you don't, before she arrived at the most solid and sensational Stardom any woman has ever had *and* arrived there by the route of becoming the all-time best Scene Stealer.

IF you can steal a scene from Greta Garbo in the first five minutes you get the Award. Marie Dressler did it in *Anna Christie*, as many of us remember. And from Jack Barrymore in *Dinner at Eight*. When Marie was in a scene the audience didn't take their eyes off her, no matter who the others might be.

In her years in the Theater, from her debut at thirteen in a traveling musical company, she suffered untold agonies from two things—a memory that made getting *her lines* a nightmare, and stage fright, which Jack Pearl—the first great radio comedian—told me had her clinging to the scenery to hold herself upright just before she made an entrance.

Thus the Movies, where originally she had no lines, and, later, scenes could be shot over if she muffed her dialogue, were heaven to her. But she had to do her usual number of Comebacks.

First she came to Mack Sennett and did something about *Tillie*. When a second picture wasn't offered she toodled back to New York.

Later, as we know, she did Mrs. Callahan—and the Irish took umbrage, which they are so apt to do in the wrong places. I've watched this in my own Irish family for a couple of generations.

But in time on the stage George Lederer told me, "There was only one entirely *Irreplaceable* woman, Marie Dressler."

And Irving Thalberg used that same word to me once at MGM when we had just seen a run of the day's takes of *Tugboat Annie*. "She is Irreplaceable," he said. "Who else is?"

Oh yes, she had run the gamut of all emotions.

She married first a man named Hopper.

Weber, of Weber and Fields, who was her Number One Fan, told me of that. "He was maybe about the handsomest man I ever saw," said Mr. Weber, as we sat in his office high above the noise of Broadway. "Like a Greek God, we used to say. All right, I guess every woman has a right to a romance with a big handsome dummy, like Gentlemen from time to time prefer Dumb Blondes. And Hopper was a big handsome dummy, and the marriage couldn't last. But Adam and Eve were made two by two and Marie was human as any woman can be—and so she fell in love again and that love lasted as long as he did."

His name was Jim Dalton—and he was already married and though he asked his wife for a divorce she wouldn't give it to him. It was a story that is all too well known, but Marie at the time didn't see it that way. She waited. She went on loving him. And finally he was in some accident that put him in a wheelchair for the rest of his life. He had been devoted to Marie, and everybody liked him because he was so kind to her. He had taken care of her, he had tried to keep her from working too hard, and he used to come to the theater every night and help her dress, and rub her feet and legs when she had grown tired with dancing.

And for many years his wheelchair stood in the wings of every Theater in which Marie Dressler starred. And she told me that she always did her show for him—she was never satisfied if she hadn't made Jim really laugh, this was her desire.

> Laugh, and the world laughs with you;
> Weep, and you weep alone.

A contemporary of Marie Dressler's, Ella Wheeler Wilcox, is remembered perhaps only for those lines. They were Marie's favorites. She could do whole Shakespeare plays for you from memory, after years of work on them, and she once sang us the whole part of Katisha in *The Mikado*, to enliven an evening at Mr. Mayer's.

Yes yes a great woman.

The greatest of all women Movie Stars.

How did she get that way?

It may be trite but there is no other way to say it. You'll find it all in the thirteenth chapter of Corinthians I. It begins, Love suffereth long and is *kind*. If I'd told Marie that I hadn't married the only man *I* ever really loved—or maybe it's better to say the man I loved most—because he had a cruel streak she would have said,

You should have married him and with Christ's help healed him of it. I'm sure she would have been right—but it's too late now.

At thirteen she went to work to support her *family*—her mother whom she adored and her sister. Hired by mail, as she so often said with a chuckle, by a road company who advertised for chorus girls. If they'd seen me . . . Marie said, but when I got there it was too late and I went with them on their travels.

At twenty, she was a favorite on Broadway, spending the intervening years with various Musical Comedy companies. Weber and Fields, who understood comedy better than anyone else in the American Theater, were bright enough to see that she was irrepressibly funny and they gave her a chance to prove it and she did.

But at thirty she was selling peanuts from a wagon at Coney Island, when there wasn't anything else to eat she had peanuts for supper. She explained this to me one day at a studio party when there were crackers with peanut butter on the hors d'oeuvre tray and Dressler turned green.

Before she was forty she led the Chorus Girls up Broadway and Fifth Avenue in the Equity Parade, at the time when actors and actresses struck against management for better pay and conditions. By that time she was well known for her Fighting Face and Abe Erlanger, head of Management forces, refused to attend a reconciliation meeting if she was there. The truth was, she had once run him out of his own theater, leaping one jump ahead of the scenery brace in her hand. She chased him down Shubert Alley, to the delight and edification of a vast crowd calling him all kinds of unpleasant names, without any four-letter words, such as thief and double-crosser and white slaver, etc., etc., etc. because he had gotten around the six-days-a-week-only clause in the Actors' Contract by calling his Sunday night show Concerts. "Simon Legree," Marie shouted as he sped ahead of her for his life.

Oh yes—she had a temper.

Inherited perhaps from her father, a bad-tempered, violent German. He was irascible and mean, Marie said, but he was also a fine musician.

Music, laughter and God, the only three things necessary, Marie said. My mother taught me about God and my father taught

me Music and I guess I got laughter from my godmother in my
cradle. Maybe she was the Comedy Muse or something. Because
my first memories are the desire to make people laugh.

The real sorrow of her life was that she had no children. "I
should have married some honest laborer and had eight or ten
kids," she used to say. But like that other childless woman Jane
Addams she tried to make up for it by being mother to hundreds
—thousands—of motherless kids. She came into my house at
Malibu one day when, besides my own, a lot of the neighbors'
children were scattering sand and seaweed over my nice clean floor
and I was shooing them back into the ocean where they belonged.

"I've missed them all my life," she said.

Of course, I remember her mothering everything on the MGM
lot, beginning with L. B. Mayer, who maybe needed it worst
—and Police Chief White who turned over the irreconcilables to
Dressler—and Garbo who didn't Go Home but went to Marie's
house and nowhere else. Marie's house by the way, was one I
rented to her—and as a landlady I had learned some odd things
about Movie Stars who shall be nameless. Like its taking two men
three days to clean the bathroom. Marie was scrupulously clean
as a German Hausfrau—and the house was filled with rich
warmth and love love love.

At fifty, anyone in the world would have told you Marie
Dressler was *Through*. Finished. Washed up. And furthermore
without a dime. The world had gone youth-mad, as it does period-
ically, especially in the U.S.A., and Dressler was acting practically as a shill in order to have one bedroom at the Ritz on Park
Avenue—and in case the word shill is out of use it means or meant
one who is accomplice to a street pedlar and starts the buying
—Marie was supposed to start traveling salesmen and such buying
the Ritz as their favorite New York hotel. But she was pretty
desperate about this, and so she decided to take what capital her
friends like Anne Morgan would furnish and start a Theatrical
Hotel for Americans in Paris. And she was about ready to sail
when her dear friend Nella Webb, then New York's favorite
astrologer, came rushing into her Ritz bedroom and said, "No,
no. No! This is wrong. You must go to Hollywood." "I've been

to Hollywood," said Dressler. "I know," said Nella, "but this time all will be different. You will become a Star." "That's an astrological pipe dream," said Dressler.

It wasn't.

Nella had signaled Frances Marion, now in a top spot in the Movies, and this time when she brought Marie Dressler to Hollywood, first for a role in *Anna Christie* with Garbo and then to play opposite Wallace Beery, it was for good. For good, meaning forever, and for good, meaning she did become the biggest Movie Star in the world.

At sixty-one, she could go nowhere except as a Royal Progress.

And, like Gable, she loved it. She received them with open arms—she made them laugh—and they began to borrow her mirth to dry all their tears.

I like to remember the last thing she said to me when she was —and knew she was—on her death bed in a hospital in Santa Barbara.

"Be seeing you," she said, and lifted one finger in a gesture that was so sure it made me smile all over.

And so I know she will be seeing me in the Tavern at the End of the Road.

And now, I have to pull up another chair!

I mean here I was, all set on my Tavern.

We know who has been invited, we know who will be there. And now just because I took down a copy of Jane Austen's *Pride and Prejudice* for its annual rereading I have to change my whole arrangement and move up that extra chair by the first and who do you think is going to be in it?

None other than Clare Boothe Luce.

The simplest way for me to understand this is to copy down the letter I found in that book.

It is from my friend and, as it were, Co-hostess Colleen Moore Hargrave, who at the moment is busy painting the ceiling of a temple she recently brought home from Thailand to install at her ranch up in the hills behind Paso Robles.

It is dated in a scrawl at the end April 20th 1967 and I'm going to reproduce it whole so as to have it on the record

Mrs. Homer Hargrave
   Cairoli 6
Piazza Benedetto
   Roma, Italy

Dearest Adela; Never as happy as here. My whole time is working and loving it. To learn is life's greatest happiness for me. I need a book. Not now, any time. I think the name is Around the World with the Abbe children written by papa who as you remember was a big time photographer. I want to use his format for around the world with Grandma, and written as if by Charlie Billy and Kathleen who I am taking around the world in 1970. Hope all is going well with your book, almost called you last evening got lonely for a chat, but it was midnite and didn't think you would relish the call. As it was I just read a little of "Tell No Man" and had my visit that way.

Clare, who we all think of as being so self-sufficient is having a *bad time*. Her last letter very *lost*. She and Harry were great friends and he was her greatest admirer. It was like Homer and me. I made speeches and like that time in London when I ran our Lilac Time at the Embassy for the Royal Academy etc. he burst with such pride tears ran down his cheeks as he watched the film. Well! Clare did all things for Harry's amazement & amusement and he was amazed and amused and would get nervous and PROUD. I have seen him. She was a constant source of interest. She has lost her best loved audience as I did. And she will pull out but she is having a rough time. Her life has been cut in two—and I think more than ever she realizes how much she depended on the partnership they had. Helping each other. They read to each other every night by the fire in Phoenix. She was always sure she would be the one to go first and finds herself really jarred aside from what you cannot help but see is a true sorrow. Also it seems to have confused and bewildered her about money as he always handled everything for her. The truth is she just doesn't know what to do without him. He advised her on every move and

listened to everything she wrote as she listened to all his
ideas and they stimulated her and now she doesn't know
what to do or say. Not, as I say as self-sufficient as we
thought and much much more kind and loving. She feels
poor and forlorn without him.

As you can see a poor and forlorn Clare Boothe Luce, in true
sorrow at losing her husband and partner in life, is another matter.
This is the heart I didn't think she had. This is the gal who after
that—after 1967—got up off the floor and did the things he
had left her to do.

So—and I find this makes me very happy because I like to
find the wings are still there on the most *successful* women—my
invitation to Mrs. Luce.

And I suppose probably finally in the end between Dorothy
Parker and her idea of Isadora's great, torn, tormented *soul*, and
Robert Thom's feeling that a personality so terrific and irresistible
as Isadora's has to entitle her to not only a seat in any Tavern but
a Throne in Valhalla—I will issue a grudging invitation to Ms.
Duncan. *As* the first liberated woman.

My Ugly Duckling once said to me, "A great woman is greater
than a great man—her spiritual wings are stronger."

So—here are my great American women, with wings, from the
past these women are. I don't think any of them ever heard the
word liberated—they naturally knew that they were and could
soar as high as they wanted to at any time and none should succeed
in saying them nay.

I wanted the modern woman to see and know what these women
from another day—a past era—did. Liberated or unliberated.

How about it?